TRANSFORMING ETHOS

TRANSFORMING ETHOS

Place and the Material in Rhetoric and Writing

ROSANNE CARLO

UTAH STATE UNIVERSITY PRESS
Logan

© 2020 by University Press of Colorado

Published by Utah State University Press
An imprint of University Press of Colorado
245 Century Circle, Suite 202
Louisville, Colorado 80027

 The University Press of Colorado is a proud member of
ASSOCIATION the Association of University Presses.
of UNIVERSITY
PRESSES

The University Press of Colorado is a cooperative publishing enterprise supported, in part, by Adams State University, Colorado State University, Fort Lewis College, Metropolitan State University of Denver, Regis University, University of Colorado, University of Northern Colorado, University of Wyoming, Utah State University, and Western Colorado University.

∞ This paper meets the requirements of the ANSI/NISO Z39.48–1992 (Permanence of Paper)

ISBN: 978-1-64642-062-9 (paperback)
ISBN: 978-1-64642-063-6 (ebook)
https://doi.org/10.7330/9781646420636

Library of Congress Cataloging-in-Publication Data

Names: Carlo, Rosanne, author.
Title: Transforming ethos : place and the material in rhetoric and writing / Rosanne
    Carlo.
Description: Logan : Utah State University Press, [2020] | Includes bibliographical refer-
    ences and index.
Identifiers: LCCN 2020024007 (print) | LCCN 2020024008 (ebook) | ISBN
    9781646420629 (paperback) | ISBN 9781646420636 (ebook)
Subjects: LCSH: Rhetoric—Social aspects. | Place (Philosophy) | Materialism. | English
    language—Rhetoric—Study and teaching (Higher) | Academic writing—Study and
    teaching (Higher)
Classification: LCC P301.5.S63 C36 2020 (print) | LCC P301.5.S63 (ebook) | DDC
    809/.933552—dc23
LC record available at https://lccn.loc.gov/2020024007
LC ebook record available at https://lccn.loc.gov/2020024008

Partial funding for the indexing of this book was provided by Sorolta Taczac, the Dean of Humanities at College of Staten Island.

Cover photo by Sohomjit Ray

For Theresa Enos

CONTENTS

ACKNOWLEDGMENTS

This book would not be possible without the help and support of many people.

First, I am grateful to all my students, whose stories and interest in writing about place and the material inspired me to keep on keeping on.

I owe a lot of thanks to my colleagues at College of Staten Island CUNY. Lee Papa, who—as our department chair—advocated on my behalf for release time and other resources I needed in preparing this manuscript. Gloria Gianoulis, for her many years of service to our writing program and for taking up the lion's share of the day-to-day administrative issues to give me the space to write. Mary Boland and Ira Shor, who read my book proposal and offered their time, feedback, and encouragement. Simon Reader, who joined the department the same year as I did and was always the best of colleagues, as I could turn to him for writing advice and encouragement. And, most especially, Harry Thorne, who always made himself available to chat about the book and who read drafts and gave a final read to the full manuscript—with his encouragement and insight, I was able to see the value of this work and believe in it more.

Thanks to Sarolta Takács, the Dean of Humanities and Social Sciences at College of Staten Island, whose office provided partial funding for the indexing of this book.

One of the key experiences in composing this book was my participation in a writing group at CUNY as part of the Faculty Fellowship Publication Program (FFPP). I am especially grateful for the feedback given by our facilitator, Carrie Hintz, and the two other rhetoric and composition faculty in the group, Lisa Blankenship and Jennifer Maloy.

Many scholars at conferences encouraged me, often coming to my presentations and offering feedback on this work, more than I can venture to thank in these acknowledgements. I'm grateful our field has so many kind people who genuinely want to nurture junior scholars. Aneil Rallin and Ian Barnard, who have counseled me well since my first year in graduate school. Patrick Bahls and Adam Hubrig, who have presented with me on place-based writing in the past and have engaged my work in thoughtful ways. Paula Mathieu, who took an hour in the halls at the Conference on Community Writing to emphasize "write the book you want to write." Stephen Parks, who offered feedback on my book proposal and sample chapters. Paul Walker, who, through his editorial direction in *Intraspection,* is working to make space for many of us in the field who value experimental prose; the journal published an article of mine that contains some kernels of ideas I further explore in this book. Elisabeth Gumnior, who always gave me fresh insight on Jim Corder and how to apply his work to the classroom.

I'd like to thank my editor, Rachael Levay, for her work on the project and her belief in the work—she was always on top of things and pushing the project forward. And, of course, the peer reviewers of this manuscript, Paula Matthieu and Stacey Waite, who made this a better book, particularly in offering advice on how to make the argument more cohesive.

This book would not exist without the dear friendship and mentorship of Theresa Enos, to whom this book is dedicated, as well as many others who helped me on my journey at the University of Arizona—too many to thank individually! I would like to thank the other members of my dissertation committee who read early drafts of this work: Ken McAllister, Keith Miller, and John Warnock. I would also be remiss if I didn't acknowledge my graduate school friends and colleagues Rachael Wendler Shah, Jessica Shumake, Jessica Lee, and Jennifer Jacovitch—all four are buoys in my life, making this book better because of their insights. Rachael, being a step ahead of me with her own book, was always willing to answer questions about what this process entails and how to move forward, as well as offer feedback on the content of this work through reading drafts. Jess Shumake, with whom I shared many hours on the phone in rigorous conversation about the state of the field, offered her smart observations, which have undoubtedly made their way into this book. Jess Lee has always been there to offer her perspective and support around teaching as we have exchanged many classroom and administrative stories, finding similarities across our underfunded institutions. Jenny, already writing her dissertation on Corder while I was just encountering his work for the first time, always had a generous and encouraging spirit—I'm thankful for the many conversations we've had about Corder, which greatly influenced this book.

I'm grateful to my undergraduate professors at Eastern Connecticut State University, particularly those who fostered my early interest in rhetoric and composition: Susan DeRosa, Stephen Ferruci, Barbara Liu, Rita Malenczyk, and Lauren Rosenberg.

I also want to thank my community of friends and colleagues who supported me as I worked my way through this writing process: Liz Baez,

Britney Bombardier, Luke Boyd, Matt Brim, Thomas Christou, Todd Craig, Ryan Cresawn, Jenna Podeswa Clarke, Amanda Fields, Becky Fusco, Katie Goodland, Sharifa Hampton, Ashley Holmes, Veronica House, Brooke Hundtoft, Matt and Kati Jones, Regina Kelly, Christine Martarana, Tom Morassini, Nicole and Mike McMinn, Sohomjit Ray, Al Riccio, Chuck and Rene Rinaldi, Sue Rocco, Rachel Sanchez, Aalok Shah, Katie Silvester, Jamie Stoops and Jon Meair, Steven Tarca, Stephanie Wade, and Danielle Zandri.

I'd like to thank Roberta Corder for her generosity in allowing me to keep Jim Corder's drafts and unpublished papers, some of which are included in this book.

This book wouldn't be possible without my loving family, whose influence can be felt—I'm sure—throughout these pages and whose encouragement allows me to be who I am today: Robert and Bridget Carlo; Rachel Carlo, Hussayn Ar Jami-Al Mahdi, and Elijah Ar Jami-Al Mahdi; Rosemary and Thomas Calamo; Bruce Carlo; Lucille Havranek; Anthony Riccio; Cathy and Ted DiPaolo; Marc, Stacey, Quentin, and Keira DiPaolo; and many others.

And my thanks to my dear Brian, who makes my life all the better with his insights, humor, and laughter. You continually ride my professional highs and lows, proofread my pages, and assure me I'm a good writer when I think I'm the absolute worst—I love you for that and so much more.

TRANSFORMING ETHOS

Introduction

RHETORIC AND WRITING FOR ETHOS DEVELOPMENT, NOT TRANSFER

*To come out of scenes like these schools [NYC public schools] and be
offered a "chance" to compete as an equal in the world of academic
credentials, the white-collar world, the world beyond the minimum wage
or welfare, is less romantic for the student than for those who view the
process from a distance. The student who leaves the campus at three or
four o'clock after a day of classes, goes to work as a waitress or clerk, or
hash-slinger, or guard, comes home at ten or eleven o'clock to a crowded
apartment with the TV audible in every corner—what does it feel like
to this student to be reading, say, Byron's "Don Juan" or Jane Austen
for class the next day? . . . How does one compare this experience of
college with that of the Columbia students down at 116th Street in
their quadrangle of gray stone dormitories, marble steps, flowered borders, wide spaces of time and architecture in which to talk and think?
. . . Do "motivation" and "intellectual competency" mean the same for
those students as for City College undergraduates on that overcrowded
campus where in winter there is often no place to sit between classes,
with two inadequate bookstores largely filled with required texts, two caf-
eterias and a snack bar that are overpriced, dreary, and unconducive
to lingering, with the incessant pressure of time and money driving at
them to rush, to get through, to amass the needed credits somehow, to
drop out, to stay on with gritted teeth?*

—Adrienne Rich, "Teaching Language in
Open Admissions"

EXCELSIOR: EVER UPWARD?

In the east stairwell of my office building there hangs a vine that has
somehow crept through an air-conditioning vent. Concrete and fluores-
cent lights surround the alien tendril. The first time I saw it, I paused
in amazement, looking twice, because I wondered how it had grown so
large without my noticing.

I'm fixated on this vine because it is a symbol of neglect, decay,
and the natural taking over the human made. Most days, the vine

DOI: 10.7330/9781646420636.c000

embarrasses me—I walk by it quickly, pretending it's not there. Other days, I'm angry at it, wanting to rip it out from the ceiling in one violent tug. Some days, I believe it holds all the secrets in the universe but refuses to tell me.

The vine almost always reminds me of the material realities of working at a city university that operates on a shoestring budget.

I want to talk about what it's like to be a writing-faculty member and administrator at an institution with a vine growing out of the air-conditioning vent. I want to convey how important it is for the field of writing studies to keep the experiences of my students at the forefront of curriculum discussions, to remember their resilience, to remember the systemically unfair ways they've been treated, to remember their struggles with schooling. I want to talk about how I perceive the landscape of higher education through the lens of my institution in the City University of New York (CUNY) system, and the ways I see a movement toward efficiency and timeliness to earning a degree—as well as an emphasis on writing as a pragmatic tool—undermining the success of our most vulnerable student populations. I want to investigate why Adrienne Rich's description in the opening of this chapter about teaching in open admissions at CUNY in the early 70s feels relevant today. I want to talk about how writing programs design curriculum and the ways I think we are ignoring the vine growing in the stairwell by not recognizing the material realities of student lives outside the university.

I want to talk about how we can recover our discipline by reexamining one of its key terms, *ethos*, and how the revival of ethos can begin to shape our thinking about writing and its teaching.

One example of advocacy for efficiency in higher education is the group Complete College America, which has now made CUNY a partner. I first heard about this group during a department meeting where a proposal for an accelerated composition course was being discussed. I looked at my colleague's PowerPoint slide with, I'm sure, that little crinkle in my brow that I get when I am frustrated. My lips remained pursed. Our CUNY students, the presenter said, take on average three to four years to complete their associate degrees, and Black and Hispanic students on the whole take longer than their white and Asian counterparts. The graphs with percentages were flashed before our eyes, and the data on the screen told a story about deficiency and inefficiency.

Colleges across the nation are reducing or eliminating non-credit-bearing remedial writing courses in favor of models such as corequisites, studios, and accelerated learning programs (ALPs). At CUNY, remedial writing classes will become almost nonexistent by spring 2021. Instead, students have the option to take non-credit-bearing courses through programs such as CUNYStart or Immersion, yet these programs are not connected to academic departments or taught by CUNY faculty; or, students can take coreq model classes offered through the English departments. Though CUNY students will now be placed in writing through multiple measures rather than testing—a major positive—writing colleagues are concerned that CUNY has brokered its promise to students from lower socioeconomic backgrounds by its imperative to "accelerate remediation" (Bernstein 2016, 92).

The Excelsior Scholarship, an initiative sponsored by Governor Cuomo and the New York State Legislature, promises free education to those CUNY students whose family income is under $100,000 and who meet certain academic requirements—one of those is to graduate on time. The solution: students must take more credits—thirty a year—to stay on track.[1] Research conducted by Complete College America (n.d.) has found that students who take thirty credits in their freshmen year are more likely to succeed in school. And, it is argued, remedial writing slows the progress of a student.[2]

I should be clear here that the loss of writing remediation itself isn't particularly distressing to me—some students will no doubt benefit from being mainstreamed into first-year writing. These models for acceleration, by and large, have been shown to be effective when measured for the outcome of efficiency. However—and this is the distressing part—"success" is only being measured through the lens of "efficiency." Measures of persistence and retention, as well as student demographic data for these variables, have not been featured as much in the discourses at CUNY or nationally. Also not taken into consideration are the ways writing curricula can encourage a sense of belonging and persistence in college though an engagement of student experience outside the classroom. There should also be a discussion around the quality of educational experience and the ways writing can foster a sense of self and prepare people to be in community. What is writing education for? Why does it matter?

In effect, CUNY's adoption of this acceleration agenda, titled the CUNY Momentum Initiative, plays into the need for efficiency in higher education and promises to move students through our classrooms and into the workplace. As Nancey Welch and Tony Scott (2016) discuss, these discourses of efficiency to "seek the cheapest, fastest route to degree" are a part of education in the age of austerity (4). They particularly highlight how the Obama administration, through its imposition of the College Scorecard, further emphasized that the solution to fixing higher education enrollment and retention, and thus creating more economic opportunity, wasn't to offer more funding to schools or students but to drown universities and colleges in discourses of *account-ability*; this has led to "changes in curriculum, pedagogy," further "tying the 'value' of a college degree to the speed of its completion and the earnings of its recipient" (10). Colleges and universities are becoming as beholden to government mandates as the secondary level. This changes the game completely, as universities must show students are meeting competencies on a predetermined rubric, which I believe furthers the ideology that education is a vocational enterprise.[3] If we consider the role of writing in this framework, I fear it will be seen as a skill and not as a way to foster learning and inquiry. Furthermore, this fast tracking of students through our doors may lead to the devaluation of other goals that cannot be so easily quantifiable, such as a students' understanding of abstract ideas like social justice or democracy. Saying that a university, or a system of universities, is doing its job because its graduates are graduating quicker and are now socially mobile only favors a particular index of success and may work to devalue or mask others.

I am trying to sort out where I stand on these issues in higher education as a professional in our field who sometimes wears an administrative hat. I don't mind the discourses of social mobility because I do indeed wish economic success for students. However, I'm distressed by these discourses of efficiency and deficiency, these discourses of measurements and certainty rather than invention and inquiry. What I am seeing too is connections between the national movements of efficiency in higher education and some of the scholarship on disciplinarity in rhetoric and composition, and how these further influence first-year-writing (FYW) curriculum design. Embedding disciplinary knowledge into the FYW class, with strategies like writing about writing (WAW), teaching for transfer (TFT), and threshold concepts (TC), has shifted our emphasis in values to align writing studies with professional entry into more advanced university work. One of the things I think is falling quickly by the wayside in higher education, and in writing instruction, is an attention to the material realities of our students and the lives they are leading outside our institutions. Also, if we focus on writing that names what we know, this focus leaves little space for uncertainty, conflict, and becoming. This focus could translate into a diminished emphasis on exploratory writing, personal writing, and writing for and about community and public issues.

Whenever we are discussing the material and place and people's experiences, whenever we are talking about ourselves in community, these discourses fall under the rhetorical concept of the ethos appeal—something I think we desperately need at the center of the discipline of teaching writing. I worry we are becoming too corporatized, or, perhaps more accurately, that we're already there. In the corporate university, there seems to be little value or time for the kind of writing I see as central to college students—reflective narratives and research investigations into local community issues.

When we focus too much on outcomes, too much on certainty and display and presentation in writing, we close the door to an exploratory writing that allows time for invention and inquiry, writing that allows us time to reckon with our contrasting ideas and selves, writing that allows us and our readers to potentially see in a new way and be transformed. This kind of writing is done through a process of slowing down, not speeding up; putting your foot on the break, not the accelerator. Like Jessica Restaino (2019) in her book *Surrender: Feminist Rhetoric and Ethics for Love and Illness*, I'm advocating "for broken methods and contradiction, for creativity and too much feeling, for blurred genres and for doing the work that scares us" (12–13). This kind of writing is hard to assess with a rubric—it's not the writing of logos; rather it centers ethos and pathos. When we write from a perspective of inquiry and openness, we dive into what we don't know, what we can't express, and we must work through that scariness and vulnerability. Writing with inquiry at its center traces where we've been, what we've thought, how we've felt rather than stripping all this away by coming to the point and announcing our arrivals.

I see how these movements toward disciplinary content in FYW are responding to institutional pressures and the need to show student success, and although I sometimes find this scholarship and ideology appealing, I still have come to believe that the momentum initiatives on the local and national level, coupled with the current disciplinary writing movements in rhetoric and composition that place faith in the idea of transfer, erase the material realities of students, especially those in precarious positions, and their experiences outside the university. They also deemphasize the magic of writing, the uncertainties around knowledge, and the emotions we experience as thinkers. I also fear we are looking to solutions proposed in Research 1 contexts and applying them to other institutions with different populations in ways that may be causing harm; for example, just because teaching for transfer (TFT) worked at Florida State University does not mean it will work at my institution in the CUNY system. These movements, in my view, ignore the vine in the air-conditioning vent. I wonder: What are our institutions of higher learning running towards and whom are we leaving behind? How are our first-year writing curriculums and learning outcomes affected by these discourses of momentum? What are the consequences for students, particularly those who attend public colleges and universities?

In class writings and in conversations, the material realities of the students at my CUNY college come to the fore. One student tells me she must move out of her apartment this month because they raised the rent by $100, a price increase she cannot afford working two part-time jobs. Another explains he is the primary caretaker of his younger sister and has trouble getting to class because he needs to see her off to school first. A mother of two debates whether she should continue her undergraduate studies or work full time when faced with her husband's recent layoff. A single mother was forced to move out of her boyfriend's apartment and is now living on her friend's living-room couch. And the stories continue to be told every semester. I remember Rich's question: Do these students "stay on with gritted teeth?" (1980, 61). I think about how the material conditions of my students' lives lead to real conflicts and challenges to learning and to completing their degrees on time. The charts I am being shown about graduation rates do not reflect these stories. These plans for eliminating remedial classes and encouraging our CUNY students to take thirty credits a semester do not account for the realities of our majority working-class, minority, and first-generation student population. Asking students to come in and be ready to concep-tualize a theory around writing practice also seems to ignore where these students are at academically. These policies and disciplinary-writing cur-riculums favor students who can prioritize school as a full-time job and those who already have a history of academic success and preparation.

In this chapter, I hope to show how the "managerial unconscious" of composition (Strickland 2011)—or our intense focus on profes-sionalization and marketing the usefulness of writing for capitalist production—is a detriment to the practice of rhetoric. Furthermore, pedagogical practices that stem from this ideology kowtow to the needs of the corporate university rather than nurturing students as authors of their stories for their future roles in community. Focusing writing cur-riculum on disciplinary knowledge(s) may further alienate working-class writers and their experiences outside the university.

TRANSFORMING ETHOS

Before I unpack some of the contemporary terminology of the field, terminology I feel stems from this rhetoric of professionalization—like *rhetorical awareness, threshold concepts,* and *transfer*—I want to pause here in this section to define and review the importance of ethos to our modern field. When our field loses its specific language—vocabulary and etymology—of rhetorical terms such as *ethos*, we lose our ability to talk about rhetoric and to practice it. The loss of words and their meaning is a detriment to literacy, specifically literacy about place and materiality, as Robert MacFarlane (2016) claims in his book *Landmarks*. His project of recovering words about natural phenomena in glossary form reminds us how terms hold "word magic" and provide the possibility for "re-wonderment" as "language does not just register experience, it produces it. The contours and colours of words are inseparable from the feelings we create in relation to situations, to others and to places" (26). In relation to the field of writing studies, the language loss of ethos—its full range of meaning and its place in the rhetorical tradition—leaves us with a hollow field of study.

How do we inspire rewonderment around literacy practice? I don't much think I have the secret answer to this question; however, I want to believe the content of this book—both theoretical and practical—illuminates another path for the field, one based on rhetoric that has a more ecological approach, considering place and material realities. The book recovers *ethos* as a key term of rhetorical practice, as this appeal is essential in communicating lived experience as a form of knowledge, returning to a kind of narrative epistemology. The sharing of life stories in writing, though a vulnerable undertaking, is one that can lead to subject development and transformation (of both writer and reader) and further allow for the potentiality for identification(s) with others.

Because I worked with Theresa Enos, I would say I am a student of the New Rhetoric. I remember her walking up to the board in seminar, her sequined heals clacking on the linoleum floor, and writing a formula on the board, Rh=Life. She explained to us that this equation meant we had to work from the world, from our lives, to build rhetorical theory. Rhetoric was something beyond the act of persuasion and the truth; it was beyond certainty and display; it was about getting at that ever-elusive idea of what it means to be "present," to represent ourselves with others. I learned from her and other scholars that the study of the word and of actions is a revealing of the "intertwining" relationships among "invention, voice, and ethos." I learned that we are continually creating ourselves and emerging through our discourses. Expressing selves, making lived experience and reflection visible for readers, is important because it is one way to create identification(s). Rhetoric is a way we "construct ourselves among others," so it is imperative that we teach how to use language in ethical ways (Enos 2013, 5).

Ethos, as defined by Enos (1994), is developed through style and voice of the writer; this voice acts as a vehicle for dialogic experience between reader and writer—in this way, ethos is connected to rhetoric's cannon of delivery (189). Using Jim Corder's writing style as case study, she shows us how a writer, through stylistic choice, can work to appeal to a reader and speak with them. She goes on to qualify how ethos can be transforming when "we see, and share, the process of transformation taking place" (186). The process of writing with the ethos appeal in mind can leave the door open to surprise and transformation.

The way writing studies defines *ethos* influences how the term is used in scholarship and teaching. If we only offer a facile definition, such as *ethos* = character of the speaker, if we try to quantify this appeal for fast consumption, the term's usage is compromised and thus loses its power and specificity. Rather, we should pay attention to how scholars have discussed ethos as an author's ability to create inviting discourse through style,[4] as Enos argues, and how others have thought about ethos in relation to democratic discourse, discussing how character development is essential to right thinking and action, as John Duffy, John Gallagher, and Steve Holmes (2018) and others have done.[5] We should also—as I am arguing in this book—pay attention to ethos's connection to habitual behavior and the practice of everyday life with others in places and with things.[6] Transforming ethos is expression of (1) character as lived experience (ethics), (2) character as expressed in text (voice), and (3) character as expressed in the material (place and objects); we've tended to downplay the material aspect of this triad, so this book highlights that the most.

My book project further develops the case for a theory of ethos that is communal, connected explicitly to the material and the geographic.[7] Ethos is not only stylistic or related to development of the voice of the writer, it is also about narrative epistemology, focusing on how our surroundings (material, natural, cultural) construct and inform a living ethos. Nedra Reynolds (2004), in the last chapter of *Geographies of Writing*, titled "Learning How to Dwell," calls for scholars to develop a richer understanding of embodied practices in place and how the classical concept of ethos helps us in this investigation. Reynolds "invites us to revisit the connections between habits and places, between memories and places, between our bodies and the material world" (141). My central argument is that when writers tell of their experiences with objects and places, they create and reveal the ethos appeal, and this type of personal writing is central to identification across difference. Writing self(ves) is a way to transform both yourself and your audience through dialogic experience. This identification between reader and writer is an essential form of communication with ethical possibility. Rhetoric without communion is a hollow shell. Education should be transformative, not just transactional.

For the purpose of this book, I forward a definition of transforming ethos that is connected to physical place, that highlights the community and the cultural practices we perform in places. Scholars and teachers must place emphasis on a rhetoric with ethos at its center, one that frames its practice as a form of dwelling—as a guidebook on how to live (with others). Responding to institutional pressures for successful outcomes, recent trends in composition studies have shifted the definition of rhetoric and its practice by focusing first-year pedagogies on academic preparation and workplace performance. These approaches, however, have led to a rhetoric centered on professionalism rather than on ethics, learning to be and think with others. Rhetoric needs its heart. We must bring forward an embodied and emplaced definition of ethos to inspire a kind of rewonderment around literacy practices.

I THOUGHT I WAS ON THE GRAVY TRAIN

As someone who went through college at public institutions on merit-based awards that covered my tuition, I desired to work to increase access for students in the ways I had experienced it myself. I believed education was a meal ticket, but also something more. I desired to give back. I saw how my journey in higher education was more difficult for me than for some of my peers and yet in many ways so much easier than for others, particularly the students I teach today. This story of access through open admissions at CUNY was the history of the field of rhetoric and composition I clung to, believing in the imperative to educate for social justice and economic uplift. Like Steve Parks (2010), I thought I was riding the gravy train. With my graduate school learning, I saw a legacy of scholars behind me in the writings of Mina Shaughnessy, Sondra Perl, and Ira Shor. As I became a professor and read further into the history of CUNY open admissions, I learned about the activist poets and writers—such as Aijaz Ahmad, Toni Cade Bombara, Barbara Christian, David Henderson, Addison Gayle, June Jordan, Audre Lorde, Raymond Patterson, and Adrienne Rich—who worked for the Search for Education, Elevation and Knowledge (SEEK) program in its early inception and the ways they advocated for a praxis that "created a space for experimental collaboration—a localized, liberatory, pedagocial process" (Reed 2013, 38) that particularly aimed to serve the program's

Black and Latinx populations.[8] The discourse of access today, however, is all about momentum and academic discourse and less about the material realities of class and race consciousness.

The lofty goals and narratives surrounding increased access—at CUNY and elsewhere—sometimes ring false. I'm left feeling a great disjunction between my original intention for signing up for graduate school in writing studies and the realities of my position as a tenure-track writing-faculty member. I think about the ways I have reaped benefits from a system that favors some identities over others. I think about my white, female body[9] as I stand in front of the classroom and in meetings; I think about the power I have as a WPA over nontenured faculty; I think about how I don't offer a form of representation for my students who are nonwhite, which is the majority. I don't think these disjunctions are something I experience singly; rather, this is a collective weight and responsibility many of us in the field shoulder—especially those who have identities with more privilege. To not speak out and admit that privilege is to be complicit in it.

Furthermore, my concerns about discourses of efficiency and transfer don't just apply to the CUNY system but extend into higher education and the administration of writing programs in particular. Writing programs, particularly our curriculum design, cannot help but be influenced by these discourses of efficiency. The focus on the material realities of students and communities that surround our schools is often masked by the need to produce measurable outcomes that point to student success. The numbers and charts I mentioned earlier that support CUNY's thirty-credit freshmen experience are "diverting attention from the contextual variables" (e.g., working-class/minority lives) and thus only focusing on results that can be easily quantified and shown to be successful. These data support the justification of the university's (and by extension, the writing program's) existence to the academic bureaucracy and others, providing "public accountability, strategic planning, and the identification of 'programs of excellence'"—all the things that assist in gaining institutional accreditation and funding of programs and projects (Gallagher 2012, 46).

To cast this story about the privileging of outcomes and efficiency as a new movement in academia is an act of purposeful amnesia. The CUNY open-access legacy, and the scholarship and ideas writers have brought forth about and from this context, runs parallel to what Donna Strickland (2011) in her history of the field describes as the "managerial unconscious" of composition studies. She discusses how the field emerged from a division of labor in English departments. This division was one of actual thought and also ran along gendered lines, as literature was "associated with 'creative,' productive work," and thus the majority of its teachers were men, while composition—a field dominated by women—became "associated with 'mechanical,' reproductive work" (44). This origin of our field, and its attendant second-class nature within English departments, led scholars at the time to be concerned about developing a discourse of conceptual, academic work around writing studies—and this discourse, Strickland details, emerged from the development of our professional organizations (CCCC and WPA), graduate programs in rhetoric and composition, and journals. This move to professionalize composition, however, led to the development of a professional class, WPAs and other PhDs, who manage writing programs and create and enforce curriculum and policy; as Strickland explains, professionalization "enfranchise[d] those involved in the administration of composition more than it has enfranchised the vast majority of teachers of composition," and, I would add, our students (54).

To continue this line of thinking, I want to analyze three particular discursive sites in our modern field that reveal a focus on outcomes and professionalization, and, at the same time, the absence of rhetorical concerns and vocabulary beyond the "rhetorical situation" of transfer in the university. These are the WPA Outcomes Statement (Council of Writing Program Administrators 2019), *Naming What We Know: Threshold Concepts in Writing Studies* (Adler-Kassner and Wardle 2015) and its attendant theory of threshold concepts, and *Writing across Contexts: Transfer, Composition, and Sites of Writing* (Yancey, Robertson, and Taczak 2015) and its attendant curricular application teaching for transfer (TFT). I think a closer analysis of these texts reveals an emphasis in value and a new professionalizing rhetoric for writing studies.

The movement of writing as a skill for professionalization is most evident in the approval and dissemination of the WPA Outcomes Statement and its updated versions. This is the document we point to for justification of our curriculum development and goals, and the one we often use to defend our writing programs from administrative oversight. It is a document by which we guide new scholars in our field and also one we use in the professional development of adjuncts. In other words, it's a foundational text that represents who we are (or want to be); yet I think many of us feel an aversion to its framing and language—particularly in how it defines rhetoric. For example, Peter Elbow (2005) reacted to its first release in "A Friendly Challenge to Push the Outcomes Statement Further," expressing unease with what the statement omits. What is absent is important because it shows what ideas are being suppressed. Elbow responded, "Insofar as the Outcomes Statement treats invention at all (and it mostly doesn't), it treats it more as a matter of finding and responding to material in readings. I see no awareness in the root ability to find thoughts and topics of your own—to write as an initiator and agent rather than as a respondent" (179–80). To cast writers in the role of respondents to other texts (voices) is to limit their potential for self-knowledge and transformation and for using their voices as a way of communicating with others. It also casts rhetorical invention as a process that comes only as a response, not as an act of creation. Furthermore, "Rhetorical Awareness"—as it's outlined in the Outcomes Statement—emphasizes that students must be good practitioners of discourses for academic contexts. Students are cast in the limited role of responders to academic texts. When we look closely at the wording of the WPA Outcomes Statement, for example, we see how rhetoric is framed as a mere set of strategies to employ in writing— "negotiating purpose, audience, context, and conventions" for the purpose of achieving personal advancement in disciplinary fields and eventually in the workplace (Council of Writing Program Administrators 2019). The WPA Outcomes Statement, to this end, puts forward three goals for the acquisition and use of "rhetorical knowledge" in first-year writing: students will learn

- the expectations of readers in their fields
- the main features of genres in their fields
- the main purposes of composing in their fields

The repetition of "in their fields" hits home the idea that the WPA Outcomes Statement casts the applications for the study of rhetoric in only a narrow way—as a tool for professionalization.

The professional movement is not just found in one of the field's defining documents but also in texts we've centered curriculum development on for both graduate students and FYW. For example, the book *Naming What We Know*, which is used in many graduate and undergraduate courses in composition theory and now has a sequel because of its success (2019), frames for audiences a too-neat kind of "consensus" among practitioners as they identify the tenets of the field in digestible mantras, or what the book's authors call "threshold concepts" (Adler-Kassner and Wardle 2015, 5). Though the book includes a few nods to rhetoric as a social practice (Roozen 2015, 17–19), rhetoric as an ethical practice (Duffy 2015, 31), and rhetoric as inherently ideological (Bazerman and Tinberg 2015, 61), it is overall too myopic, framing rhetoric as a *discipline*, not as a way of dwelling, not as a way of life. Its many sections focus on the cognitive and reflective dimensions of writing as far as these can be used to help students become effective writers for the purpose of advancement in their college careers. Also, the second part of the book talks about how to base curricula around the threshold concepts theory, one section particularly on first-year-writing (FYW) curriculum. The book, like the WPA Outcomes Statement, reeks of professionalization.

Writing across Contexts and its spin-off curriculum are part of the movement of professionalization in composition studies at the level of implementing TFT (teaching for transfer) in the FYW curriculum. The reader is placed in an ideological framework that supports the notion that FYW "help[s] students develop writing knowledges and practices that they can draw upon, use, and repurpose for new writing tasks in new settings" (Yancey, Roberts, and Taczak 2015, 2). Students, it is argued, need to learn how to write about writing, how to theorize the process of writing—only then, its authors argue, can students learn to meaningfully transfer writing across contexts. This idea, on the surface, looks to be one that would create writers that respond to the rhetorical situation, but the book and its curriculum only measure writing transfer in a narrow setting, that of future university writing tasks beyond FYW. The fact that this pedagogical approach was born of an R1 institution and has been adopted wholesale across different contexts (like community colleges) is further cause for concern, as the assumption is that all these contexts are magically the same, normalized under the R1 banner of excellence.

Furthermore, *transfer*, as a key term, presupposes that the only writing that "counts" is writing in the university. An "expressivist" class is discussed in the study (Yancey, Roberts, and Taczak 2015, 77–82), and the authors found that the writing done in that class didn't transfer to the other writing done in the university—and, to be honest, I'm not surprised that was the conclusion. My question is, did the writings in this expressivist class transfer to other contexts, to students' lives outside the university? Did the writing and thinking done in that class transform the writers, in that it allowed them to see themselves in a new way and to communicate to others in a new way? We don't know. These questions, though, are important. They are questions of character development because they involve different places and times beyond the walls of the university.

As a professional in the field reviewing this body of scholarship, and as someone who serves an administrative function in my writing program, I feel caught between the overarching narrative of the managerial unconscious and the other alternative, progressive histories of composition I was exposed to as a graduate student (Parks 2011; Rice 2007; Sirc 2002). I remember furiously reading Geoffrey Sirc's (2002) *Composition as a Happening*, inspired by the early practitioners of the discipline of writing studies who, in a way, brought the funk, creating classroom spaces that "allow[ed] the inhabitants a sense of the sublime, making it a space no one wants to leave, a *happening* space" (1). And, in some ways, I think I'm trying to bring the funk to my classroom, but once we all leave that space, well, the rest of the university is pretty ticky-tacky at best. I am torn—many days I believe in my work as an administrator and a writing teacher and that I help students move forward to become better writers and potentially better leaders and critical citizens. There's a feeling of hope for a chance at advancement. But some days, I have this sinking feeling that I am upholding an institutional hierarchy in which I play a role as a middle manager and that I am championing, or at least complicit with, a system that perpetuates racial and class inequality through its focus on success and efficiency. Throughout academia now, higher administrators are calling on writing programs to kowtow to the needs of business rather than to the needs of community. Certainly, I am not the only one who feels a bit jaded in my professional role.

My professional title actually reads: Rosanne, the Accidental WPA. Yet, I read scholarship like the edited collection, *GenAdmin*, and I find some colleagues who "came to see administration as a core component of their professional and intellectual identities, and who pursued or accepted administrative roles before tenure to satisfy personal or professional needs" (Charlton et al. 2011, xi). The WPA generation, of which I am a part given my time in graduate school and my role as an untenured WPA, is the result of the barreling agenda of professionalization in the field. In fact, some graduate programs are producing a type of scholar-teacher that may only have a surface knowledge of the practice of rhetoric and its theories (re: ethos = character); rather, these new scholars are well versed in assessment practices and measures and quantitative methodologies. Yet I argue that the latter form of generating knowledge needs the former type of theoretical frame to inspire critical thinking about the results of such pedagogical and programmatic studies, and both ways of knowing must be emphasized in graduate work in the field. Sometimes I fear we overspecialize on the graduate level and create a false schism between the people who run writing programs and the people who do the rhetorical theorizing. I'm grateful in many ways to be working only with students at the MA level, which affords me distance from preparing grads for an oversaturated and ever-shrinking academic job market; however, I know many of my readers must feel pressure to place PhD graduates. There is a temptation to fast track grad students into WPA roles, but do we really want young colleagues to take up administrative roles before tenure? Is the professionalization agenda even good for our junior colleagues? How does perpetuating a schism between rhetorical theory and WPA administration affect the running of writing programs?

This isn't a critique of WPAs (as I said, I am one—accidental or not). I'm also not saying the role is one that always already attracts scholars who are, or become, obsessed with success and outcomes at all costs. Some of the very best WPAs have worked for the rights of contingent faculty and students. Some WPAs do amazing jobs of creating community and professional-development opportunities for the people they serve. Some WPAs have advocated for expanded curriculums with community concerns at the center. The truth is that many of us in the field serve in administrative roles, so administrative work is not just something we can push aside given the nature of our field. It's something we must approach thoughtfully, using our skills as students of rhetoric and our knowledge of best practices for teaching writing.

I do think the members of *GenAdmin* have, for various reasons—mostly due to institutional pressures—adopted an intense focus on assessment and learning outcomes for writing studies that creates a disciplinary rhetoric centered on professionalism, with *transfer* as its key term. It *is* important, as a WPA, to ensure a curriculum that is more unified across sections to show a "first-year experience" and to justify that what we are doing in FYW will impact students positively as they write in their advanced classes; transfer pedagogies allow us to make these claims, by and large.

When I was first writing this chapter, I was honestly doubtful of the connections I was developing in my head among our emergent "disciplinarity," the emphasis on *GenAdmin*, and the pedagogical movements that advocate for the professionalization of FYW—and by this, I mean FYW as having disciplinary content (i.e., TFT, WAW, and TC). However, the edited collection *Composition, Rhetoric, and Disciplinarity* (Malenczyk et al. 2018) contains several articles that bridge these ideas as well. I particularly want to focus on Leanne Roberts and Kara Taczak's (2018) contribution, "Disciplinarity and First-Year Composition," which argues that we cannot become a full-fledged discipline until the content of our introductory course aligns and has a singular purpose: transfer (198). They argue that the field is "un-disciplined" because we allow for several pedagogical approaches in FYW curricula, and our lack of unity makes our colleagues in other disciplines perceive our discipline as less serious than theirs (192). We are ignoring, they claim, very important and defensible research on transfer and putting "values" over what is proven to be true empirically—that transfer pedagogies work in developing more rhetorically savvy and competent writers.

I see this research as rooting out all the vines, and I'm not going to lie that this sometimes totally appeals to me. Some days, I definitely do not want to be "un-disciplined." There are negative consequences for being "un-disciplined." I want a body of research to defend what I know about good writing and its practice. I want to believe in this idea that we can produce amazing writers who can know how to respond to all the writing situations within our university walls. I want to believe what transfer research is arguing. I want to prescribe to something that tells me to believe in the results of hard research with charts and graphs and a reproducible methodology. But, inevitably, there is a small voice in me that says "Wait." I think this voice is there because of my training in rhetoric, and I don't wish to silence it. "Wait." Wait; is this research really applicable to all learning contexts? Wait; is quantitative work even the best methodology for writing studies? Wait; what are the consequences of adopting a transfer curriculum at my university, and others like mine, where the majority of students are struggling writers from working-class and minority backgrounds? I can't run toward this new paradigm because I'm unsure I want to leave where we've been as a field.

The "old values" Roberts and Taczak (2018) are asking us to put aside, I believe, are those associated with narrative and story, the qualitative side of life that dares to enter the university and our writing and writing process. The "old values," maybe we can call them *exhausted topoi*, are "writing is a practice, is individual in expression, is learned by doing, and is inclusive" (198). I have trouble putting these values to rest, and I hope others in the field feel the same way. The heart of the trouble with transfer pedagogies, to me, is their conception of rhetorical invention—all the possibilities for writing and expression available to students. In the transfer frame, rhetorical invention must be limited by the demands of disciplinary genres; these have important contexts, purposes, and audiences all their own. So, a kind of rhetoric is central to transfer, but rhetoric is only applied in a certain way because the other, older values of rhetoric, like individual expression—maybe we can even extrapolate this term to mean voice or ethos—no longer fit within the transfer-writing schema. More accurately, the voice we want students to learn is that of an expert in their discipline (Yancey 2018, 25), not the voice that speaks about their material conditions or their struggles that derive from class, race, or other identity markers. Transfer does, most certainly, value rhetoric and principles of invention; however, the important thing to hold on to is that transfer is just one terministic screen though which to understand the practice of rhetoric, and it happens to be the one we've decided to hold up as valuable today. Transfer is, as Kathleen Blake Yancey (2018) describes, part of a new turn toward "disciplinarity" (18), and, like most of our "turns" in the field, I think it merits a critique.

To channel a *Queer Eye* reference here, transfer pedagogies are like the French Tuck of men's fashion—super in, super sexy—but are people still going to be dressing that way in fifteen years? Is this the best way for everyone to dress/write? Is the transfer movement going to go the way of, for example, 70s and 80s cognitive talk-aloud protocols?[10] A more lasting staple for writing studies, like a good pair of black pumps, is to show how the connections among ethos, materiality, and place are powerful instruments for writing and its teaching—an anchor that insists on the relational and multimodal aspects of writing and makes prominent its inherent ethical considerations and possibilities.

Our field has cozied up to the idea of transfer, basking in the warm glow of one form of disciplinarity and rhetoric and thus defining a purpose for writing studies in the first-year experience to ourselves and our higher administrations—that purpose being its disciplinary content: writing about writing, proclaiming what we know, and writing as a means to learn in other disciplines. At this point, it is hard not to agree with Ann Larson's (2016) proclamation that "Composition's Dead"—or at least on life support. Larson explains that we have focused on our disciplinarity as a way of advancing an elite group of scholars to tenure-track and tenured positions, but we have not done much in the way of improving working conditions for nontenured faculty (166–69); the next step in the chain of logic, I think, is that we have advanced a form of disciplinarity to the detriment of our students, arguing for a way of teaching writing that casts writing as merely a tool for disciplinary advancement and later professionalization.

We should be careful how we frame and teach rhetoric and writing. As Adrienne Rich (1980) tells us in "Teaching Language in Open Admissions," the ability to use language is one imbued with a certain power; likening it to a weapon, she says language can reflect, criticize, rename, and create (68). Educating students, she claims, releases them into language so they can use it rather than be used by it; however, this liberatory pedagogy hangs on the idea that students are "not simply learning the jargon of an elite, fitting unexceptionably into the status quo, but learning that language can be used as a means of changing reality" (67). Rich, of course, means a reality in which justice is central. As a field, I think we've replaced the idea of language as a way to liberatory justice and instead see disciplinarity as the way to teach a professional rhetoric.[11] If we are indeed teaching a rhetoric of disciplinarity, our rhetoric becomes entrenched in the institutions where we teach, which many in the field have reminded us reflects a privileging of standard English, whiteness, middle classness, maleness.[12] As Carmen Kynard (2013) argues, the context of literacy learning has a "white center," and the field has not done enough to interrogate "deep political and ideological shifts that have left structured inequalities and violence firmly in place" (64). For example, disciplinary rhetorics, and a focus on professional genres in particular, could further the ideology of code-switching, enforcing a kind of segregation that upholds racial superiority, as Vershawn Young (2009) describes in his article, "'Nah, We Straight': An Argument Against Code-Switching" (51), an argument also reiterated by writers in his edited collection on code-meshing (2018). Fast forward a few years since this influential article to his call for papers for the 2019 CCCC. The debate that ensued on WPA-L after the release of the call was an unmasking of the façade of "acceptance" of student home languages.[13] Rather than being inspired by Young's call to performance, many of our field's practitioners quibbled over whether his use of African American Vernacular (AAV) was appropriate for the call—because CFPs, after all, are a particular genre with its own conventions and no deviation in language or creativity need appear. We continue to experience strife on this professional listserv today with the posting of overt hate speech. When I consider the graduate students coming up in our ranks, particularly those students of color, I feel the field must do more to invite them in. When we agree that the work of composition is teaching the disciplinary knowledge of writing for students to transfer to other disciplines, we may be opening a Pandora's Box that spews out white supremacist, violent rhetorics[14] I think many people in the field do want to stand against.

I keep hearing Audre Lorde's (1984) warning that "the master's tools will never dismantle the master's house" (112); though this phrase appears in a speech she delivered to a group of feminists to remind them to be more intersectional in their movement and to include the voices and experiences of women of color, it is a warning that fits all contexts where language and pedagogy are being wielded to maintain normativity. As Lorde explains, it is only with deliberate inclusion and acknowledgment of differences that we can build "a fund of necessary polarities between which our creativity can spark like a dialectic." She continues to explain how this creative energy, the dialectic of difference, values an interdependency that can lead to a state of "power" that shows us "new ways of being in the world" (111), ways not connected to the patriarchy and the master's tools. If our pedagogies work to uphold a disciplinary discourse that reflects back to us whiteness, middle classness, and maleness, we strike down difference and potentially eliminate it. Pedagogies that value difference, such as those based in narrative epistemologies or those with an investment in code-meshing and translingualism, give us some hope for making a world—or at least classrooms—in which we can all flourish.

Considering the narrative about higher education and rhetoric and composition I've sketched out in this chapter, I now look to my own student demographic at the College of Staten Island CUNY. We accept 98 percent of those who apply to our school, and our population is made up of about 53 percent nonwhite students (the citywide average for CUNY is 80 percent), many of whom are the first in their families to attend college. Also, according to data provided by CUNY Central as part of a grant for moving to Open Educational Resources (OER), "Nearly forty percent of CUNY's students come from households with annual incomes of less than $20,000, spending an average of $1,200 per year on books and other supplies is too often an insurmountable barrier to academic success." ("Open Educational Resources"). Given the student demographics of the system where I teach, I become very uneasy championing the discourses of disciplinarity and transfer and the rhetorics of efficiency.

I desire a different way forward, a new rhetoric for writing studies, which, admittedly, might have some of the vestiges of the old rhetoric from the 60s and 70s. These questions underlie my concerns and are the impetus for writing this book: How can we define the work of writing studies to others without relying only on a positivist ideology? Can we think of more creative ways, breaking free of the transfer discourses, to administer writing programs and to develop curriculum? And, even more important, can we think of ways to engage local and material realities in our work? Can we look to the work happening in universities that serve working-class students as models for practice?

A NEW RHETORIC FOR WRITING TEACHERS[15]

I came to the study of rhetoric because it offers a way to talk about language as inherently ideological and because it reveals the ways society is stratified and the inequalities we experience (or don't) because of this.

Theresa used to say often, "I don't mind being retro." Sometimes, we have to step back to move forward. In many ways, I think we skipped over some important movements that could be at the center for writing studies—I hope to show that one of them is the focus on place-based and material writing through the study of ethos.

I see this book as a clarion call for a way to structure composition studies around ethos-constructive practice, ethos as a way to think about curriculum design, to engage student stories and experiences, and to discuss and write about socially and ecologically relevant topics. Similar to Derek Owens (2001) in *Composition and Sustainability*, I am reacting to "faculty members and administrators [who] are obsessed with various assessment mechanisms," and I am earnestly calling for us to "confront our collective failure as educators in building a sustainable culture" (34). Owens's book offers a framework for a curriculum centered on the idea of sustainability, arguing that first-year writing is ripe for developing "sustainably-conscious thinking" (7). His book lays out a way for educators to incorporate place-based writing, work reflections, and analyses of current and future social issues into the composition classroom. He excerpts several student reflections as well that show us the kinds of writing and ideas his students produced throughout the semester. The fact that *sustainability* has not become as much of a key term for our field as *transfer* is all the worse for us.

Nedra Reynolds's (2004) book *Geographies of Writing* also offers our field a way to talk about and write about place, and it sets out a transformative vision for the field as she highlights how the study of place reveals social inequalities. In her last chapter, titled "Learning How to Dwell," she calls for scholars to develop a richer understanding of embodied practices in place. She mentions how the classical concept of ethos helps us in this investigation and "invites us to revisit the connections between habits and places, between memories and places, between our bodies and the material world" (141). This work of being in place and taking note of our relationship to it and to others is an important part of studying rhetoric—ethos is the substance of rhetoric because it provides an ethical center.[16] When we investigate place and the material, we are at a starting point for "understanding difference, otherness, and the politics of exclusion," and this understanding allows our writing to advocate for "critical literacy, social justice, and liberatory education" (3). In general, when students are led to think about their embodied performances in place through considering their own identity markers alongside others who share the space (and their attendant identities), they form a critical literacy and a way for understanding and working through difference. In other words, ethos brings to the fore issues of inequality in our society and can make students aware of how to write about those issues and advocate for themselves and others.

A more recent study of ethos and calls for its return in the discipline are found in the edited collection *Rethinking Ethos: A Feminist Ecological Approach to Rhetoric* (Ryan, Meyers, and Jones 2016). In the introduction, the editors show how ethos is related to ecology and ways of being in the world, separate from the Aristotelian notion of it as only related to "character" or "credibility," and further talk about how studying ethos through a feminist lens brings to light "new ways for interrelationality, materiality, and agency" (viii). The collection is organized by three guiding principles for how a feminist ethos can work as an appeal that allows for interruption (of the dominant discourse/hegemony), advocating for others, and relating to others. I'd like to focus specifically on Stacey Waite's (2016) chapter in the interruption section as she reminds us that ethos isn't about communicating an essential self but rather must focus on "location, positionality, and dwelling" as key terms (72). The relation of ethos to place, time, and being allows us to think about how rhetoric circulates and the ways we can work to interrupt dominant discourses that divide or exclude. In the case of *Transforming Ethos*, I am forwarding the need to begin to disrupt dominant discourses of our field (i.e., transfer) and on a national level (i.e., efficiency). Ethos, like the self, isn't fixed but rather something we construct provisionally with others and with places and things. As Waite reminds us, queering the term *ethos* takes us out of the fixed sense of identity and allows rhetoricians to "as Emily Dickenson might put it, 'dwell in possibility,' to see not only from our own limited positionalities, but to see from elsewhere, to cultivate the ability to imagine elsewhere or otherwise. A queer ethos can interrupt normative ways of looking" (72). This imaginative leap rhetoric can foster, the "being elsewhere or otherwise," is a kind of future-making, one that can be transformative for the speaker and listener—I focus on this idea extensively in chapter 1. Thinking about recovering ethos for the field, I'd like to position the discussion less around an Aristotelian notion of fixity in the binds of credibility and character and more around seeing the formation of the appeal as a relational and multimodal (e.g., encompassing people, places, and things) process that creates ethical possibilities. In this sense, chapter 1 of this book searches for a transformative definition of ethos that can throw open the constraints of space and time to allow for a "being elsewhere and otherwise" and tries to sort out how we can apply this definition to our theory and our pedagogy.

Because this book relies on the idea of dynamic character, of transformative ethos, of tracing ideas rather than announcing certainty and conclusions, I experiment here with form and voice, balancing the theoretical with the personal. In this book, I share parts of my identity and reveal the moments in places and with things I believe are important to its construction. This "interruptive" narrative writing is in the service of the theories about ethos and identification I am working to develop. I am inspired by the writings of Corder; I believe his scholarly oeuvre is timely, as his personal, performative style challenges paradigms of objectivity and cognition, embracing the emotional and the uncanny. Further, Corder theorizes ethos beyond style as he values the personal (his sacred objects and places in West Texas and working-class background); he believes communicating these facets of identity is ethos.

When Theresa introduced me to his work, Corder's voice and writing appealed to me because, moving from Connecticut to Arizona for graduate school, I felt the same kinds of displacement from my own geography, and my Italian American heritage, that he describes in relation to West Texas. I had finished my undergraduate degree, I was twenty-two, and I put this naïve faith in the idea that things would work out for me if I just worked hard enough. I remember a mentor from my undergrad program advising me to go to graduate school far away because, in the logic of the academic job market, "You're more likely to be able to return to the East Coast if you go out to Arizona."

I was the first person in my immediate family to go on to graduate school—and the first woman to earn a BA—so there was definitely this culture shock.[17] I felt I had to assimilate, to learn different ways to present myself, dress, and speak. These lessons weren't easy. For example, I remember before I took my comprehensive orals, one of my professors told me in a private conference that my written exams were spot-on but if I really wanted to do well, if I really wanted to earn distinction, I had to learn to articulate myself without using sentence fillers: "like," "um," "yeah," and "you know." I had to be more assertive in stating my arguments. This was definitely something, he said, that I needed to learn before I went on the job market. People wouldn't "take me seriously" in academia if I kept these speech patterns; patterns that are linguistic markers of my generation, my legible gender, and my ethnic and class identity. I have no resentment, though the experience was painful—he was offering me his insight into how academia functions. I worked on my speech like Eliza frickin' Doolittle, "The rain in Spain stays mainly in the plain," but I definitely wasn't singing, or happy about it. I earned distinction on my comprehensives. I have contradictory feelings about memories like these, about my own advancement in the academy. I think many of us do. My story, given my positionality, does not even skim the surface in representing the ways people of color have felt harmed by the academy.

Academia—by its nature—forces many students to feel displaced, as they are often taught to adjust behaviors, speech patterns, and ways of being. Even more, students sometimes must move to other locations, sometimes hours or days away from those they love, for the promise of the job ahead, if it ever comes, or to be ready to pick up when the job offer(s) arrive. This root shock is heightened when we consider the dimensions of class and race and the way academia demands assimilation into a white, upper-middle-class habitus. Harm is further perpetuated when we consider forms of linguistic oppression that privilege Mainstream American English and create racist attitudes of anti-Blackness (Baker-Bell 2020). Academia is classist and racist, and by extension, so is our writing pedagogy and assessment.[18]

The stakes get higher and higher, the displacement greater, as students advance further into this academic life. Our FYW students certainly experience this shock when they come to us—even more so when they come from working-class and/or minority backgrounds, when they deviate far from that white, upper-middle-class habitus. It's not just about working hard enough—the game is rigged.

By some talent and hard work, by finding a mentor and friend in Theresa, by a lot of luck, and because—I'm sure—of my white ethnic identity, things did work out for me in academia. I ultimately got a tenure-track job on the East Coast; I got to return to my family and friends. That kind of outcome was and is not open to a lot of my peers. I made genuine friendships in graduate school, found a love and appreciation for the Southwest, became more independent, and earned a credential and now a salary that allows me to be middle class. Yet there's also all this lost time, these lost moments with my elderly relatives who died while I was in Arizona or shortly after I returned, and also this loss of an earlier self I ache for even though—you know—I'm not her anymore.

When we deal with loss, with death, and with displacement, we have to keep finding threads to piece ourselves together in a different way in order to move forward. We must write from a subjectivity that is fragmented and unfolding—as Corder did—as I do in these pages ahead. As Restaino (2019) asks in her book *Surrender*, "How might we render our writerly subjectivity in ways that *surrender* its palatability or wholeness?" (132).

When we write from a place of memory, about our places and our people and our things, when we trace the origins of our ethos, we must reckon with a lack of wholeness and a shifting sense of subjectivity and writerly self. As Corder (2004) writes in "Varieties of Ethical Argument," a person with an ideal ethos "lives in a space large enough to house contradictions" (79). Surrendering certainty and adopting a tentative stance are par for the course—this ethos allows for readers to inhabit our worlds, to know our multiple, contradictory selves.

Many desires drive this book—to build a material and place-driven theory of rhetoric and writing that casts ethos in a central role and pushes the field to imagine pedagogies that reflect this vision, to talk about the material conditions in city and state universities and pay attention to the realities of our students' lives, to dive into my memories and offer an example of scholarship that reads as personal, to highlight Corder's contributions to the field, and to memorialize my dear friend and mentor, Theresa. These desires stem from different times in my life, from different places, and are inspired by many people; they make me restless, force me to write, demand and compete for my attention. I write out of all these emotions, love being perhaps the most salient. These desires and emotions make up the very fabric of this book's being, and they also work together to—at once—ravel and unravel, reveal and conceal my character as its author. Though we may wish for a whole and complete text, a whole and complete theory for rhetoric and writing, a whole and complete self, it seems that all we can offer is the desires, the parts of the whole. Certainty about what we are and know is a lie. All we can hope for in rhetoric—as writers and as audiences—is a willingness to work through the imperfection, to labor and love, despite the holes, contradictions, and disparities.

READING AHEAD

The following chapters synthesize philosophy, rhetorical theory, and composition theory to clarify for readers the role of ethos and its potentiality for identification(s) and pedagogy that may illuminate a new way forward for the field. The chapter summaries below offer a more specific vision of the place-based and material applications of the ethos appeal. Furthermore, the book also contributes to our discourses in the field in the following areas: (1) identification, particularly the role ethos plays in that process, (2) multimodal applications of composition and rhetoric through engagement and composition with material objects and places, and (3) personal writing as essential to scholarly and student inquiry.

The structure of the following chapters moves the reader from high rhetorical theory to its application. The middle three chapters rely on a theoretical framing for understanding ethos and its material and geographic applications. In these chapters, the works of theorists such as Roland Barthes's *Camera Lucida: Reflections on Photography* (1980) and Walter Benjamin's *The Arcades Project* (2002) are examined as case studies. The last chapter considers how we can apply place-based curricula in classroom practices and thus analyzes student examples. Though *Transforming Ethos* draws upon key philosophical and rhetorical works, its use of narratives by myself and other writers—as well as its discussion of classroom applications—makes high theory more accessible to readers.

The book intends, by its focus on the term *ethos*, to show how the appeal is essential in communicating lived experience as a form of knowledge and how the sharing of stories, though a vulnerable undertaking, is one that can lead to subject development and transformation, and further to the potentiality for identification(s) with others (readers). This idea should undergird our approach to rhetoric and curriculum design.

Chapter 1, "Finding a Transformative Definition of Ethos," relies less on a contemporary discussion of the discipline and higher education and more on the theoretical approach I think we need to adopt to achieve these expressed goals. The goal to humanize rhetorical practice and pedagogy, I think, requires a leap into the works of theorists that focus on aesthetics and spirituality, almost the reverse of works by extreme pragmatists that focus on datasets and outcomes.

In this chapter, I argue that the ethos appeal is often misunderstood or oversimplified in contemporary usage when scholars and teachers define it solely as character expressed in a text. More important, the definition of ethos has material consequences and cultural connections. When we think about a speaker's character, we must consider their material and geographic realities and experiences as part of the development and emergence of subjectivity. Ethos, when expressed by speakers through material and geographic means, acts as a vehicle that creates an opening for a threshold, or passage, that allows for emergence of the subject among the self, others, and the material world. This chapter describes how *ethos* is a key term in Burkean identification, or the ways in which the outside becomes interior and how subjects relate to each other. In this first chapter, I explain the theoretical foundations for this theory of ethos through contemporary and ancient discourse on the term in relation to time (kairos), space (gathering place), and Martin Heidegger's concept of dwelling, relying on his theories on the call of language.

Chapter 2, "Finding and Collecting: Stories on Material Objects and the Ethos Appeal," explains how the human impulse to find and collect material objects is a practice of rhetoric, particularly related to ethos development. The chapter relies on current scholarship and ancient writings in material studies, linking texts such as Jane Bennett's *Vibrant Matter* (2010) and Lucretius's "De rerun natura" (2008) to forward key principles for materialist rhetoric. The chapter asks teachers and scholars to analyze narratives about material objects, construct their own, and invite students to write on theirs. The chapter uses cases studies from professional materialist writings, such as Benjamin's "Unpacking My Library" (1969), Barthes's *Camera Lucida* (1980), and Corder's *Lost in West Texas* (1988).

Overall, the chapter argues that an engagement with the material—investigating our own and others' affective relationships to it—has the potential to further our understanding of rhetorical ethos and to build relationships between the self and other(s). If we can see the things that matter to others and the reasons they matter, we have a whole new way of identifying with the other. When we understand that inhabiting the world is a process others undertake through their objects, we begin to see others' values and their characters emerge, creating identification(s) through ideological, racial, and other differences. Identification doesn't necessarily require a collapse of difference, or normalization, but rather sees difference as essential to meaningful relationships with others.

Chapter 3, "Movement: The Possibilities of Place and the Ethos Appeal," argues that the continual process of getting into place is inescapably linked to rhetorical ethos. Place-making requires a continual attunement to place (see Thomas Rickert's [2013] *Ambient Rhetoric*), often achieved through movement—movement is further discussed as a rhetorical practice. Reflecting on place allows people to understand and communicate their experiences and their knowledge(s). Additionally, subject/object divisions between the self and the environment/other(s), through this lens of rhetorical place-wandering, are recognized and worked through as a process that allows for potential identification(s).

Throughout the chapter, I propose that rhetoricians and teachers of writing consider place through the Greek term *chôra* rather than *topoi* because the former term places more of an emphasis on subjectivity and emotions; it connects the idea of place to spatiality, discourse, and the body. Rather than describing love of place as *topophilia*, the chapter proposes the term *chôraphilia*, as the latter accounts more for our embodied and emotional connections to places. The chapter furthers the connection people have with place(s) through the concept of the fold, which, I argue, can occur through embodied and mental acts of wandering through places. Writings from the scholars Corder and José Esteban Muñoz are examined as case studies for rhetorical-movement practice and for seeing place as essential to ethos development.

Chapter 4, "For an Affective, Embodied, Place-Based Writing Curriculum: Student Reflections on Gentrifying Neighborhoods in New York City," is a practical application of the theoretical groundwork laid in 2 and 3, as it argues for an affective, embodied, place-based rhetoric in the writing classroom and offers a critique of contemporary seminal texts in rhetoric and writing studies, such as the WPA Outcomes Statement (Council of Writing Program Administrators 2014), *Writing across Contexts* (Yancey, Roberts, and Taczak 2014), and *Naming What We Know* (Adler-Kassner and Wardle 2105), that diminish the role of rhetoric as an ethical practice and shift instructors away from critical pedagogies. Through its case study of a curriculum at a public university in New York City, the chapter argues that place-based writing works to instill what Ira Shor (1999) calls a "critical literacy" in students as they work through their positionality (identity) in the world and recognize this identity in relation to the communities they are a part of or live alongside. In other words, students develop an ecological perspective through place-based writing assignments. Furthermore, cultivating a heightened rhetorical awareness in students of self, place, and audience is one of the most important parts of rhetorical education because it allows them to contribute to public discourse and debates across difference.

In the place-based FYW curriculum outlined in chapter 4, the assignments encouraged students to move from personal reflection to public debate on gentrification and its effects on New York City (e.g., rising rents, displacement, business closures, and so forth). Throughout the semester, students reflected on their own experiences in NYC neighborhoods, engaged perspectives on gentrification through analyzing oral histories, wrote a researched opinion essay on a case study of economic development in Staten Island (the borough where their college is located), and, finally, created a public multimodal argument on gentrification. This place-based writing curriculum, I argue, fostered a sense of local, critical literacy, allowing—as Linda Flower (2008) asserts—for students to speak with, for, and about the community surrounding the college as they composed. In many ways, the curriculum asked students to analyze what Robert Brooke (2015) refers to as "the commonwealth" of New York City, a point of view that supports an ecological interpretation because it sees the city as "a mutually interdependent system of relations," a system that creates "a cultural entity: a network of mutually interdependent cultural systems that work together within a particular political entity" (28). The chapter offers a way we can and should educate students to see the social issues that come out of their places and the ways they can advocate and write about these issues. There is also an appendix with further detail as to the assignments and readings for this FYW course.

If I can venture to summarize the overarching argument in this book, it is that the ethos appeal—at once textual and beyond textual—expands space and time to create the conditions for identifications that both value and recognize diversity. I want to understand how our living—our things, our places—helps us construct and also somehow reflect our process of understanding ourselves. This work is informed by rhetorical theory, particularly seeing ethos as an appeal in classical rhetoric, its revival in the twentieth-century New Rhetoric, and its continued study as habitual and emerging in objects and places in the twenty-first century. I continue to ask how our worlds create our values and ourselves, and then further how we communicate this process to others, and then—even further—how others identity with our ways of being so they feel, as Kenneth Burke describes, "consubstantial with" us. Studying the ethos appeal is consequential to our modern discipline, as it casts rhetoric—and its teaching—as a relational and multimodal (e.g., encompassing people, places, and things) process that creates ethical possibilities.

Thinking back to the vine in the air-conditioning vent, I now admire its ability to thrive. I don't wish to rip it out anymore. If we cut out our students' lives, if we don't offer occasions for writing that engage their experiences in our pedagogies, we're ignoring their contexts and the issues that spring from them. We are not helping them respond to those issues in their own voices. We need these student voices to listen to and learn from in our public discourse, voices that will advocate for and show us a way to a better world.

1

FINDING A TRANSFORMATIVE DEFINITION OF ETHOS

WRITING CAN INSPIRE TRANSFORMATION

Logic is chancy, emotional values vary wildly, and no single rhetoric can bind us all together. Ethos is what there is for us in our speaking, and ethos is never completely achieved. It is always emerging, and it can reach us without offering gratification if it speaks a commodious language, creating a world full of space and time that will hold our diversities.

—Jim W. Corder, "From Rhetoric to Grace: Propositions 55–81 about Rhetoric, Propositions 1–54 and 82 et seq. Being as Yet Unstated; Or, Getting from the Classroom to the World"

Theresa told me that in a private conversation with Corder, he admitted to her that he spent his entire career trying to answer one question: Why do we listen to some voices and not to others?[1] I, too, am pursuing this inquiry. I can't always seem to explain why some voices, some speakers, attract me. I want to know how a sense of intimacy is developed between a speaker and a listener, and how worlds are created and doors are held open by language. I want my students' voices to be taken seriously—I want people to hear about their experiences and to learn from them. I want our public discourse to be transformed by the voices of my students.

This force, or attraction to a speaker, is a form of persuasion, but more. I am reminded of Burke's (1969b) caution on the limitations of the use of *persuasion*, as it is not an accurate term for "describing the ways in which the members of a group promote social cohesion by acting rhetorically upon themselves and one another" (xiv). The word Burke uses to describe this feeling beyond persuasion is "identification." Of course, Burke spends an entire treatise defining what identification means, but one description stands out, particularly when we are referring to the attractiveness of a voice: "Only those voices from without are

DOI: 10.7330/9781646420636.c001

effective which can speak in the language of a voice within" (39). The context in which this passage appears in the book argues that rhetoric is a social—and socializing, and perhaps even moralizing—process. This section also elucidates how a listener becomes acquainted with the "communicative norms" of their society or group and begins to identify with other speakers (39). I understand this passage to mean that the voices of others call out, but only those who can speak in the language of the voice developing within reverberate in our marrow.

Yet Burke (1969b) does not always address how identification comes to be; often, in fact, he uses words such as "transcendence" and "mystical" and "mystery" to describe the process of identification (326). Identification, at many turns, is described as a type of courtship between speaker and audience, and Burke talks about how there is often a collaboration happening here, and additionally how a certain style—of speaking, of being—is needed to involve an audience in this act of ascension (58). What is most concerning here is how identification is seen as a counterpoint and as reliant upon a feeling of division and that extreme cooperation always already implies division at every turn (23). No rhetoric—as Corder asserts in this chapter's epigraph—can unite us all. But when this uniting does happen, how does it happen and why? Why do we listen to some voices and not to others? Rhetorical ethos is essential in processes of identification, and studying ethos gets us ever closer to answering these questions.

I believe ethos is the appeal that truly allows listeners to see the speaker's words as their own, to fold the voice of the outside in. We must pay more attention to the development and expression of the ethos appeal and the power of identification. It is no coincidence that Burke's theories came out of a time of great division, as he was analyzing the rhetoric of Hitler and the dehumanization of the Jews and the resulting world war and its aftermath. We are also living in a time in which divisive rhetoric is reaffirming white supremacist attitudes, and this is very dangerous. Identification can be harmful if it leads to forms of hatred, violence, and genocide. Yet, identification, if it is possible across space and time and difference, can lead to respect and love and an advocacy for justice. If we leave ethos out of schooling, out of the practice of rhetoric, I fear we'll see more insidious kinds of identification in our society.

However, ethos, and its definition, is contentious. James S. Baumlin and Tita French Baumlin (1994) discuss in the introduction of *Ethos: Essays in Rhetorical and Critical Theory* that, even in ancient discourse, ethos was debated because it was seen by some (Plato; Isocrates) as embodied, a part of a person's living, and by others (Aristotle) as constructed, created by words in a speech. The line of division here seems to be a question of whether or not ethos as an appeal is something beyond a textual phenomenon. Is ethos to be seen as an appearance the speaker creates, as Aristotle asserts (xv), or is it to be seen as something that precedes speaking, a possession of the speaker that they bring to light in truthful discourse, as Plato and Isocrates contend (xii)? Of course, these questions are superseded in our contemporary time by the postmodern question of whether or not our words are even our own, whether we are indeed the authors of our discourses and ourselves (Barthes 1977; Foucault 1969).

I don't know whether I can resolve these ancient and contemporary debates in one manuscript, but I do think I can begin to parse some of these lines of inquiry into ethos and to create an image for my reader of what it is and what it can mean and become in our speaking and writing and teaching, and, further, why it contributes to the process of identification. One purpose of this book is to expand the term *ethos* beyond the Aristotelian definition—beyond a constructed appeal through words—and out into a theory of transforming identities. I want to understand identity formation through a rhetorical lens, and I believe one of the ways to do that is to explore the term *ethos* and to see how our living—our things, our places—helps us construct our character. I don't think ethos is something intrinsic to us completely, or related to the idea of a soul, as Plato might suggest. Rather I mean to ask how our worlds create our conceptions of our values and ourselves, and then further ask how we communicate this process to others, and then—even further—ask how others identify with our ways of being so they feel, as Burke describes, "consubstantial with" us. Or, as I'm trying to show here, the ethos appeal—at once textual and beyond textual—expands space and time to create the conditions for identifications that value and recognize diversity and can unite us even in division.

This theory of transformative ethos I am building, though one would call it largely positive, isn't asserting a form of identification that makes us all sing and hold hands in a circle. I don't mean to erase division or to cover over historical oppressions or to deny the righteous anger of those who have experienced injustice. Sometimes identification across difference cannot happen. Perhaps it is because the potentiality for identification across difference and space and time is so rare that so many others and I are attracted to the study of rhetoric, and the term *ethos* in particular. Furthermore, I think the study of ethos can bring forward a rhetorical tradition that values the expression of self with others.

Ethos is a rich term because it is—all at once—in text, in person, in time, in place. Ethos exists in a liminal space between the organism and the outside world, "this 'somewhere between' being none other than a discourse whose language is in part one's own but in equal part a possession of one's time and culture" (Hyde 2004, xxii), and, I would add, one's context, or place. Additionally, ethos is never static, and because it relies on language, it must then always be emerging. As Corder (1989) explains in "Hunting for Ethos," "We make *ethos* from the words we find, but some word finder is leaving us words to find, telling an *ethos* towards us, altering ours in the process" (216). This assertion is deceptively simple. It encapsulates a complex understanding of ethos as both possession and dispossession. It also implies that "finding" ethos is a process we attune ourselves to and actively work toward—very similar to ways of understanding how identities perform themselves. If ethos is always emerging, from where is it emerging? What is the origin of ethos? How does it aid in creating identification(s)?

In this chapter, I contend that *ethos* as a rhetorical term acts as a vehicle that creates an opening for a threshold, or passage, that allows for the speaker to cross through to understand and be with others. Transformation takes place in the writer and listener with the ethos appeal. This, to me, is relevant for any conception of social justice. Crossing the threshold is a metaphorical representation of identification, as the outside becomes interior. In this first chapter, I explain the theoretical foundations for this theory of ethos in relation to time (kairos) and space (gathering place) and Heidegger's concept of language beyond discourse.

One important mantra for this book, perhaps the missing threshold concept in Linda Adler-Kassner and Elizabeth Wardle's *Naming What We Know* (2015), is this: writing can inspire transformation for both the speaker and the listener. In fact, *transformation* is a large part of what Jan Meyer and Ray Land envisioned when they sought to define the theory of threshold concepts. It's the part of their theory I find most salient, and it's the one I think we should hold on to if we wish to forward the idea of threshold concepts as a field. For my purpose, I suppose that if students can learn to understand the ethos appeal and its application for their own speaking, writing, and reading practices, they might develop a "shift in perspective [that] may lead to a transformation of personal identity, a reconstruction of subjectivity" (Meyer and Land 2003, 4). The image of the threshold is a powerful one, whether we are describing a process of learning—moving from a novice to an expert of a discipline—or, more abstractly, describing a process of identification, learning to dwell with others in language. Rhetoric has the potential to transform a speaker and a listener.

Therefore, we need to meditate on how ethos has been defined and used in rhetorical discourse in order to fully understand its application to us today and how the appeal can be transformative. In his book *Ambient Rhetoric* (2013), Thomas Rickert challenges scholars in his first chapter by asking, "How can we augment and rethink ancient and contemporary rhetorical theory?" (11). This book, in part, responds to this call by examining one term—*ethos*—and identifying its threads of meaning in ancient and contemporary conversations in order to augment our understanding of this term and to contribute to rhetorical theory, particularly theories of identification, and to pedagogical practice, particularly to the development of first-year writing curriculums.

DEFINING ETHOS

Aristotle's (1991) definition of rhetoric as an "ability" to identify "the means of persuasion in any given case" (36) and to "argue persuasively on either side of the question" (35) offers us insight into how he understood ethos as a central discursive appeal—a means the rhetor applies through their speech. As Nan Johnson (1984) notes, Aristotle understood rhetoric as a deliberative art that aids in decision-making, and additionally—when seen through this lens—ethos then becomes "a pragmatic strategy which serves practical wisdom in human affairs" (103). Ethos as pragmatic strategy does not involve the speaker's actual embodied and lived character. Aristotle (1991) is careful to distinguish ethos as a "kind of persuasion" that "should be achieved by what the speaker says, not by what people think of his character before he begins to speak" (36). The content of character, then, is created by the speech act and not by lived experience. Character is thus a textual construction.

Although Aristotle (1934) takes great pains in discussing character development in the *Nichomachean Ethics* as a form of *hexis*, or way of being developed by habit (29, 34), he does not discuss how this character-building labor can translate into a form of practice in his treatise *Rhetoric* (1991).[2] Aristotle only claims that rhetoric has the potential for harm and good depending on whether the ability is used "justly," and he warns the student of rhetoric that "one should not persuade what is debased" (34–35). But beyond this one remark, there is very little commentary on the ethics of rhetoric. Thus, the *Rhetoric* suggests ambivalence on the part of Aristotle to discuss the importance of developing the ethical character of the person who is speaking. Remember, character (ethos) in the *Rhetoric* is discussed only as a textual appeal, a pragmatic strategy. Ethos is certainly valued in the Aristotelian system, but it may be argued that it is seen as less important than logical proofs and arguments based on probability (the enthymeme), as Aristotle writes, "There are three reasons why speakers themselves are persuasive; for there are three things we trust other than logical demonstrations. These are practical wisdom [*phronesis*] and virtue [*arete*] and good will [*eunoia*]" (121). This triad of *phronesis, arête,* and *eunoia* was important to Aristotle, but these ideas are discussed in the treatise much less than are logical proofs. He does not theorize ethos in the *Rhetoric* in terms of its relation to the formation of ethical speakers or how it can foster better, more cooperative communication practices—practices that indeed lead to rhetorical identification.

Both Plato and Isocrates were concerned with developing the character of the speaker in rhetoric, seeing ethos as an appeal beyond a practical strategy. Rhetoric would be a hollow and false art if it did not—at its center—account for the speaker's character prior to the act of speaking. For speaking should reveal a truth of character, not create character or a persona for the rhetor. Isocrates writes in the *Antidosis* that "the man [*sic*] who wishes to persuade people will not be negligent as to the matter of character; no, on the contrary, he will apply himself above all to establish a most honorable name among his fellow-citizens" (quoted in Baumlin and Baumlin 1994, xiv). Character is outside the speech act here—it is not a strategy only, but rather a prerequisite to effective persuasion. Plato (1913) adds his view in his dialogue *Phaedrus*, where he critiques the Sophists especially for their relative stance toward truth and adds that the study of rhetoric should be an enterprise that seeks to heal and develop the soul, as medicine works on the body. A rhetorician in Plato's estimation must "become a lover of wisdom or of beauty, or who will be cultivated in the arts and prone to erotic love" (113). These descriptions of the character of the rhetor show how Plato wanted to see rhetoric as an art that directed "the soul by means of speech" (127). Rhetoric, then, should not be seen wholly as connected with persuasion toward one side; it has a deeper implication of fostering a just outlook in its speaker, constantly reminding them of the good and the need to speak for the good. Ethos, then, is about revealing the character of the speaker and not about constructing it for the audience.

There is a sense of conflict in the ancient perspectives on ethos—whether character exists as something constructed or revealed, something intrinsic to the soul or wholly of the text. Ethos, I suggest, should be seen as three pronged: (1) character as lived experience, (2) character as expressed in text, and (3) character as expressed in the material (place and objects). All these threads of ethos matter and play an important role in rhetoric, particularly in identification. Michael Halloran (1982), in a piece on rhetorical ethos, identifies the appeal's potential to exist beyond an Aristotelian notion of ethos as textual. He connects ethos to cultural knowledge, as the speaker is "a kind of living embodiment of [their] heritage" (332); this definition explicitly links the ethos appeal to place and time and living. Ethos, then, is a part of a tradition in which rhetoric is seen not only as an ability but as a way of life, of being—rhetoric is not only discourse but tied to the world where we feel, move, and interact with people, places, and things. Ethos, then, must be a part of a rhetoric that is viewed both as ontological and as epistemic—a theory of rhetoric that works to understand the creation of worlds where people can live together.

As Halloran (1982) further explains, ethos is what we have to offer another in our world of increasing "fragmentation and isolation;" ethos is the appeal the speaker uses to "articulates his [their] own world, the degree to which he [they are] . . . willing and able to make his [their] world open to the other, and thus to the possibility of rupture" (332, 339). Ethos, as Halloran and others describe, is a vehicle for world sharing, one that allows the audience to take a glimpse into that speaker's living space and time. The idea of a rupture in the distance between the subject and object in this description is one I wish to return to later in this chapter; however, I use a different metaphor for this moment, instead describing the ethos appeal as creating an open and inviting threshold, or passage, into the world of the speaker. Rhetoric is no longer an abstraction whereby speakers gain assent to an idea—it is about creating a shared reality;[3] as Halloran notes, "If . . . rhetoric is the means whereby the self and its world are constituted, *ethos* is the measure of one's willingness to risk one's self and world by a rigorous and open articulation of them in the presence of the other" (339). The ethos appeal is not only a pragmatic strategy but also a point for the genuine emergence of selves. Halloran is right to align the ethos appeal with the idea of a risk; to me it is the only appeal that reveals to others the lives we lead and our beliefs. Emerging in the presence of another is always a risk—even more so when the act is happening across a difference in opinion or identity marker (race, class, gender, sexuality, etc.).

Ethos is not just a construction of character; it is representative of our living space and time. As Halloran (1982) notes, ethos—in ancient Greek thought—was seen as a way for creating a gathering place for community. This broad understanding of the term means that any character or credibility shown through the ethos appeal emerges "from a way of life that is itself already embedded within locations, communities, societies, and environments and hence 'spoken' by them even as we create and transform them" (Rickert 2013, 222). This returns us to the origin of ethos. If it is a gathering place, it must be something dependent upon our dwelling.[4] The culture, the landscape, our objects, all must be involved in the emergence (and origin) of ethos. Michael Hyde (2004) suggests, in his edited collection *The Ethos of Rhetoric*, that a theory of rhetoric must have ethos at its core—that it is indeed the most essential appeal because of its relation to virtue, moral character, and ethics.[5] Rhetoric, then, must be a project of world revealing; as Rickert (2013) notes, speakers are responding to others' perspectives and putting forth their own "through affective, symbolic, and material means, so as to (at least potentially) reattune or otherwise transform how others inhabit the world to an extent that it [rhetoric] calls for some action" (162). The idea of self/other/world transformation is important here, as it suggests rhetoric plays a role in mutual cooperation and building of the future. Only the appeal that speaks from the perspective of world-dwelling, ethos, can be evoked for this kind of transformative action. The future is not just imagined as future success in the workplace but a future where community and the good are at the forefront.

Ethos as rhetorical appeal, then, allows speakers and listeners to "transform space and time into 'dwelling places' (ethos; pl. ethea) where people can deliberate about and 'know together' (con-scientia) some matter of interest. Such dwelling places define the grounds, the abodes or habits, where a person's ethics and moral character take form and develop" (Hyde 2004, xiii). The transformative potential of ethos—its ability to hold open space and time to create a world where identifications can occur—is a subject that needs further attention, particularly more concrete descriptions as to how this can happen, which I attempt to explain in the next section.

TRANSFORMATIVE ETHOS IN SPACE/TIME

If one wants to picture ethos as a transformative appeal that works to create rhetorical identification, it is essential to imagine the appeal as having a generative, inventive quality—ethos is, indeed, always emerging and dynamic, just as rhetoric is always reliant on variables such as context, audience, and speaker for its meanings.

The constructive and revealing properties of the ethos appeal also cannot be separated from a prophetic conception. Although I was somewhat hard on Burke for his characterization of identification as "mystical," I don't think one can divorce the ethos appeal completely from a feeling of anticipation and attunement on behalf of the audience and a show of goodwill, experience, and world-revealing on behalf of the speaker. Ethos is most affective when the audience has a sense of preparedness and openness to receive a message, when they feel they are being invited into a created world and are then called to enter into that world and to respond. On the other side, ethos is most effective when it is carefully developed and cultivated in the speaker, when the speaker owns their experience and risks giving it to others.

A complex theory of rhetoric must acknowledge the full meaning and significance of the ethos appeal—one that accounts for ethos as something that reveals a process of living and world-building. As Hyde (2004) argues, rhetoric is "a 'hermeneutic' and 'situated' practice, an art that informs and is informed by the way human beings dwell on earth" (xxii). This conception of rhetoric as a part of dwelling is one that is both reflective and generative in the sense that it both reveals a world and creates a world. This is why Corder describes ethos as emerging, for both dwelling and character development are continual processes. We're continually homemaking, as Rickert (2013) notes: "Dwelling is an ongoing and never stilled process of attunement, disclosure, and building" (248). Attunement is the way we try to understand and receive the messages from the world around us, disclosure is our continual search for the right words and symbols to share our world with others, and building is the continual effort to make a better world with others, to flourish with others.

"Generative," the word Corder uses as a qualifier in his discussions of ethos, relates to the idea of ethos as emerging. Corder (2004) defines generative ethos as always being "in the process of making itself and of liberating hearers to make themselves. In this form of ethos there is always more coming. It is never over, never wholly fenced into the past. It is a speaking out from history into history" (30). Corder's use of the action word "liberating" shows the transformative potential he places on this form of ethos. There is also a sense of how time is transcended through generative ethos at the end of this passage, something I discuss further in this chapter in a section on the Greek term *kairos.* Another important aspect of the idea of generative ethos is its ability to create an opening to the speaker's world; this opening is created through language, but beyond language as we traditionally think of it. Language is often associated with the idea of closure, what is said is said. But generative ethos relies on the idea of making and invention, so language too must not be thought of as a closed system; rather we must see language as a vehicle that "shove[s] back the restraints of closure, like a commodious universe, to stretch words out beyond our private universe" (189). In this way, the writer is consciously thinking about their relation and presence with the audience; they are working to emerge to the audience (in and through language) as a voice, one the audience needs to be in dialogue with rather than ignoring or talking over it. This creation of ethos is a labor on behalf of the author, and it also asserts that their character (world-creating, life experience) can be found in their texts. The writer/author/artist emerges as a presence.

This work in the work, this expression of generative ethos in writing and art and other texts, is the key component of what I am calling *transformative ethos* and also at the heart of a theory on rhetorical identification. I am particularly interested in Martin Heidegger's (2008) understanding of art as disclosure of truth, that art creates an opening into a world that invites its audience to participate in it and dialogue with it, perhaps to even feel consubstantial with it. The text communicates a way of being, a type of opening up to a world, a "disconcealing" of that world so that "in the art work, the truth of what is has set itself to work" (38). Heidegger further describes how this world-making in the text is about space, the creation of space in the work for the audience: "A work, being a work, makes space for that spaciousness. 'To make space for' means here especially to liberate that Open and to establish it in its structure. . . . The work as work sets up a world. The work holds open the Open of the world" (44). Again, notice the use of the word "liberate" as a verb for how a generative ethos works in a text; liberation here is connected with invention and creation of a world, and similar to Corder's view, it is about the invitation it extends to an audience to make themselves a part of that world of the text.

These assertions about the work of art as opening, as inviting, still seem too abstract. I want my readers to imagine their interactions in the past with a speech or a painting or a poem or a play. Have you ever felt invited into the world of that text, into the world of a speaker? When I think about my favorite play, Eugene O'Neill's *Long Day's Journey into Night* (2002), I can see the oppressive fog rolling in—the thick kind that develops at night near the shore, the kind that makes you unable to see your hands as you extend them in front of you. I can hear the foghorn in the distance. I feel the sense of being trapped in that house with those characters and their traumas and their addictions. Edmund's soliloquy in act 2, his description of being a hand on a sea ship, a moment of freedom and escape from his family life, moves me to tears. I am in that world, with them, I dwell there—it's a difficult form of identification but a form nonetheless. Some of my identifications with texts and worlds are less difficult, even pleasurable. Heidegger (2008) describes his own affinity with van Gogh's painting of a pair of shoes, black work boots. He says that the "painting [speaks]" and that when we are near the work of art, we feel as if we "[are] suddenly somewhere else than we usually tend to be" (35). That moment of being somewhere else—that feeling—is one I can't seem to describe fully, but it's a transformative experience. It's entering into a reality not your own. Would I be the same person if I had not read *Long Day's Journey Into Night?* Would Heidegger have been the same if he had not interacted with the van Gogh painting? These openings to another world, and entering that world even for a while, are connected to some form of living beyond our own space and time. These experiences must be connected to ethos development, the transformative kind I am trying to sketch out here in this chapter. Heidegger labels this experience of identification a form of truth, one that deals with the "unconcealedness of being," or what the Greeks called *aletheia*; it is a type of work in the work of art that offers "a disclosure of a particular being, disclosing what and how it is" (35). This being (from the work) must tell us something about our own being in our reality, especially if we feel consubstantial with it.

To be someone who creates inviting language or images and to also be someone affected by the world of the text and the words of others is to be, in some way, connected to the other worldly—perhaps one could say there is a relationship between identification and the divine. Not in the sense that the artist or writer or audience is disconnected from the earth, from the here and now, but rather that identification requires an act of looking up and out. Heidegger, in his later work, forwards the idea that poetry tells us something about our being, that it helps us map out and understand the dimensions of our presence in the world. It is important to note that poetry is not exclusively to be thought of as lines and stanzas but rather in an expanded sense to include its root in the Greek term *poesis*, "to make." *Poetry* is a verb because it involves, as Heidegger asserts, a form of measure-taking, not in the sense of a scientific process, but rather "measure-taking gauges the between, which brings the two, heaven and earth, to one another. This measure-taking has its own *metron*, and thus its own metric." Poets, in other words, bridge the real and the material to the beyond, to other worlds—and Heidegger would go as far as to say—to the divine. This measure-taking reveals to the poet "the breadth of his [their] being" (Heidegger 2013b, 219).

Poets, those who make, see beyond what is here and now; they show us a "sense of the trace of the fugitive gods"; they "stay on the gods' tracks, and so trace for their kindred mortals the way toward the turning" (Heidegger 2013c, 92). This description is mythic, certainly, and it reminds us of how always operating in the real can limit our potential for something other—for seeing something other, being something other, creating something other. The real can be routine or violent or oppressive. It can suffocate. Yet, there is a message here about how turning out yonder helps us to turn back and to continue to build in the here and now. When humans understand being in relation to others and to existence and to the beyond (however one conceives of that), they can sing the song of being, or "be present in what is present itself" (135). Being present ties us to reality and allows us to move and make ethical decisions in that reality. Words and making can plot out a future, and the poet can "sing the healing whole in the midst of the unholy" (137). Being present to local realities is what our curriculums need to foster rather than being mindful of the goal of university success and eventual career preparedness. No one is going to heal the world because they wrote a theory of writing in their FYW class, but assignments that actually ask students to look yonder to the issues in their communities might inspire them to engage in activism further down the line.

These descriptions, I admit, are somewhat highfalutin'. Certainly the world isn't always brokenness, and additionally, poetry, or the act of making, will not always heal or fix. And, one can see how Heidegger is entrenched in a discourse reliant upon a spirituality that searches for grace in the aesthetic as a way to access the divine. This poetic theory is not without a theological grounding, and there is no way to escape that foundation. And, I'm sure, a reader can critique this orientation toward being for this reason. Tarrying in the prophetic is not the typical discourse of the academy. But, I draw upon Heidegger because his descriptions of poetic and artistic experience model a process of world-making that investigates how we build better relations with each other and our environment. Dwelling, he claims, is reliant on the poetic. Those of us who study rhetoric are often attempting to explain how the word grounds us and shapes our reality. Heidegger makes explicit for us how the poetic is a prerequisite for building, not only in the sense of growing things and raising buildings but also through finding meaning in our existence with each other, creating sustainable structures of dwelling (and being) that can house our diversities—poetics is one way of creating identifications (Heidegger 2013b, 225).

Although Corder never explicitly cites Heidegger, I see some similarities in his writings on generative ethos because he too discusses how language is central to a process of world-making and identification. I am reminded of his essay "From Rhetoric to Grace" (1984) especially because in this essay he creates propositions for rhetoric to show readers how its study can help us understand our identity, or how we come to know ourselves and be in the world. Coincidentally, Corder talks about this process of world-making—as Heidegger does—in a spiritual way, explaining that rhetoric is a process of reaching toward grace. Corder's spiritual grounding is explicitly in a Judeo-Christian framework as he understands grace to be a state of total love and forgiveness, something that cannot be attained by human means but rather must be sought after, again and again, by turning toward all of creation, the source of all language.

For example, at the end of the article, Corder (1984) creates a metaphor for the rhetorical term *invention*: "Invention is God, the site and origin of Grace" (27). He describes invention as a miracle, a way to unbind time in order to access the past, present, and future of our experience and speaking. He says invention is how we find words to describe our living experience. Invention is every possibility for speaking. It is the richness of creation. We cannot even tap the whole of the inventive world. In some ways, we can think of invention as essential to making and poetics. Corder believed spoken and written language are inadequate mediums for expressing all our inventions because we are forced to choose what to say; we create a structure through our speaking or writing, and thus we leave out other possibilities. For we cannot say two words at once. So we must order and structure our inventions, sectioning off a part of reality to present to a listener; "Possibilities," says Corder, "are greater than actualities" (55). Structures create meaning through their order. Corder sees the structuring of language as related to style, and he sees stylistic choices as related to personal identity and to the habits we learn in our living. Style is an enabling capacity, Corder explains—it helps us move in the world. And in our writing, it is how we communicate our being to others. Corder believes rhetoric to be a generative process as we cycle back from invention to structure and style, from opening to the richness of creation to closing through speech and language. He sees this process as an ability to bring us closer to self-awareness and to developing an ethos that has our lived experience behind it. Corder saw ethos as habit, and he believed the habit of expression through speech and writing could lead us to understand more of invention. Striving for grace is a process of recognizing the limitations of closed speech and turning again toward the openness of a new invention.

It is important to note, too, how these theories of world-creation through the work—poetic, artistic, rhetorical—are reliant on a particular way of understanding time beyond a linear conception. Corder's idea of "unbinding time" as part of the act of invention, for example, reminds us of how engagement with language can disrupt the present time in which we operate. Heidegger additionally describes his theory of the unconcealedness of beings as "never a merely existent state, but a happening," which further shows how time, or more accurately timing, plays a role in how we attune ourselves to the world and the works we encounter in it (2008, 52). Rhetorical identifications, as I want to discuss and understand them, are predicated on the concept of time as *kairos*. Many scholars have written on the multiple meanings of this term (Hawhee 2004; Kinneavy 1979; Miller 2011). In sum, kairos has been characterized as relating to timeliness, or seizing the opportune or critical moment; practicing due measure, discretion, and appropriateness; experiencing moments of insight or connection, and additionally being able to harmonize opposite perspectives and select among alternatives; and finally, knowing when to speak and when to be silent.

When I consider these definitions, and the ways they apply to how we relate to the world and each other, I see kairos as offering a framework for understanding ways of (1) being, (2) seeing, (3) experiencing, (4) knowing, and (5) creating. Kairos is concerned with both ontology and epistemology because it orients us to our own being and reveals to us how we come to know the world and others. Being sensitive to timing allows us to move in the world in more meaningful, and, hopefully, ethical ways. It is important to understand our existence as a part of temporality, or how our "existing orientations, as dispositions that have already been formed in us, . . . must always already be at work in our Being, in our potentiality for Being, and in such a way as to find their appropriate attunement, their fitting measure, in a particular system of action" (McNeill 2006, 90). When I consider this idea of "orientations" or "attunement," I can't help but feel there is also something lurking here about an emerging ethos essential for rhetorical identification. Does ethos not rely on a past stance, a present happening, and a future potentiality? Even this last question implies a linearity in time that may not stand, for kairos suggests a disruption in that linearity, as we can experience the future of the past, the present-past, the future of the present. One need only recall the disorientation of a moment of déjà vu to know how skips in linear time are disruptive to our normal routine.

Thus, kairos is beyond the schema and definitions presented earlier for understanding time; it is largely—I think—a feeling. Kairos strikes us with force, it is a "transitory moment" that opens a passage for us beyond linear time, one in which "the passage of this time of the present comes from the future to go toward the past, toward the going of the gone" (Derrida 1996, 28) or in which "Dasein's futural existence depends on its having been: the future is a carrying back to a time to which one has always already come" (Wyschogrod 1998, 158). However one describes time disruption, it has large implications for how we understand our existence in relation to each other and our environments. Our lives—our histories—can no longer be measured or told on a straight continuum but rather must be like, as Benjamin suggests, a constellation of flashing moments (Sieburth 1989, 24). How do we identify a kairotic experience; how does a flashing moment feel? Kairotic moments loom large in our memory; to me they are the moments we recall to tell the story of our identity; they are defining.

One metaphor I have entertained in understanding kairos is through the concept of time in the Christian liturgical calendar: kairos is the meaningful break of Lent in a chronos sequence of Ordinary Time. Lent is a forty-day time of reflection on the sacrifice of Jesus, practiced through dedicated prayer and fasting. Lent is often a time for repentance and renewal—it is a transformative pause, like a caterpillar spinning in its chrysalis. Kairos is this same type of pausing of the everydayness of life—it is a time out of time, one in which reflection can be practiced. Kairotic moments may even be a necessity it terms of moving forward in our lives, in choosing the right course of action and response.

Kairos reminds us of how time flows through and around us—how the past, present, and future intersect to affect us. Additionally, we experience a type of displacement in kairotic moments because we *feel* time as its own entity—both connected and yet separate from us. In other words, kairos is not just to be thought of as a moment a person seizes; rather we should also see kairos as something at once connected to us and yet also beyond us in our engagements with other people, places, and things (Rickert 2013, 83). Kairos is not necessarily an act of will—is time ever something we solely have control over? Surely, kairos is about attuning oneself to time, and there is an element within its meanings that speaks to a person's ability to respond and to act accordingly. Yet I can't also help but feel, as Rickert (2013) does, that "the kairos does what it does to us, with us, and alongside us" (90). There is a dialectical relationship here as we imagine kairos as a part of both the interior and the exterior. Kairos is then to be thought of as a happening that leaves an impression upon us—a *feeling*, one that may be disorienting, one that may give us a new perspective, certainly one that prepares us to move forward and to take action.

There is a type of transport beyond the here and now in the kairotic moment. Perhaps the feelings that accompany a kairotic moment, particularly disorientation, are linked to our relationship with space. By this I mean to consider how kairos is not only a concept of time and timing but a spatial concept as well. Can kairos also be material, or perhaps inspired by the conditions brought about by the material? Time and space are not separate; they are dependent, even isomorphic (Wyschogrod 1998, 148). And when we consider rhetorical ethos, and even more broadly rhetorical identifications—and the conditions that create those identifications—we operate in a paradigm in which there is an expansion in space and time, space/time. For world-making to occur, the normal flow—the ordinary time—of space/time must be somehow disrupted. These ruptures in space/time that allow for rhetorical identifications are created through language that is open and inviting, a key facet of transformative ethos. The following section further explores how we may consider language's participation in acts of identification.

THE CALL OF LANGUAGE

Burke (1993) reminds us "language is an abbreviation radically" (45). Indeed, we can certainly think on the ways written and spoken discourse truncates our thinking. Language, as understood in a traditional sense, forces a closure through its structure and, at times, its inability to transcend its monovocal nature (particularly in its written forms).

Barthes (1980) additionally discusses how, as a writer, he felt uneasy because he was "torn between two languages, one expressive, the other critical," and the critical language—from various academic disciplines, like sociology and semiology—felt reductive rather than freeing. He writes, "For each time, having resorted to any such [academic] language to whatever degree, each time I felt it hardening and thereby tending to reduction and reprimand, I would gently leave it and seek elsewhere: I began to speak differently" (8). This dilemma addresses how authority in language can prevent possibilities for what can be said. Academic language is certainly a form of abbreviation. Barthes recognized the limitations of language and was looking for ways to circumvent the abbreviation.

Corder (2004) also often muses on this problem of abbreviation, including a version of this line in many of his manuscripts: "Language comes out of us a word at a time; we cannot say everything at once" (51). This unique problem of language makes us particularly careful and reflective about the words we do choose to communicate our ideas. Additionally, writing (speaking) can be an arduous process, particularly if a person wants their audience to identify with an experience or a particular issue. Language is one medium we have for creating identifications, and yet it is so woefully imperfect. How can we communicate our character, insight, and experiences to each other? Corder's answer to this is a process of repetition—speak to speak again:

> We have to open ourselves to experience and insight and evidence and say what we can, but what we say will invariably be incomplete. . . . Language forces a closure. . . . To be sure, having spoken—or written—we can open ourselves again to experience and insight and evidence and try to say it all again. But what will come out will be fiction. We cannot make all that *was* into *is*. Whatever we can get into our heads we will make into narrative that will be our truth until we learn again. (51)

The problem of the abbreviation of language is somewhat alleviated through the idea of circling back to see what was left out. As mentioned previously, turning back toward all of creation and language potentiality moves us forward to explore placing our thoughts into new structures. The pieces keep revealing themselves through this process of incremental repetition and addition. In the latter part of the passage above, Corder (2004) additionally speaks to the problem of authority in our statements. When I further consider the ethos appeal as one reliant on showing credibility, it is hard to believe we can reach such authority in our speaking and writing. We cannot capture all our living space and time for another. If authority or finality is to be abandoned, in other words, "if we can't be good, or thorough, or authoritative, then what enabling capacities [for identification] can we hope for?" (53).

Perhaps one answer is to abandon the concept of authority in language altogether. If the language we encounter—in speech and in writing—is abbreviated, is only "the residue of a speaking long past" (Heidegger 2013a, 192), its authoritativeness seems questionable. We must move forward, I think, with a sense of language as contingent and contextual, just as we understand our self(ves). But do we also abandon the author as we move away from authority? What of rhetorical ethos, an appeal traditionally understood as authorizing speaker credibility? Some scholars absolutely agree with the displacement of the author, others say no; I agree with the latter. Further, I think the question leads us to consider a way to move forward and to shift our perspective on language and its uses. Stepping away from authority, from codified ways of speaking, can open up doors for rhetorical identification. We must then adopt a provisional stance in our speaking and writing.[6]

It is important to note that the possibilities of language exceed actualities, in whatever form of spoken or written discourse. Heidegger (2013a) is on to something when he notes that "speaking does not cease in what is spoken" (191). Further, we should shift our understanding of language away from the actual and more toward the possible—in other words, spoken and written expressions are only one form of language, but language as a concept is indeed much larger. Language is something that calls us to respond. We must shift into a more abstract understanding of language to fully appreciate its force in our communication practices and in rhetorical identifications. Language is not rational in this conception; it is not a system of subjects, verbs, and objects. The abstraction, Heidegger (2013a) explains, can be thought of through the passage in the Gospel of St. John: "In the beginning the Word was with God. The attempt is made not only to free the question of origin [of language] from the fetters of a rational-logical explanation, but also to set aside the limits of a merely logical description of language" (191). We all know language is logical, and yet as practitioners of language, we should also know it is not—language is an appeal, expressive and individual, and yet it is also related to a larger network in which we find ourselves situated. Language is creation, and the Gospel of St. John aligns this inventive capacity with the figure of the Godhead. To speak of language is, at once, to deal with all of its meanings, literal and abstract.

Language, Heidegger (2013a) argues, is what calls us into being—allowing us to relate to the other (person, place, or thing) in space/time and thus to also know ourselves, "our own gathering into the appropriation" (188). One metaphor many scholars cite is his description of language as "the house of Being"; he writes, "The nature of language does not exhaust itself in signifying nor is it merely something that has the character of sign or cipher. It is because language is the house of Being, that we reach what is by constantly going through this house" (2013c, 129). In other words, language is not just related to the systems of sign and signifier—these are the abbreviated forms of language, the forms we see as part of addressing each other, language that is contextual—but rather language is all that is unsaid, is said, has been said, will be said, and this timeless quality of language imbues it with an ontological function. The house of Being is the larger picture of language, and spoken and written language is an enabling capacity to explore the whole of the house; language is prior to human speech. Rickert (2013), who uses Heidegger's work as a theoretical frame in his own analysis on ambience and its implications for rhetorical practice, coins the word "rhetoricity" to refer to this view of language as house of Being. Rhetoricity implies

that there is "always ongoing disclosure of the world shifting our manner of being in that world so as to call for some response or action"
(xii). *Rhetoricity*, or whatever term one assigns to this act of disclosure
of the world, is the bedrock of rhetorical identification. The expansion
of space/time cannot happen unless language exists as both rhetoricity
and rhetoric; or put another way, identification is reliant on rhetoric,
and rhetoric is reliant on language, spoken and written, and language
is reliant on the house of Being, which is the source of creation. Of
course, this last explanation is reductive and sets up a chain of reasoning that perhaps I do not intend. For just as worlds disclose, we must
also be receptive to the call of their disclosure, and this receptivity is a
kind of open stance that is actively practiced. This attunement "indicates
one's disposition in the world, how one finds oneself embedded in a
situation," Rickert claims, allowing us to see the activity of rhetorical
identification as dialectical rather than merely an agent being acted on
or agency being exerted over a situation (9).

These situations to which one is called by language are invitations
to worlds that can be both real and imagined, or some combination of
the two. Identification, as I asserted earlier, requires imaginative leaps
in space/time. As philosopher Ernesto Grassi (1994) asserts, "Rhetorical
speech is an imaginative language which brings ideas before our eyes"
(92). And thus language—written and spoken—derives from language—
the house of Being—to allow for a "calling [that] calls into itself
and therefore always here and there—here into presence, there into
absence" (Heidegger 2013a, 196). This miraculous act of language that
brings what is only idea into presence for listeners is what underlies rhetorical identification. Heidegger speaks to how language can bridge the
"dif-ference" in space/time through its calling and gathering function.
An imaginative leap, he explains, is created through the reading of a
poem by Georg Trakl called "A Winter's Evening": "Snowfall and tolling
of the vesper bell are spoken to us here and now in the poem. They are
present in the call. Yet they in no way fall among the things present here
and now in this lecture hall. Which presence is higher, that of these present things or the presence of what is called?" (2013a, 196). This question brings to the forefront an orientation toward the world that asks
one to see beyond the potentiality of current space/time. It additionally
reminds us of the functions of language that report and reflect material
reality and those that move us beyond that reality.

How I want to understand identification is through this idea of the
call of language. This call is one we must ever attune ourselves to—it
requires an open, listening stance. The house of Being is a call that

gathers—sometimes invites, sometimes commands—us and the "world and things into the simple onefold of their intimacy" (Heidegger 2013a, 205). I'm interested further in this image of the onefold—the gathering of the subject/object. In the following section, I discuss more about how the concept of the threshold and its crossings can explain rhetorical identifications and the role of rhetorical ethos in this process.

THRESHOLD

I continue to extend my inquiry into identification: How do we explain identification in more concrete ways? What are the conditions in space/time that allow for identification? How does rhetorical ethos relate to moments of identification?

When Burke discusses identification in *Rhetoric of Motives* (1969b), he writes of the relationship between subject and object—this description both upholds and deconstructs the notion of separation. He writes, "In being identified with B, A is 'substantially one' with a person other than himself. Yet at the same time he remains unique, an individual locus of motives. Thus he is both joined and separate, at once a distinct substance and consubstantial with the other" (21). This condition of being joined and yet separate is one that continues to engage my imagination. As mentioned earlier, it is the rarity of identification across difference—whether in space/time, positionality, or ideology—that makes this act particularly engaging. In continuing my inquiry into identification, I've found that in order to say anything meaningful about these phenomena, one must accept, reject, or continue to wrestle with the notion of subjectivity and its attendant implications for unification with the Other, and my project too cannot escape this quandary. I'll show my hand and say I prefer to wrestle with the concept of subject/object relations. When I consider this act of holding the middle ground, I am reminded of Josh Gunn's (2008) assertion that rhetoric is "the promise of a coming relateability that never arrives" (150). The notion of promise is essential here—it implies an everlasting effort to reach toward the other, despite the impossibility of literally being one with the other. A stance of openness is essential in wrestling with subject/object relations—and with theories of language and rhetoric that value this stance, and we can name many that do move forward this important discussion on potentialities of rhetorical identifications that recognizes rhetoric as a promise of relatability (Blankenship's [2019] rhetorical empathy; Burke's [1969b] identification; Corder's [1984] emergence; Foss and Griffin's [1995] invitational rhetoric; hooks's [1994] radical openness; Hsu's [2018] alternative rhetorics; Lugones's [1987] world-traveling; Young's [1992] Rogerian rhetoric—the list probably goes on and on here). An essential commonality—despite the differences across these theories—is that they support the continuous production of language through dialogue. An open stance, too, creates a space where multiple meanings exist. This ambiguity in meaning creates a type of spaciousness that, ideally, allows for a valuing of multiple subjects/subjectivities without the erasure of selves. In other words, when we practice a theory of rhetoric that values this open stance, perhaps subject-object relations become subject-subject—a shift occurs in terms of how we perceive the Other, not as completely ourselves but not objectified; Others become, for lack of a better description, fellow world explorers.

Burke's (1969b) description of being "substantially one" remains unsatisfying to me because of its lack of specificity about *what* this actually means and *how* this happens. This book project endeavors to provide a clearer lens through which to understand rhetorical identifications. This last section of this chapter in particular sets up a metaphor for identification through the visual imagery of the threshold—imagery I largely pull from the works of Heidegger. I'm using this imagery to further explain the process of identification and its relation to the call of language and the ethos appeal more specifically. To summarize, I am arguing that there exists a threshold between the inside and outside—subject and object—and that the crossing of this threshold is an act of practicing a form of transformative ethos. Transformative ethos creates disruptions in space/time—creating the threshold where subject/object meet and cross. Crossings are specific metaphors for Burke's concept of being "substantially one."

The condition for identifications and crossings, however, cannot come to be until we are brought into a moment in which we recognize the threshold—or our essential separation, for identification cannot happen without division. To further understand the threshold, I want to reference the earlier idea of the call of language and return to Heidegger's example of the two presences—the here and now of the lecture hall and the winter evening described in the poem. The separation between these two locations and times is evident, yet there exists, too, the potential for a threshold to exist between them. Heidegger describes the threshold as "the ground-beam that bears the doorway as a whole. It sustains the middle in which the two, the outside and the inside, penetrate each other. The threshold bears the between" (2013a, 201). The threshold exists because multiple worlds and spaces and times also exist, often simultaneously. Our imaginations, because of the call of language, can access worlds/spaces/times beyond the one we happen to inhabit. The threshold, then, stands as a reminder of both literal separation and the potential for imaginative—and sometimes literal—crossings. As Heidegger continues, there is an "intimacy of world and things—their difference [is what] appropriates them to one another. What unites opposites is the rift, the *Riss* (cf. 'Origin') that has become the dif-ference, the pain of the threshold that joins" (2013a, 202). I think Heidegger's question about which "presence" is stronger, that of the literal reality or that of the language of the winter evening, is an acknowledgement of how the threshold bridges two very present realities. To exist at the threshold is to be affected by both worlds at once. It is also important to remember that the threshold is not just place bound, though this happens to be the example given here; it can also be a threshold between people and objects.

The threshold, though a helpful concept and one I build from here, does not—I think—complicate the experience of straddling the inside/outside. Heidegger emphasizes how the threshold is dependable, stating that "the middle must never yield either way" (2013a, 201); thus he does not consider how thresholds can collapse to create new thresholds or even how one can be fully present on one side but be changed forever by the encounter of the threshold. If the threshold is dependable, and does not change, it doesn't seem like a particularly exhaustive metaphor for rhetorical identifications. The threshold must account for the shifting nature of space/time; thus I want to consider how the subject moves beyond the middle of the threshold—we can't always be in stasis (or liminality) between the inside/outside.

Gilles Deleuze (1986) describes the fold as a figure that represents an infinite set of possibilities for the relation of the inside to the outside (97) just as we understand rhetorical identification as having many possibilities of occurring between subject and object. Because the outside keeps changing (people, places, things, language), we cannot help but be changed as well. The outside cannot help but become the inside through a conversion of far to near that "construct[s] an *inside-space* that will be completely co-present with the outside space on the line of the fold" (118). The fold, as a concept, reminds us of all those outside influences—all the thresholds we have stood in and crossed. The fold can be seen as a type of topography that traces all the connections and differences "between lived bodies, material objects, *scientia* and the passions" finding them to be, in essence, "a mesh of enfolded territories" (Munster 2006, 32). The creation of the fold is brought forth by our interactions with language, other people, and environments. And, to me, the fold thus shows how all these things are on one plane, and, I argue, this oneness is achieved by rhetorical ethos.

And so, we have made our way back to rhetoric. Transformative ethos is indeed the catalyst for thresholds/crossings because of the appeal's ability to widen our conceptions of space/time through its definition of gathering place and dwelling. When language, the material, and the environment affect us—and we experience the ethos appeal that speaks to us from the experience of living (whether our own or others')—we are drawn into the threshold of another's world and begin to create our own subjectivities in relation to each other. The thresholds we continue to make in our lives—the attempts to bring the outside in and to project the inside out—are a way to understand our character development.

Subjectivity is a continual struggle, one in which we are always encountering difference and variation; and the ultimate impossibility of being one with the other can be transformative (Deleuze 1986, 106). Experiencing identification(s) is not something that can be forced but that relies on affect and attunement to space/time and a willingness to see differently and perhaps live differently.[7] And, additionally, when we consider the lives of others, we may feel "substantially one" and "consubstantial" with them—an affinity often created through recognizing that their life experiences and attitudes (character developments) align with our own. In other words, when students are taught to see ethos in this generative way, if ethos is seen as an essential term and threshold concept for the field, I think students can further see the transformative potential of speaking and writing.

When I consider this chapter in the scheme of this book, I recognize how some readers may find it to be too reliant on the classical rhetorical tradition and its revival in the New Rhetorics, too reliant on the Western philosophical tradition, too reliant on the work of DWM (dead white males). That's a fair critique. The intention of this book, however, is not to invoke this classical work to revive it wholesale but rather to see where the rhetorical tradition has come and to plot out together where we think we might be going in our scholarship and teaching. To know the etymology, history, and debates around a term like *ethos* wrests it from the reductive formula of ethos = character. This knowledge further wrests rhetoric from the work of neoliberal, capitalist skills development that is becoming the center of first-year writing.

What is rhetoric for? I keep coming back to this question. I don't think it's merely a tool for success in school. I don't think it's all about creating a theory of writing about writing. I don't think it's all about transfer. I can't accept such narrow definitions for a way of knowing I hold at the center of my life. I can't help but see rhetoric as a way of bringing our realities into existence, a way of listening to the realities of others, a way for being with others and moving forward with them. So, I'm staring at a disjunction between what I understand in theory, what I practice in my personal life, and, on the other side, what I think the field is doing in practice through its pedagogies and curriculum design. Writing this book presented a way to move forward past this discrepancy in my personal and professional life.

In the following chapters I further ruminate on the ethos appeal and how it is developed through our interactions with objects (chapter 2) and places (chapter 3) and how writers express the appeal to others. Both chapters are theoretical in nature, but unlike what I explore in this chapter, I offer readers analyses of professional, more contemporary writers who are fond of materiality and place as subjects, such as Barthes, Benjamin, Corder, José Esteban Muñoz, and bell hooks. These writers' voices persist for me—they are the voices I listen to and meditate on often; perhaps I feel drawn to write about them to find out why they hold my attention, why I feel "consubstantial" with them in some way. Chapter 4 offers application of this transformative theory of ethos to our first-year writing curriculum design.

These chapters illuminate a way forward for teachers and scholars who wish to include personal reflection and local research in the classroom and in their own scholarship, for teachers and scholars who hope to practice and teach a rhetoric with an ethical center—one that offers the possibility of transforming both readers and listeners so they see each other and embrace each other, and perhaps love each other.

2

FINDING AND COLLECTING
Stories on Material Objects and the Ethos Appeal

PART I: BUILDING A RHETORICAL THEORY OF MATERIALITY

If you put your ear to my work and you strain to listen, I think you will hear—behind the theory of ethos—the music of Wooster Street in New Haven on summer nights during the Feast of Saint Andrew. And you'd hear my Ozzie laughing as she makes a pot of sauce. And the clanging of the sewing machine in my Nonie's apartment.

And you'd probably hear the tension(s) between the language of the academy and the ones spoken at home. And you'd maybe hear questioning as to the value of formal academic writing and also skepticism toward the narratives of "advancement" that circulate around literate practices. And you'd certainly hear a lament, a longing for connection to the people and the places and the things that a person becomes uprooted from—sometimes violently—when they start to walk down the road to Parnassus (academia) and away from Wooster Street.

I came to this work because I encountered Corder's creative nonfiction and scholarly writings in Theresa Enos's themed course Beyond Postprocess and Postmodernism: The Spaciousness of Rhetoric in graduate school. I understood how Corder felt displaced from his roots and thus worked to create a theory of rhetorical ethos that allowed him to trace them—I unpack this assertion later in this chapter. For now, it is important to know that Corder shows readers how a writer can understand the term *ethos* beyond a stylistic interpretation. Corder believes communicating identity is a part of ethos. He values bringing the personal in his writing—he shows us his objects: photographs, sketches, rocks—from landscapes in West Texas that literally signify and mean the world to him. His writing about objects shows us his emotional work with them; he emerges as a presence and we become closer to him as readers because of this.

I knew I wanted to write scholarship like Corder's someday—to write in order to trace my own ethos, to show the people, places, and things

DOI: 10.7330/9781646420636.c002

that mattered to me, to investigate how this ethos material work could be found in the writings of others, to theorize why we listen to some voices and not to others. When you explore what Barthes called the *punctum* of an image or object—the thing that strikes your personal sensibility, that gives you a wound or prick, similar to the idea of pathos in our rhetorical vocabulary—you have to "give yourself up" to a reader, and that act can create a kind of vulnerability that shows your fallibility as a producer of knowledge (Barthes 1980, 78). Theresa warned us that these desires to change the nature of scholarship—to pair the personal with the scholarly, the private with the public—happen all the time when graduate students read Corder's work. This observation, however, was always issued with a warning: "You don't get to write like Corder until you have tenure."

Restaino (2019), in her book *Surrender: Feminist Rhetoric In Love and Illness,* dramatizes this conflict when she writes about Elizabeth Ervin—Corder's student. In her memorial for Corder after his death, Ervin struggles to write about him because she sees the limitations imposed by academic discourse as "'ridiculous'" because by its nature it doesn't allow for "'multiple narratives, roles, and identities'" (quoted in Restaino, 135); Restaino claims Ervin is haunted by Corder and "in memorializing him she traces our disciplinary limits, our ongoing refusals of both/and in the academic and the personal" (137). Ervin wanted to break down these barriers between the personal and academic, but she was stymied by the field of her time. Restaino cites Lisa Ede's memory of Ervin advocating for the personal in scholarship at the first Feminisms and Rhetoric Conference in 1997. Ede writes that the senior scholars at the time—though they were sympathetic with Ervin's cause—couldn't support her desire for challenging academic norms because "we all knew the realities of tenure and publishing" (quoted in Restaino, 139), hence Theresa's warning.

The field has made gains since then, of course—largely due to the movements of feminist rhetorics. This book, by a female untenured professor, would not be possible without this turn toward the personal as scholarly. This project isn't about outlining those changes in scholarship, but I share the above anecdote because it is important to keep in mind that when we dive into the personal, when we make knowledge from our positionality, when we "give ourselves up," it's a kind of writing that houses contradictions, that explores that which we don't know—the limitations of knowledge. If we believe a discipline is about naming what we know, we reify the boundaries and limitations of what is "scholarly," and this affects what can be written and published and, at the same time, what can be taught.

Like Corder and Ervin and Enos and Restaino, I'll not tarry in the "ridiculous" binary but choose to produce scholarly work in personal ways. I offer my story here as an example of the type of writing that asks us to be present to readers and to reveal our places and things to them. If we learn to speak a commodious language that traces the origins of our character development (ethos), perhaps we then open a threshold to our worlds that allows others to enter. And, if we value this type of writing in our scholarship, it will translate into our classroom teaching practices.

Sometimes I dream of my great-aunt, Ozzie. She died when I was in high school.

She comes to me in the small kitchen of her two-bedroom condo that she shared with her daughter, only a few steps away from Wooster Street in downtown New Haven. This is the Little Italy section of town, with Pepe's Pizzeria and Lucibello's pastry shop and St. Michael's church.

I remember many details from that kitchen. The way the dining room chairs swiveled and twisted on their wheels, seemingly low to the ground with bodies shaped like eggs. The way the room brightened as the sunlight came in from the windows and the screen door overlooking their small, fenced-in yard. The beige wallpaper with orange, green, and yellow flowers. The large, white hutch with glass doors that opened on a slider.

Ozzie was always moving about, checking on the food or serving coffee. My favorite time to visit was Easter morning. She would be preparing her family's afternoon meal. The smells of an Italian kitchen—fresh tomato sauce and the soup she made with the little meatballs—would be in the air. All mixed with the strong, bitter smell of Italian coffee and the zest of lemons.

The places and the people of my childhood are gone. I can never go back to that kitchen, except in my dreams. It's hard to feel connected to the past, to the history of my family. The connection to the Italian language, and in many ways to the Italian culture, died with my Nonie's generation. How does one move forward after great loss?

When I reflect on my life, I feel the sacrifice of the generations of women before me. All my great-aunts and my Nonie left grade school to work in garment factories. I got to move on; I lived in new places, I travelled, I earned several degrees. I'm no longer defined solely by my childhood. I'm not working class. I don't think I can ever really return to my family.

Ozzie comes to me because she was the family storyteller. She updated us on the scintillating neighborhood gossip, the news from the garment-workers union, the latest national political controversy, and the goings-on of everyone in the family. Ozzie talked to everyone because everyone loved her and she loved everyone, so she knew everything.

She used to make little clicking noises as she talked, her tongue touching the roof of her mouth in excitement. When she was engrossed in a story, her mouth formed an O, as if it were sucking in the air of the room, and at the same time, it seemed, she let out a long, high-pitched "Ooooo." Her eyes behind her thick glasses were always scrunched, a wide smile on her face for her listeners. Her balding head added to this picture of serenity and calm. She moved her hands through the air, her arms flapping. She was a short woman, but large in body, thick. Her arms were usually left exposed through the cutout sleeves of her moo moos. I watched her arm flab wave as she talked, as if it were disconnected from her body. When I sat next to her, I used to play with her arms—poking them, jiggling them, squeezing them like loaves of Italian bread. She used to laugh at me, saying things like, "You like to play with Ozzie's arms, bella?" and "Don't flap them too hard, I may just fly away."

I have my Ozzie's arms. I am aware of them flapping as I talk and gesture in class. I also have her penchant for telling stories.

My godfather, Uncle Tony, recognized Ozzie as a storyteller, recording and transcribing her words and stories in his book, *The Italian American Experience in New Haven*. As with his other interviewees, he included a picture he took of her with his old black-and-white film camera (Riccio 2006, 179). He felt the need to archive our ethnic experience, to hold on to the stories of his interviewees and to preserve their memory. His mother and father were dying and their generation was dying and some sense of our Italian American culture was dying too.

Uncle Tony's son, Al, and I were in middle school when he was doing the bulk of his interviewing, and we used to tease him about the project, which to us was a seemingly long, never-ending quest. I can see my Uncle Tony as he was then—in his early 40s, thin, slightly balding, jittery, and joyously running to interviews with his notepad and tape recorder in hand. He put on hold anything and everything, and everyone, for a chance to talk with whomever it was whose story he felt was absolutely important to get down. As a writer now, I understand this passion all too well. But then, as preteens, Al and I were always in the background, snickering, shouting things like, "Oh no! I better interview Angelina before she dies!"

"No! Not Angelina!" (fart noise mimicking the sound of death)

Needless to say, I was a little shit.

His book was published a decade later, when I was in college and Ozzie was already dead. I remember opening the book for the first time and quickly looking for her name, Antonette Sicignano, in the index so I could read all her stories first. It was an odd feeling to see her words in print and to see her picture with her wide smile and balding head. This strangeness, I think, was because I was encountering Antonette Sicignano as a text. I imagined other readers who never knew her—who never heard her laugh—being let into this world of her stories. To be honest, at the time I didn't know what the subjects of her interviews were; I just knew Uncle Tony interviewed her several times while writing the book. And so, in some ways—as an adult, as a budding intellectual—I was meeting Antonette Sicignano for the first time.

At the same time, her words weren't just a text to me. I also felt a sense of intimacy—as if the dead were speaking to me. I can hear her voice, imagining where she paused and the ways she pronounced words in her accent and where she may have exclaimed or laughed. I remember reading her story, "How Beautiful They Looked," in which she describes how she had to leave school to work in the shirt factory:

> I didn't go to graduation. I was only thirteen years old, now I'm eighty-eight. What a difference! My mother used to do like this. Because we were a lot, my father was a sick man with bad asthma; he died when he was in his fifties. If one daughter wanted to get married, the other one's got to be thirteen, fourteen years old. She used to say, "You can't go to school, you got to find a job." My sister got married that September. I found a job. I had to go work in the shirt shop; that's how I started working in the shirt shop. But I didn't graduate; I wanted to graduate. Because there was going to be a room, just for all the girls. They had no boys; they had all girls. And I went to see the graduation the year before, the ones that graduated. I loved it. They were all in white for graduation with all big flowers. How beautiful they looked. And I sat there watching them and I said next year I'll be up there on the stage. We had a stage at Greene Street school. But I never went. No, I couldn't. School closed in June; the week after I went to work. (Riccio 2006, 50)

Though my great-aunt left formal schooling, I see how she is a writer: setting up the situation in her family, using her mother's voice, including imagery and description, and employing strategic repetition and her emotional response. I see the stage, the girls in white, the big flowers. I feel her longing to be up on that graduation stage the following year. I can't breathe normally when I read her words. To share this story seventy years later, it meant something to her; her story also came to mean a lot to me. It reminded me to honor whom and where I came from.

Many of us in academia can trace our rhetorical lineage to women like Ozzie. These are the people who ground us. Ozzie and her sisters, including my Nonie, worked hours in poor factory conditions,

conditions they fought to make better through creating a union and joining together in protest for workers' rights. They gave up so much so their family could move forward.

It's hard to balance this sentimentality toward the past (and the people in it) with my education that has taught me to be critical of the patriarchy, white supremacy, and other conservative ideologies, all of which my family has reproduced through its generations. Who would Ozzie have been if she had been given the opportunity to go to college, like her brothers?

I circle around these questions as I try to reckon with the past in the present: What does it mean to move forward after loss? What kind of future do I construct for myself? What does my Italian American heritage mean to me? What about growing up with others who were working class? What does it mean to claim to understand those identities now?

This is my material story, about Ozzie, my memory of her, and my relationship to my family. It's about constructing an identity in the now and the future given the past.

Ozzie's granddaughter, Nicole, became my instant friend. We grew up together, she being only a year younger than I. She was the leader in our hangouts, though, assured and confident. She had tight-curled brown hair, springy; she was beautiful, thin, and copper skinned. She used to smile at me with mature, knowing eyes. She told me everything about fashion, music, and boys. I liked to follow her. When she got married, I was in the wedding party. I was going to buy her a gift off her registry, like everyone does for wedding showers, but I found something so much more meaningful—a way to bring Ozzie into our celebration. I know she would have loved to be there for Nicole.

In recent years I have become someone who stalks antique shops for hours in search of the things that strike me as important. Perhaps this habit is because of my reading Corder, though I always had collections as a child—pogs, baseball cards, model Volkswagen Beetles. I had a special drawer in my nightstand where I kept things that mattered to me. The collecting has become less focused now, though, as my runs to the stores, flea markets, and estate sales have been more about intrigue than certainty. In Tucson during grad school, I often drove to the familiar corner of Speedway and Rosemont to "get lost" in an antique mall half the size of a football field with hundreds of individual venders. It has now closed, another place I can never return to. The visits to Copper Country were always events, two-hour investments at least. I became a finder, a hunter of antiques.

On this particular trip, the one when I found Nicole's gift, I was in the back room of Copper Country, Fred's Thrift Shop—where all the bargain prices are to be had and haggled. There they were, resting on a shelf, eye level, arranged just so—pieces of the desert-rose pattern china set. I was transported back to Ozzie's kitchen again, remembering the Italian cream pastries she served on these plates and how she filled my teacup with milk so I wouldn't feel left out as the adults drank their coffee. I ran my finger along the teacup's handle, painted to resemble a stem—the cup was light, funnel-shaped. I believed these dishes were here for me. I believed Ozzie had a hand in my finding them for Nicole. This was my first time seeing a complete set of four in a junk shop. These were the old-model dishes too; Franciscan Ceramics, the distributors, continue to make this pattern, but the newly manufactured ones look slightly different—their flowers are larger and the colors are more muted. I saw the dishes' past—as if they belonged to Ozzie, as if they were the ones she once used. Perhaps some grandmother did serve her meals on them. I became euphoric as I gathered the dishes in a box and prepared to buy them. I imagined Nicole's face as she opened the present; I imagined her using the dishes—serving food on them during the holidays as Ozzie did. If the dishes were with Nicole, I believed, Ozzie couldn't be gone from our lives. To me, this is a form of "rescuing" an object, of giving it a new home and thus a new life, projecting the past into the future.

I have the tactile instinct of the finder and collector, the craving to touch, to be inspired. The dishes hit a nerve with me that day. They called to me. I wrote the dishes into my life narrative—my affect toward them was one built from memories, from a place of nostalgia for the time in Ozzie's kitchen.

Some things you have to hold on to, and some things you have to let go of—this applies to material items as well as lessons learned. I'll hold on to the feeling of comfort Ozzie always gave me when I was in her apartment in New Haven, and I'll remember her stories and her love for telling them; I'll let go of the attitude that women must serve their families as part of their duty. I haven't answered all my questions about who I am and what I stand for; this is a continual project, one I do alongside and with objects. The force of the material is ever present and cannot be denied as a rhetorical construct in our lives, particularly related to ethos development.

I believe objects have the ability to "touch" us, but those of us devoted to the study of rhetoric don't yet have an exhaustive vocabulary to describe the intrinsic power of things, or the myriad ways they affect us, or additionally, how we assign meaning to objects through narrative. We don't yet have the vocabulary to describe the motives and emotions of finders and collectors. We don't yet have an understanding of the key role materiality plays in the construction and expression of ethos.

This chapter is an attempt to build a theory of materiality that focuses on the positionalities of the finder and the collector. I want to synthesize the material work of philosophers (Barthes 1980; Benjamin 2002; Bennett 2001, 2010; Derrida 1996) with the work of rhetorical scholars (Corder, "A Portable Flea Market"; Kinneavy 1979; Shipka 2011, 2015), and the work of literary theorists (hooks 1994, 2009; Sontag 1973; Stewart 1993). This synthesis of scholarship considers a humanistic as well as a posthuman perspective on materiality, working to value the ways humans interact with their material environments, yet also to value how the material exists without human intervention. The goal is to create an understanding of the material that is more spacious, one that accounts for the process of meaning-making across space and time, considering the give and take of the object and subject—the material and the organic.

I argue that an engagement with the material—investigating our own interactions with things and others' affective relationships to objects—has the potential to further our understanding of rhetorical ethos and even work to create a threshold between the self and Other and eventually fold the subject-object. Material engagement is another way world-making can occur, and this chapter wants to account for how the material world contributes to character development and how it could further be a catalyst for rhetorical identification. So, this study has two prime motives: (1) to reconcile the divide between the self and the material and (2) to see how this reconciliation can help us recognize other humans who live and work through their own materiality—a process, of course, linked with character development (ethos) and identification.

I want to assert here that I am seeking a theory of materiality that first and foremost explores ways of "being with" objects; as my opening narrative shows, I'm attempting to explain the impulse to find, own, and collect objects. I want to situate the reader in a discourse of affect, to bring emotions to the forefront of this inquiry. I think emotions toward objects are the force that drives people to find and collect them. Consequently, I do not shy away from affective experience in this chapter. I want to bring this theory of the material more to the ground of the familiar, the everyday, because the work we perform with objects is one that is not necessarily an abstract and theoretical engagement.

My hope for this chapter is to take my reader on an exploration of what the material reveals to those sensitive to its call, and, by extension, to offer analyses of writers who are materialists and to analyze their stories for common threads. I also want to connect the obsession with the material to the study of rhetoric, which I believe will further help us understand the relationship between the material and the subject, as well as our living relationships with others who work with objects alongside and with us. With this motive in mind, I keep asking the following questions: Who is the materialist, or the person who is affected by the material? What is their relationship to materiality? Can we find the materialist among their effects? How might this study of the material be important to rhetoric, specifically to the development of a theory of ethos, of identification?

Objects signify. They have a rhetorical purpose. Objects humanize and beg for a narrative, though one may never be supplied. Rhetoricians need to come up with a particular rhetorical vocabulary for describing how people relate to objects and additionally how objects potentially reflect their owners (present and past and future). The groundwork in chapter 1 describes the generative possibilities for the term *ethos* to be constructed through our dwelling places and things, and by extension, our actions in places and with things. When we understand that inhabiting the world is a process others undertake through their objects, we begin to see others' values and characters emerge. So, we must start studying the material and the way it "rhetorics"—material rhetoric is not a noun, but a verb.

Rhetoric and composition as a field has been interested in the material as archive even as early as Robert Connors's (1992) description of historical research as an "August mushroom hunt" through the available data saved from the past (23). *Rhetoric Review* has provided a venue for several issues called *The Octalogs*, in which scholars have contributed to the discussion of methodology and historical research in rhetoric and composition. Now scholars are paying close attention to the process of research and material interactions with artifacts—I am particularly thinking of edited collections like *Beyond the Archives: Research as a Lived Process* (Kirsch and Rohan 2008) and *Working in the Archives: Practical Research Methods for Rhetoric and Composition* (Ramsey et al. 2010). Additionally, the CCCC has sponsored workshops on archival research, as has Rhetoric Society of America during its summer institutes. The conversations here have tended to highlight more traditional spaces for research—the archive in special collections, the library, the museum, the historical society—and also seem to frame the materialist as an academic.

There is a stark contrast, though, between my opening story about Ozzie, which frames material objects as connected to rhetorical ethos and the lives of their owners, and the—sometimes-sanitized—ways we discuss studying the material in rhetoric and composition; in other words, the field often approaches studying the material as a research method rather than as an experience and a communicative act.

Jody Shipka's (2011) work illuminates the latter interpretation of material analysis—as experience and communicative act. In *Toward a Composition Made Whole*, she reminds us that communication is a process that is a "dynamic, embodied, multimodal whole—one that both shapes and is shaped by the environment" (26). Throughout the book, Shipka offers practical examples of the multimodal compositions of her students. These compositions break the fourth wall of the screen (digital writing) and take on a tactile dimension. In other words, Shipka's work taught the field to see ballet shoes as a communicative act with rhetorical force (3). In her later work on "found objects" at estate sales and flea markets, Shipka (2015) creates video compositions to show how these objects have a kind of "life" by "giving voice" and "new potentials for meaning to these strangers [the previous owners] and their largely silent life materials." Her remixed compositions—with videoed objects, environmental stills, and narrative—bring attention to how the lives of objects are intertwined with their environment (nonhuman) and with human life.

Shipka's scholarship is aligned with terms like *memory, kairos,* and *ethos* as she recovers and gives meaning to objects. She shows how objects are indeed deeply connected to understanding identity, to finding a place to be situated. The material is closely related to our ways of being and dwelling in the world and, most important, to rhetorical practice.

In an unpublished work, Corder, like Shipka, discusses his need to go to flea markets and estate sales in order to understand the time in which he lives, to find artifacts meaningful to his existence. He aligns the material with a type of survival after death. He writes, "Still, if I locate the particulars I've sometimes lived with, maybe I'll be found among them, or alongside them. Perhaps they will situate me. Anyways, I can remember. If we don't remember, who'll save our daily blessings and curses, who'll find us in some archive?" ("A Portable Flea Market" n.d., 19). In Corder's few sentences, we already see how materiality is connected to a rhetorical vocabulary—specifically, the ancient concept of kairos. Like Corder and Shipka, I want scholars to see the generative possibilities of an expanded notion of time that resists linearity and how it can be fortuitous to the study of the material as an experience/communicative act. The past, the present, and the future are fluid; they give way to one another in a moment. This blurring of the common boundaries of time is most felt in Corder's injunction to work toward a project of remembrance in the present, "If I locate . . . I can remember. . . . If we don't remember;" a call to consider the places and things of our pasts, "I've sometimes lived;" and a gaze toward the future of a legacy, "Maybe I'll be found. . . . Perhaps they will situate me. . . . Who'll save. . . . Who'll find us . . ." (19). This grammar indicates to the reader that the meaning(s) of the material continue to be absent and yet present to us, for the creation of the archive—which Corder is very concerned about in his last question—signals that we must preserve what we have, and yet what we have often reveals what is missing (or *who* is missing) or yet to be found. This can be thought about metonymically; an object stands for a whole history that lies behind it or is obscured by it.

Indeed, the absence-presence of material meanings gives way to a posture of longing; we wait and wait for the meaning of things to be revealed or for inspiration to create something new from them, as Shipka does in her compositions. We wait for something—or perhaps someone—to return, if only to shine light on one aspect of life from a time past or a future yet to be experienced. This continued search is a hope for the future, as the materialist believes that what is lacking will eventually become present, will materialize and act in the world. To be someone who interacts with objects—finds them, collects them, archives them—is not necessarily to align this work with the remembrance of the past or the knowledge of the present, though the work may do that, but rather, the impulse to find and collect and archive is also for the future.[1]

Essayist Rebecca Solnit (2005) describes the idea of an anticipatory future as an open door, relating to readers her childhood memories of Passover. In this celebration, Jews leave out a glass of wine and keep the home door open to the prophet Elijah in anticipation of his return. She describes the nights of Passover as time to embrace the unknown, "the door into the dark," because the dark is "where the most important things come from, where you yourself came from, where you will go" (4). Standing near the open door in the dark is to be in the position of someone open to the possibility for transformation, or even to be transformed. Solnit describes this readiness for transformation as taking an unknown risk. She writes that the things we want most in life require stepping out into the unknown of night: "Love, wisdom, grace, inspiration—how do you go about finding these things that are in some ways about extending the boundaries of the self into unknown territory, about becoming someone else?" (5). The self as someone else, I imagine, gestures toward a transformative process of identifying with others different from us. The material provides an open door for rhetorical identification(s). As scholars in the field, I think we must cross through the threshold and talk about the material not just as a method but as an experience.

In this sense, this chapter builds a theory of material rhetoric based on experience through analyzing the works of writers who focus on the material, such as Corder, hooks, Barthes, and others. By identifying key terms related to the material as experience, and then tracing the expression of those concepts in the selected writers' reflections, the chapter hopes to ground discussion in the material in a discourse with affect, ethos, and identification at its center.

A JACKLEG HEURISTIC FOR THE STUDY OF FINDERS AND COLLECTORS AND THEIR THINGS

When considering the scope of this project and the reach of the possibilities for inquiry, I desire to mark for the reader the points I explore and synthesize about materiality, finders and collectors, and the potential avenues of study these present to scholars and teachers in rhetoric and composition. This chapter aims to will help us think about how materiality relates to character development and identification(s) and the importance of encouraging this work in our scholarship and pedagogy. In this spirit I share six key terms for the study of material rhetoric.

No doubt there is more to be said about the material and finders and collectors than what I offer here. In the article "Jackleg Carpentry and the Fall from Freedom into Authority in Writing," James Baumlin and Corder (1990) assert that we must make structures in our academic writing that will hold for our present purposes; they compare these temporary academic structures to the work of "jackleg carpentry," a building usually made from the scraps of wood lying about. They describe a "jackleg text" in this way: "'Well, there it is, by God—it ain't much but it'll hold us until we can think of something better'" (18). An academic reader could balk at this description, especially in the context of a book project; it appears "folksy," and perhaps it is. However, I think Baumlin and Corder and develop a good argument in the rest of the piece about academic writing, for it is through the jackleg perspective that scholars will resist dogmatic claims of authority in their writing and instead embrace a sense that theories are provisional and always have room to grow. Scholars in rhetoric and composition, in their discussions of the material and finders and collectors, should consider how we already apply the key terms below and have yet to apply them—leaving room in our conceptions of the material for

1. thing-power,
2. affect,
3. character,
4. narrative,
5. time, and
6. becoming.

Thing-power: The dialectical relationship between self and object is one that rhetoric and composition as a field is highlighting in scholarship, especially in its turn toward the posthuman with the work of scholars like Jane Bennett (2001, 2010), Thomas Rickert (2013), and Christian Weisser and Sidney Dobrin (2001). These posthuman scholars are often writing from a perspective of revising or creating a new ontology, a new way to understand our being in open systems of matter and ecology—in other words, to see how human agency is not above the material. Often, these methods move beyond the discursive. One recent book that clarifies this intellectual movement to me is an interdisciplinary edited collection, *New Materialisms: Ontology, Agency, and Politics*, edited by Diana Coole and Samantha Frost (2010); in their introduction, they claim that materiality should be seen as "something more than 'mere' matter: an excess, force, vitality, relationality, or difference that renders matter active, self-creative, productive, unpredictable" (9). Matter shapes our everyday lives and our perceptions; it's not merely something we act on, but it also acts on us and with us. When I index the idea of thing-power in this chapter, I mean to account for the intrinsic power of objects themselves, to explore how agency is distributive between the subject and object, and to flatten traditional hierarchies that privilege the subject.

Affect: Rhetoric and composition has a tradition of considering affect and its relation to rhetoric and the teaching of writing.[2] Scholars such as Laura Micciche (2007) claim the field is in an "affective turn," as we have focused our energies toward thinking through the relationship between emotion and inquiry in the process of meaning-making, particularly in the formation of argument (15). Emotions are an activity that we share. And emotions are also a force for movement in the world. Emotions, too, are in process. As Micciche writes, emotions are "technologies for doing. . . . [Emotions] have to do with consequences and effects, interpretation and judgment, change and movement"; therefore, emotions are rhetorical activity (14). Although the field has traditionally thought about affect in discursive and argumentative contexts, we can forward this discussion when we consider the ways we interact with objects, which involves an analysis of the motives of material acquisition and collection. Some of these motives are chiefly related to the impulses to memorialize and to mourn—and impulses may lead scholars to develop a discourse on nostalgia.

Character: As outlined in the previous chapters, this book explores for readers the term *ethos* beyond the common contemporary understanding of demonstrated character in texts. Although this usage of ethos is important, it flattens the definition of the term and divorces it from its other, older, and perhaps more significant, meaning—ethos as related to habit, to the habitual, to the practice of everyday life with others. Of course, Halloran's (1982) work on *ethos* points us toward the latter definition when he describes the term beyond individual character; rather, ethos can be seen as a "habitual gathering place" where Halloran believes public life and culture develop (60). We can think of ethos, then, as related to physical and material space, created habitat (see Reynolds's "Ethos as Location" [1993]) Interestingly, *ethea*, its plural form, refers to "haunts" or "abodes of animals and men" (Miller 1974, 310). It is a leap of the linguistic imaginative to see how the older definition of habitat would then be viewed as habit and then habitual and then habituation and then character—the changes in connotation actually lie in the stress on the first letter of *ethos*, the epsilon, in reference to habit, and the eta in reference to character (309). This textured definition of ethos is the one that should guide our disciplinary inquiries as several scholars have argued in the recent edited collection, *The Ethos of Rhetoric* (Hyde 2004). As Hyde writes in the introduction, this fuller appreciation of ethos allows scholars to see rhetoric as a "'hermeneutic' and 'situated' practice, an art that informs and is informed by the way human beings dwell on earth" (xxii). As my chapter suggests, our dwelling—which is mostly material—is certainly made through the objects we surround ourselves with. Therefore, we must consider the ways material objects reveal character, which involves a careful examination of how collectors see objects as somehow representing them and their values. The material term *character* is then most explicitly tied to rhetorical ethos.

Narrative: Rhetoricians, as far back as even Aristotle and his interest in Greek theater, have conjectured on the structure and meaning of narrative in our lives. One scholar of the New Rhetoric, Walter Fisher (1989) wrote several pieces on what he called the "narrative paradigm," or a storied view of reality, in comparison to a rational paradigm that relies on facts; additionally he argued that the use of narrative opens up an interpretive and complex worldview. Corder believed we are narratives, and as such, our life stories shape our ideologies and literally make us embodied arguments—this is the central premise in his "Argument as Emergence, Rhetoric as Love" (1984). In Susan Stewart's *On Longing: Narratives of the Miniature, the Gigantic, the Souvenir, and the Collection* (1993), she makes an important bridge between the significance of narrative and objects. She argues that constructed narratives give objects meaning for us. In fact, the telling of an experience of acquisition, she says, "cannot be generalized to encompass the experience of anyone; it pertains only to the possessor of the object," and thus it is a way "to reconcile the disparity between interiority and exteriority, subject and object, signifier and signified" (136–37). Narratives, then, are bridges of constructed meanings that collapse the distance between subject and object, in this case between a collector and their possessions. Scholars, then, should learn to acknowledge the important role storytelling plays in signifying the meaning of objects to us; indeed, narrative serves as a bridge between thing and experience. Scholars then must consider travel narratives, flea-market findings, and discussions of the thrill of acquisition from collectors and tourists as primary texts for analysis.

Time: The linear conception of time, *chronos*, unfolds before us as events are ordered from beginning to end, not one event being privileged over another, almost like a never-ending chain. But kairos, as Bernard Miller (2011) writes, is not just a concept of time, but an experience: "It is the way we measure our lives on the basis of critical events that disrupt the normal sequence of chronos" (169). Kairos is a disruption of linear time. It is something to be encountered and felt. Deborah Hawhee in *Bodily Arts* (2004) gives an overview of the history of the term *kairos* and its usage from Hesiod to Poulakos; however, her description of kairos as a "force," as something felt in the body, stands out to me as informative when we consider the role of kairos in our interactions with objects (66). The object indeed has its own force (as described through the idea of "thing power" with the theories of the new materialists), but when I reference kairos in this chapter in relation to the keyword of *time*, I mean to explain the moment the object affects the subject, what it does to the subject, and then how that, in turn, affects the life of the object. This kairotic phenomenon between subject and object again collapses the distance between the two, like narrative. This moment, this call of the object to the subject, reveals something about our being—what Heidegger refers to as the *Augenblich* (see William McNeill's *The Time of*

Life: Heidegger and Ethos [2006]). Rhetoric scholars, then, must foster a greater attunement to the object in relation to time, theorize a kairos for the object; more specifically, we must see how the object can become present to the subject in a moment and simultaneously reveal the past, present, and future. In other words, the linearity of time is disrupted in the subject/object interaction.

Becoming: This key term is most explicitly tied to the idea that the object (and the subject, for that matter) is always in a state of becoming with other people, places, and things. Bennett discusses this developing capacity of the material in *The Enchantment of Modern Life: Attachments, Crossing and Ethics* (2001), as she pulls from the work of Lucretius and Deleuze's later work on the "swerve"—or a change that emerges from repetition: "From the twists and swerves of spiral repetitions are born new molecules and new viruses but also new images, new identities, and new social movements," and Bennett's contribution in her book specifically—new vital relationships with objects (38). The swerve implies a movement in objects the eye cannot always see. Corder refers to this key term in regard to people's identity construction as emergence or "unfolding"—through a repetition in the building of a narrative world, identity keeps revealing itself in surprising forms. Whatever name one attaches to this phenomenon, it suggests a networked sense of the material. This is closely related to the key term of *time* because a state of becoming, as others and I understand it, assumes a radical departure from time as chronos. Lucretius (2008) understood this well; for example, he talks about the swerve as putting the body in motion toward a desire, perhaps even toward an ideal state of being. He writes in *Of the Nature of Things*, "Whereby we step right forward where desire / Leads each man on, whereby the same we swerve / In motions, not as at some fixed time, / Nor at some fixed line of space, but where / The mind itself has urged?" Becoming relies on a nonlinear sense of time, a kairos, and also a nontraditional way of conceiving space—again, this theory is built upon an atomistic vitality of objects that are not passive in their interactions with people.

These explanations of the material key terms echo many of the ideas posed in chapter 1 about ethos and identification. It is important to align the material with these discussions because scholars and teachers should consider character development as tied not only to written or spoken language but also to the larger, more abstract conception of language as Being. Things ground us in the world, and though they cannot speak, they contribute to our inventive capacities as we speak of them and for them.

I will keep returning to these material key terms throughout the chapter. Though it might be most orderly and obvious to further unpack each key term in its own subsection, relying on the voices of the theorists whose writings guide me, I feel such a separation creates a false impression, for these key principles are essentially interconnected in our work to make meaning with objects and each other. Instead, in the second part of the chapter, I analyze the narratives of materialists and build these toward theory. This form of laying out the argument takes seriously the assertion that narrative is the bridge connecting thing, experience, and signification.

Therefore, I start with the stories of other materialists, of people who may consider themselves as being receptive to the "call" of objects.[3] In the case of all these narrative illustrations, I am working from a corpus of essays by each scholar. This approach does not mean the narratives, and my analysis of them, does not include theory, but I argue that they—and I—start in experience and interaction with the everyday, with objects and people and places, and move into theory. I feel as if I am "closing in" on the stories that illustrate the theories, on where the affect lies in each of the scholars' works. I am trying to get to the heart of the relationship between the material and the finder and collector, to feel its pulse.

So, each following subsection zooms in on the stories of the four theorists (Barthes, Benjamin, Corder, and hooks). And in each one, I read the narrative illustrations through the lens of the key terms I have set forth in this first part of the chapter. This work is in the hope of identifying the main ideas in the discourse of the material and synthesizing them in each piece, and, even further, adding a rhetorical dimension to discussions of the material through the key terms of *ethos*, *kairos*, and *memory*. Again, the overall goal is to create an impression of how people (specifically finders and collectors) relate to objects and how recognition of this relation between people and their objects can bring people together through this commonality.

I begin with Corder's work—the starting point for my thinking on the material and the lens through which I find myself reading the other theorists. This is not because his work is the most influential—no, I believe the other names might be more familiar to contemporary rhetoric scholars, actually—but his work is the most storied and relies least on theoretical claims, though they certainly influence him. Indeed, Corder's narratives illustrate his theories. Consider Corder's (1985) most influential article, "Argument as Emergence, Rhetoric as Love," and his bold claim that we are narratives and that we live and act in the world by the ways we understand and craft our stories (16). Corder's orientation toward the material, through narrative primarily and theory secondarily, is one that actually best illustrates what I am trying to say about the material and the development of an ethos grounded in the practice of everyday life. Corder was already trying to make the connection between the material and the development of ethos, though his work on this connection was either published posthumously or not at all. He is also the most explicit scholar of rhetoric amongst my storytellers. The other three—Benjamin, Barthes, and hooks—are not primarily concerned with the study of rhetoric and do not necessarily begin their conversations on the material through its vocabulary and method. That is not to say I don't find their stories compelling, their work essential, or their affect any less palpable in relation to the material—it's just that the lens of rhetoric must be constructed around their work through my analysis.

Benjamin's, Barthes's, and hooks's narrative illustrations are essential because they account for the fact that material stories[4] can be told in many ways by diverse people, and each writer, I believe, emphasizes different terms. In hooks's work, we can see her narratives about segregated Kentucky and the lives of her grandparents as a display of affect and becoming, as she writes about her present and future through the past of her ancestors; Benjamin's profile of the book collector and his narratives of acquisition best illustrate the key term *character*; Barthes's reflection on the death of his mother and his search for the photograph that best captures her essence is primarily a story of affect and time; my own narrative at the beginning of the chapter best illustrates the key terms *time* and *becoming*. Every material story most likely contains all six of the key terms outlined above, but they do not value or emphasize the terms equally. And that's all right. The terms aren't meant to be exhaustive or equal, at least in the sense that a scholar can plug in any story of the material as a case study to illustrate each and every key term well. Burke's pentad is informative here as it serves as a model of a spacious heuristic and accounts for the rhetorical situation. As Burke describes (1969a), not every situation analyzed through the pentad necessarily involves all five terms equally; in fact, a situation lends itself to be read through a certain term or ratio of terms more than others.[5] This is also true of the six key terms I have forwarded here in relation to the study of the material. So, it is with this jackleg heuristic I have built this chapter, sturdy for now but ready to become something other than its being, to be molded and shaped by past, present, and future thinkers on the material and its significance.

PART 2: MATERIAL STORIES FROM FINDERS AND COLLECTORS

Reflections from a West Texas Materialist

Corder's deep relationship with the material was not the first thing that stood out to me as a reader of his work—though I guess it should have been; it's there, in fact it's everywhere—in every piece he wrote. I was always enamored with his style, his theories of rhetoric with their basis in love and grace, and his way of envisioning rhetorical ethos. It wasn't until his widow, Roberta, invited me to visit her home that I was literally confronted with the idea of Corder as a materialist. It was then that I realized he and Roberta were finders and collectors, that they valued the possession of objects. Their house was like a museum, with shelves of figurines, dolls, stuffed animals, old cookie tins, baseballs, souvenirs from their travels, and all other sorts of ephemera. Things were ordered and shelved and hung by genre, theme, and size; there was a method to this collection that revealed small truths about their lives and interests.

Being in that house, with his things, affected me. I may not be describing this experience well; I feel the words are eluding me as I compose this idea, but it was a form of knowing or being with him, though at a distance. His objects incited intrigue. I imagined him among his things—drinking coffee, smoking his pipe, writing on his typewriter—though I logically knew he never lived in that house; I knew Roberta had moved years after his death. I knew he had died almost fifteen years earlier. But, nonetheless, I imagined him there, in that house. I think he might have been there. I experienced a haunting feeling. I began to think more on the material and the ways it affects us.

Being among his things made me remember all the times he indexes objects in his writing and the ways he connects the material with his identity. Corder often begins his writings with an object and a story connected to it—the reader, at first, doesn't always see the significance of the narrative, but then, by the end of the paper, the object and the story become essential to the argument he is developing. I discuss this technique further in this section when I closely read Corder's unpublished "A Portable Flea Market." In this article he describes his fixation with rocks he collected from his grandfather's farm, asserting that they are a symbol of his identity. I argue that his writing about the rocks reflects his thesis that the material is an essential part in our development of ethos. One added contribution to analyzing his work is to say Corder not only thought about creating ethos through discursive means but also conceived of ethos as a part of our dwelling places, particularly the objects with which we surround ourselves.

Furthermore, I assert Corder has a great understanding of how the material seems to pull us out of our present as we imagine the past and the future, the narratives and histories that surround object(s)—whether these narratives and histories are our own or someone else's. I experienced this same imaginative play when looking through Corder's personal effects. This engagement with the material is a direct reference to key term *time*. These imaginings can be seen as a rhetorical practice because they highlight our separation between subject and object, between past and present, even between self and other. As Gunn (2008) describes, all rhetoric is trying to reconcile the presence of this "terrible, yawning gap" (2). The fantasy of the gap's being bridged between self and other, or the hope of it's being bridged, or perhaps the belief that it can be bridged, is not one I want to let go of, at least not yet—Corder didn't want to let it go either. This is the open door in the dark.

Through this new lens of reading Corder, I realized how he was trying to create and enact a theory of material rhetoric throughout his many writings, scholarly and creative, which he later—in both published and unpublished works—refers to as a practice in "remnant rhetoric." When I was at Roberta's house, I found three unpublished manuscripts: "A Portable Flea Market," "Little Sorrows: An Essay on Changing Rhetorics," and *A Remnant* that explicitly deal with the material and rhetorical study. I believe all these manuscripts were composed in the 1990s. For Corder, the remnant, as he explains in *The Remnant*, is both embodied and material, for a person can become part of a remnant through their survival of a cataclysmic event—some large-scale examples he gives are the Israelites in exile from Egypt or the survivors of the Holocaust; however, he also believes every person experiences what they perceive to be cataclysmic events in everyday life, on a personal scale: divorce, death, and moving. Being on the other end of great change is to become part of the remnant (1992, 23). Corder tries to explain the remnant's significance in his life, in the lives of others, and in our cultural imagination, citing examples from the Bible, history, and literature. He concludes, "Perhaps, after all, the remnant draws some or all of us because we know, in one way or another, that each of us is always becoming a remnant, the last of our tribe, some tribe" (*A Remnant*, 2). The distinction between the old way of life and the new, between the past and the present, comes to the forefront of these writings.

And yet, the remnant is not just embodied, but material. What artifacts, he muses, carry us, the remnant, back to the old world, to new worlds? Corder writes, "People, places, things, grocery lists, songs, books, magazines, garage sales, the miscellany in our pockets, the detritus and the loves of our lives shove us, even if momentarily, into other worlds" (*A Remnant*, 8). This listing of objects is unique to his style of writing, as he always seems to be cataloguing and archiving the detritus—finding the artifacts that have the most possibility for transport to his past or an imagined future. One can see how he ties the material to lost worlds, past worlds. There is a lament that rises above Corder's words on the material, too. Baumlin (2003) discusses how Corder's work changes in tone when we compare his early writings to his later ones; Baumlin calls these stages "heroic" and "tragic." I am suspicious the clear dichotomy Baumlin draws here, but I cannot deny how the later writings carry with them a gravity, an overwhelming nostalgia, and in some ways, as Baumlin notes, Corder meditates on rhetorical practice as "a crisis of ethos, communication, and accommodation" (27). This lament is principally concerned with the subject/object divide, a divide Corder saw as becoming increasingly larger because of modern technologies, competing interests and ways of life, and an abandonment and/or revision of places because of economic development—all this also seemed to be coinciding with an ever-diminishing sense of agency in rhetorical scholarship, what Corder perceived as a loss of voice, or textual ethos, in the service of theories of reader response and postmodernism and poststructuralism.

We can see why, through these crises, Corder clung to the material. As he saw it, and as many others have seen it, the material has the ability to transport us to other worlds, to places we construct through our memories and our imaginations. This orientation toward the material places the scholar firmly in the key terms of material study I mention in the previous section; we are moved to investigate our affective relationship with objects, the selves we construct with them, the ways we relate to them in space and time, and the stories we tell about them and ourselves.

This is Corder's material story.

Imagine living in a two-bedroom house with your mom, dad, and older brother on the edge of the Croton Breaks, a rough countryside in West Texas that opens up and out, surrounded by nothing. Red rock. Dirt. The closest town, Jayton, has a population of 750. Your father works at a mill and at other odd jobs—whatever supports the family. It is 1937 and you are an eight-year-old boy. And for Christmas you just got your first baseball glove, the only gift that came that year.[6]

This is the setting, the starting point, for many of Corder's narratives, both in his academic writing and creative nonfiction. I particularly like how James Baumlin and Keith Miller (2008) describe Corder's frequent obsession with his childhood home, objects, and places. They assert that his move out of Jayton, and up the social ladder in terms of getting his

PhD, was painful, "nor, indeed, was the uprooting ever complete. In his mature writings, Jayton remains both psychologically distant and hauntingly present" (174). Corder's essays remind us that childhood lessons and memories are formative in our identity development; it is as if he is asserting they help us trace the people we have become.

As I mentioned, there are many pieces in which Corder deals with the material. I want to focus this analysis on one unpublished piece in particular, "A Portable Flea Market." The copy I am reading from is half hand written, half typed on a typewriter. It is a piece in process, one would say. "A Portable Flea Market" is first and foremost a reflection on the material. Corder focuses on his cherished photographs of the landscapes in West Texas and his desire to draw these landscapes from their images; he also discusses the objects he keeps from the time past—these photos and objects comprise the homemade "flea market." He cites some scholars on the material too, in particular Stewart's *On Longing* (1993) and Susan Sontag's *On Photography* (1973).

It's a beautiful piece, part scholarly and part theoretical, because it tries to account for the affective experience of those who find and collect, especially feelings of nostalgia collectors sometimes have in their engagement with objects. In some ways, it reads as an impassioned explanation of those who are enamored with the material, or at least a reflection as to why this may be so. At one point, Corder responds to Wiley Lee Umphlett's assertion in *Mythmakers and the American Dream* that nostalgia is a social disorder that brings materialists into a world of dreams and makes them long for a simpler past. Diagnosing these materialists as suffering from nostalgia neurosis, Umphlett dismisses affective experiences with the material as pathological and negative, and he also sees nostalgia as one of the primary reasons for disengagement in political life (quoted in Corder, 19 "A Portable Flea Market"). Corder backs away from these claims, aligning himself with the camp of people who are affected by objects. He reclaims nostalgia when he writes in "A Portable Flea Market," "But if I am after all merely nostalgic, I don't mind. I don't feel embarrassed. I'm glad enough to be among those who search flea markets and antique malls and garage sales to find what they lost, or missed altogether. I don't think nostalgia is a disorder. It's human. I can't avoid that, and don't want to" (23). The identification Corder makes with finders here has a warm tone—it's an admission of belonging in the group and accepting his identity as a finder of lost things from a lost past. But even more interesting is his gesture toward the idea that the impulse to find and collect objects is human, inviting all into this community. This material story, then, is one that gives a motive to the finder and collector as someone who restores lost things and by doing so constructs a world for themself to inhabit. This reflection serves as an illustration of the material key terms of *affect* and *character.*

Furthermore, Corder describes in this piece his process of rummaging: "I rummage through my pockets across the piled shelves of my office and of my study at home. I rummage through the piled shelves in my mind." I believe Corder views rummaging as a form of work that gives the finder "local habitation" and a desire to continue the hunt for the objects and photos they cannot find ("Portable Flea Market," 7). Corder's description of the finder is one of a person always in motion, always in a state of flux and becoming; they are perpetually getting situated, never fully attaining this goal.[7] For nostalgia always implies longing, and longing is an activity that involves work. I think there is a challenge being issued to readers that nostalgia is not a form of "dropping out" but rather a very serious engagement with the present—with an eye to recovering the past for the future.[8] He suggests this desire when he writes, "I expect that we all ought to draw our pictures. Otherwise, who'll save our daily blessings and curses, who'll find us for the archives?" (14). Both these questions provoke us to see the importance in such a project of preservation. The orientation of this passage, moving from the "I" to the "our" and then the "us," implies a shared investment in the material present. The future is for the archivist, the anonymous "who" that will be the person to find the objects and the images.

When I think about it, I believe Corder knew his papers would be found some day after his death by future researchers—how could a scholar so cognizant of time and the material not know, or at least not hope? In fact, Roberta repeated several times during our visit that he would say, near the end of his life, "I have to die to be discovered." It was he who put in order the paper stacks in Roberta's basement; he made several copies. This effort is no mistake to me; he wanted to be found for the archives. The fact that "A Portable Flea Market" is not published, that it is now an item in some collection of his papers, is an irony not lost to me. Of course, Corder wrote this piece with an eye to publishing it—most academics do—but the act of writing was, I think, even further intended to save the images—the drawings and photos—he loved so well. For lack of a better expression, the double irony is that these images—as he wanted them placed in the piece—are lost to me as the researcher. Many of his drawings survive in his published works, but I ache a little to know which ones were intended for "A Portable Flea Market." What pictures and images were supposed to be in this flea market he was sharing with imagined readers?

But let's return to the key terms of *character* and *affect,* for Corder is always positioning his material engagement in the service of developing rhetorical ethos. Corder (1995) placed much value on the "blessed particulars" of everyday life to reveal character in his writing (103). However, if we think about what "blessed particulars" are and what that phrase means, we cannot help but imagine the objects and places that exist in the world beyond the page. Corder cannot only be found in the stylistic tropes and the imagery his words inspire. He also is in the images and in the objects and in the hand-written draft of "A Portable Flea Market." Materiality makes the writer present to us through their personal effects.

Let me share a story behind the story. Corder wrote about a handful of white rocks he took from the land of his Grandpa Durham's farm somewhere out in West Texas on one of his return trips; the land was sold by the family and then abandoned, and then many of the buildings were demolished. The rocks make a brief appearance in "A Portable Flea Market" when he writes, "They [the images in the flea market] are scraps. They are notes from the world. I finger them, as I finger the white rocks in my pocket" (31). The rocks are amulets—they ground him in the world and they remind him of his identity; he is the boy from West Texas. While I was doing research at his wife Roberta's house, she and her daughter Alice—Corder's stepdaughter—sat down with me one afternoon and shared their memories of Corder; some talk of his idiosyncrasies and his rituals came up. Then Alice cried, "Remember how he used to carry around those rocks!" The rocks were real! That was all I could think about after her comment. The rocks weren't a literary device; they weren't a metaphor or trope in some paper—the rocks were real! And, it was explained that he would carry them in his pocket every day and take them out at night and place them in a small dish on his nightstand. The rocks were real. The dimension of tactility mattered to me. These things, the rocks, form our habitats. The engagement with objects, the rocks, shapes our characters.

The main argument in "A Portable Flea Market" is about ethos, not surprisingly; it's not just a naval-gazing reflection on some photographs or hand-drawn images or even some rocks, it's a manifesto for a way of being with objects and each other. Corder writes: "The daily domestic particulars of our lives give us texture, identity; they give local habitation to our histories. If you come toward me showing me the things of your life that gave you residence, perhaps I will see you. If you can see me in my local habitations, perhaps I existed there. I was, among these things, though I can't catch them all" (5).

The passage brings the reader back to the argument I make in chapter 1 about the need to see ethos not just as residing in the text but as connected to our dwelling places. Corder's words also resonate with the argument that the process of unfolding our histories, emergence, can lead to a greater sense of identification between subject and object. And yet, we must go further to see how the passage values the power of things (this chapter) and places (chapter 3, the next) in this process of emergence between the subject and the object. Corder is always aware of the tenuousness of such a material existence and the efficacy it actually has in appealing to a resistant listener or reader. But there is hope for the future in the phrases "perhaps I will see you" and "perhaps I existed there." Corder reminds us too of the right timing such a communicative endeavor requires, the kairos that will reveal the material to the other with force and meaning. The last sentence, too, reminds us that the collection of things will never be complete—that we will always be searching for the story behind the story or the object behind the collection, just as I will continue to search for the images that accompany "A Portable Flea Market" or long to touch the rocks from that farm in West Texas. The collection, like us, is in process.

I marvel at how such a simple sentence, prose, creative in genre—not academic—could encapsulate all the key terms I outline in the previous section. As scholars of rhetoric, we are perpetually looking to theory to answer questions about the material, and yet we can find these answers so clearly in narratives of our living experience. I want to believe in the power of the material story, passed down to generations of listeners and readers. I want to believe that the rocks matter, too, beyond the writing—that they existed and that they too tell a compelling story. Next I'll offer more narrative illustrations that exemplify material key terms and show readers a way of being with objects and each other.

UNPACKING THE COLLECTOR: BENJAMIN'S MATERIAL STORY

Reading Benjamin's *The Arcades Project* (2002) for the first time was a chore. I did not understand why the author had piled quotation after quotation on top of each other in an endless chain. I knew, after reading the section assigned, that I was supposed to become acquainted with the profile of the nineteenth-century Parisian figure of the *flâneur*—a man of leisure who roams the streets, as if in his own home, seeking the comforts of commerce, architecture, and other walkers. The writing style was unlike any I had encountered—and its uniqueness of quotation usage and form stayed with me. I kept returning to this piece and others in the book because I sensed I was reading a work in process, a collection of quotations—still not completed—that had been meticulously gathered, hoarded even, to create for the reader an impression of nineteenth-century Parisian life.

Every quotation is an object placed on a shelf, juxtaposed with others, to create this collection. Benjamin is its architect. As Richard Sieburth (1989) writes, Benjamin is a materialist historian whose main objective in *The Arcades Project* is to collect quotations on related themes—often about people, places, and things in nineteenth-century Paris—in order to, like a surrealist painter, offer an image—though somewhat garbled—of life as it was then. Sieburth describes the positionality of Benjamin as a writer; preferring "to let the documents he has collected speak for themselves, Benjamin vanishes into the intertextual murmur of the Archive, present only as the invisible hand that attaches quotation marks to the past or sites its passages into new constellations" (32). In a way, this work is one of reconstruction. The quotations, Sieburth suggests, are remnants of past life (34). History is chaotic and the remnants that reveal it to us are scrambled—just like the quotations in the subsections of Benjamin's book. History, Benjamin believes, is not neat and certainly not progressive or teleological. In the section on methodology in *The Arcades Project*, Benjamin (2002) describes his project as a critique of this historical narrative of progress and decline; "The pathos of this work: there are no periods of decline. . . . No belief in periods of decline" (458). Further, history is not chronological, but kairotic, its moments of importance a constellation that lights the way from the past to the future to the present to the past. Through the idea of passages—of moving from one space to another, one time to another—Benjamin holds up a metaphor for exploring history through objects and places in time. The material historian must wade into the chaos. Benjamin describes the collector in *The Arcades Project* as someone whose motive is to "take up the struggle against dispersion. Right from the start, the great collector is struck by the confusion, by the scatter, in which things of the world are found" (211). To collect these quotations is to catalogue them and to put them in the subsections, or some sort of "proper place"; the hope is that each quotation, side by side, will create a chain of meaning, a constellation in the chaos and lost debris. Like an archeologist, Benjamin digs through the ruins of a lost past; as Sieburth (1989) writes, "Benjamin's Arcade turns its face toward the past—where, page after tiny page, its writing gradually takes on the shape of a permanent catastrophe and assumes the eloquence of a giant ruin" (34).

Benjamin acutely knows we can never wholly return to the past but can only explore it as if walking through ruins. His later works are born from forced exile from Germany to France, and one cannot help but hear a sense of longing behind the words in the text—for it is no accident that Benjamin writes so meticulously of nineteenth-century Paris in twentieth-century Paris. This sentiment is most felt in his posthumously published *Berlin Childhood around 1900.* I keep returning to the image of a displaced mollusk, which he describes twice in the text; "Like a mollusk in its shell, I had my abode in the nineteenth century, which now lies hollow before me like an empty shell. I hold it to my ear. What do I hear?" (2006, 98, 132). The image of a lost home that was destroyed, now hollow, that can never be returned to but still lies ahead, a remnant, asking to be studied, is how Benjamin views his past life. Benjamin follows the call of the nineteenth century, holding it to his ear: copying it down, quotation by quotation, in *The Arcades Project*, reconstructing it, memory by memory, in *Berlin Childhood around 1900*, and unpacking it, book by book, in "Unpacking My Library: A Talk about Book Collecting" (1969).

It is the last article I wish to focus on in constructing Benjamin's material story. As the article was written after his exile from Germany in 1932, I assume this move was an opportunity for him to reflect on his collection of books. Benjamin (1969) does not write a story about the books themselves—only very briefly mentioning a few titles here and there, in fact; rather, the article is about collecting and the profile of the collector. What strikes me in this narrative is Benjamin's belief in the role of the private collector as a steward of their artifacts; in fact, he celebrates the idea of a private collection over a more official museum or archive. He writes that "the objects get their due" only in the private collection (67). Although a public archive would make the rare book more accessible to many, the private collector spends more emotional energy in acquiring, displaying, and researching their find. A history of ownership in regard to a book can contribute to its value as well, for when a book comes to a museum, it is the book's last owner.

Additionally, I think Benjamin (1969) means to show the book still has a "living" history when it is on a private collector's shelves, writing, "I am not exaggerating when I say that to a true collector the acquisition of an old book is its rebirth" (61). The book comes alive on the collector's shelves, gaining a sense of freedom (64). This stance toward the material is one that values a narrative of ownership, positioning the owner as liberating the objects—relating most explicitly to the fourth material key term *narrative*. The collector brings the object back to life through meticulous care—care that involves research and an intimate knowledge of its past ownership. As Benjamin writes, "Everything remembered and thought, everything conscious, becomes the pedestal, the frame, the base, the lock of his property. The period, the region, the craftsmanship, the former ownership—for a true collector the whole background of an item adds up to a magic encyclopedia whose quintessence is the fate of his object" (60). The collector spends much time engaging the history of their objects. This process is one that assigns meaning and value to the object—it may make the object seem more rare or desirable to the collector. Another factor, which Benjamin does not mention in this specific passage but does reference later in his narrative about attending a book auction, is condition (64). The collector longs for items in mint condition, untouched and as close to the original as possible.

The idea of ownership in Benjamin's work (1969) has a mystical element, which he uses to show the potentiality of objects to transport their owners through time and, additionally, to reveal the affect and character of the collector. The collector's attitude toward their objects is further discussed. For example, the collector's obsession with condition is not related to use; in fact, it is only when an object is stripped of its "functional, utilitarian value" that it can become a part of the collection. Instead, the collector "studies and loves" an item not for its value but as an experience, "the scene, the stage of their [the object's] fate." To the collector, finding the object is fortuitous. Desiring objects is an experience for the collector, one Benjamin believes causes "profound enchantment," as the collector locks the "items within a magic circle in which they are fixed as the final thrill, the thrill of acquisition, passes over them" (60). The imagery of the experience of acquisition as enchanting, magical, and thrilling makes the collector appear to be a person who is greatly affected by objects—they are able to see in the objects and feel through them—an ability that perhaps a noncollector cannot understand or appreciate. Collectors are attuned to the power of objects, and they are moved. Benjamin writes that when the collector experiences the moment of touching, of possessing the object, "As he holds them [objects in a collection] in his hands, he seems to be seeing through them into their distant past as though inspired" (61). The collector is a medium in this description, a vehicle through which the object can communicate its past. The use of the word *inspired* here points to the collector as clairvoyant—not in the sense of predicting the future but of having the ability to see the past clearly. Benjamin even goes as far as to say that the language of the collector is "whimsical" (62), and in *The Arcades Project* (2002), he likens the experience of the collector discovering a find to that of a dreamer, as "the rhythm of perception and experience is altered in both in such a way that everything—even the seemingly neutral—comes to strike us; everything concerns us" (206). The collector as a dreamer shows again how they can be visionary, or at least separated by people in waking life. Perception and experience are heightened, almost extrasensory. In Benjamin's material story, collecting is described as a sensual experience, especially appealing to the visual and tactile centers of the brain.

The motive for the collector is not only sense experience, though this does play a large role, but the collector is also searching for a way of knowing the past in the present. The collector is sensitive to time, but not in a linear way, as they strive to bring the past into the present, or perhaps the present into the past. Benjamin (1969) writes, "To renew the old world—that is the collector's deepest desire when he [*sic*] is driven to acquire new things" (61). The paradox of renewing the old is a complex one. I don't necessarily think this impulse is to deny the present world but rather to bring the old into the new. This stance toward the past is one that doesn't necessarily involve nostalgia, though it might. The idea of rescuing objects for the present and the future is related to the material key term of *becoming*. The collector's process of renewal is to bring a version of the past into the present, which means the past is in a state of becoming for the collector through the material. Collecting is an effort not every person appreciates or has the time and means to do. Benjamin himself describes the collector as a "man [*sic*] of leisure"—it takes time to search for your collection, for example, attending auctions, going to antique stores, picking estate sales (67). Even if a collector does not have the means for a purchase, they may sacrifice to collect, pawning off other valuables, as Benjamin does for a special book he won at auction (64).

Benjamin (1969) ends his material story with a disappearing act, one in which the collector is literally subsumed by their objects. Mystical imagery is again used to describe the affect of the collector: "For inside him [*sic*] there are spirits, or at least little genii, which have seen to it that for a collector—and I mean a real collector, a collector as he [*sic*] ought to be—ownership is the most intimate relationship that one can have to objects" (67). It is interesting to me to see how Benjamin seems to want to validate the affect of the collecting experience, which he claims is genuine and ideal. Collecting, for Benjamin, is certainly an activity done by a select few, which is important to note, as this is one material story among many. Benjamin's description of collecting as a spiritual experience may only appeal to a select few collectors, but for him, the intimacy of the collector with their objects is communal, as

they "[live] in them." The objects, then, become a home for the collector, like a mollusk shell. Benjamin's drive to collect created a world for
himself, or perhaps more accurately, collecting renewed an old world
from which he was displaced in exile. Benjamin "erected one of his [the
collector's] dwellings, with books as the building stones" for readers, so
when he exits the page "disappear[ing] inside, it is only fitting" (67).

PHOTOGRAPHIC WOUNDS: A MATERIAL STORY
OF FINDING A LOVED ONE'S ESSENCE

Barthes's *Camera Lucida* (1980), his last published work before his death,
stays with me. I've read many of his other books and articles, but this
stands out, as it reads as intensely personal and moving. The book is
his eulogy to his deceased mother; furthermore, the writing is also a
reflection on photography and the ways photos affect viewers through
their details and timing. After Barthes's death, the diaries he wrote
alongside composing *Camera Lucida* were published. In these pages
the reader encounters the voice of a writer who must work through his
mourning. Not surprisingly, the text is called *Mourning Diary: October 26,
1977–September 15, 1979* (2010). Two entries especially stand out to me
as a recognition that Barthes saw the writing of *Camera Lucida* as connected to mourning his mother; in fact, he even saw this as a labor,
his writing a form of production in the work of mourning. He writes:
"March 23, 1978: My haste (constantly verified in recent weeks) to
regain the freedom (now rid of delays) of getting to work on the book
about Photography, in other words, to integrate my suffering with my
writing. Belief and apparently, verification that writing transforms for
me the various 'stases' of affect, dialecticizes my 'crises'" (105).

Rarely do we get a glimpse into a writer's process or intentions for
their work. When reading this passage, I find it hard to resist saying that
the motive for writing *Camera Lucida* was tied to suffering. Writing, in
some ways, provides Barthes with a sense of purpose—it is transforming. When reading *Camera Lucida*, one can't help but note the ways
affect is constructed as it shifts from the sentimental to the macabre to
the frantic to the exacting to the insistent. The reader of *Camera Lucida*
can see the process of labor Barthes puts forth through his investigation of photographs, a point I wish to further highlight in the telling of
his material story. For now, though, I want to return to *Mourning Diary*
(2010) to share the other entry that more insistently reveals the book as
a work of mourning: "It's not solitude I need, it's anonymity (the anonymity of work). I transform 'Work' in its analytic meaning (the Work

of Mourning, the Dream-Work) into the real 'Work'—of writing. for: the 'Work' by which (it is said) we emerge from the great crises (love, grief) cannot be liquidated hastily: for me, it is *accomplished* only in and by writing" (132). When reading this passage, we cannot help but see that the work of mourning, for Barthes, is writing. Can we not say the production of the text, of *Camera Lucida*, is the evidence of this labor? For all Barthes's protests of the existence of the author, it is interesting to note his emphasis on solitude here. Throughout this diary Barthes wrestles with the phenomenon of the work of mourning, at once calling it common, banal even—a process that is generic (everyone mourns), but yet there are moments in which he concedes that mourning is intensely personal and unique (no one knows my suffering). It is this same dialectic between the public and the private that drives Barthes's inquiry into photography.

Barthes's terms for the analysis of photography, *studium* and *punctum*, indeed highlight the separation between a public and private discourse through the ways a photograph is received and discussed by its viewer.[9] The studium of a photograph is a function of its artistic merit as one contemplates the choice of subject, the angle of vision, the composition—this language of the photograph is public, academic. However, Barthes (1980) believes the punctum is what makes a photo powerful; it is a feeling the photograph inspires—the pathos of the image. Barthes furthers this definition: "A photograph's *punctum* is that accident which pricks me (but also bruises me, is poignant to me)" (27). The accident of the punctum is described in two ways in this book: in part 1, Barthes describes it as a detail that appeals to the viewer and makes it so they cannot look away—the photo, then, becomes arresting; in part 2, the second accident is more complicated—it relates to the photograph taking the viewer out of time, as they must battle through the image of the past in the present. It relates to the key term *kairos*. I want to expand more on these "accidents of the *punctum*" through Barthes's material story of finding his mother's photograph after her death.

What concerns me most in *Camera Lucida* is Barthes's (1980) insistence on the work as having a phenomenological method,[10] one that starts from experience—that acknowledges the ways emotions are evoked at the viewing of certain photographs. The language of the punctum is subjective; in fact, he writes, "Hence, to give examples of *punctum* is, in a certain fashion, to *give myself up*" (43). There is a real sense that Barthes places affect at the forefront of his analysis on photography, and he gestures here that an engagement with photographs reveals something about the self—an experience, a narrative, a way of being in the world. This connection to the material and character is a strong one in Barthes's analysis. Perhaps my obsession with this particular book has to do with the fact that I learn more about Barthes as a writer. He no longer exists as a "neutered" voice; it cannot be denied that he is the unique author of this text.

Camera Lucida (1980) recalls the process of finding a desired object; in Barthes's case, it is a just photograph of his deceased mother.[11] He describes this task as "a painful labor," one in which he must examine each photograph in his collection, "straining toward the essence of her identity" (66). He examines each photo "one by one, under the lamp, gradually moving back in time with her, looking for the truth of the face I had loved" (67). But the process seems to be a "Sisyphean labor," as he cannot find her essence and must begin again with each new photo (66). Barthes's loss is profound because he lived with his mother and nursed her through her illness. The loss of a parent seemed to affect Barthes more than it might affect others because he did not have children—his family line ended with him, and he felt this immanence. He explains, "My particularity could never again universalize itself (unless, utopically, by writing, whose project henceforth would become the unique goal of my life). From now on I could do no more than await my total, undialectical death" (1980, 72). Barthes's queer positionality leads him to see his writing as a production of himself. Does he feel it is not enough? I can't really say, but I think he believes this work, Camera Lucida, memorializes both mother and son.

One photograph of his mother does pass this test of authenticity; the photo is from her childhood, before Barthes knew her, but he claims it reveals her essence. She is standing in a Winter Garden in Paris with her now deceased brother. Barthes (1980) writes that his mother lent herself to be in this photograph, an act of grace that gives the photo punctum. He describes this act on his mother's part as a type of air, "as an act of grace, stripped of any 'importance': the air expresses the subject [his mother], insofar as the subject assigns itself no importance. In this veracious photograph, the being I love, whom I have loved, is not separated from itself: at last it coincides" (109). This photograph, he believes, gives his mother life. Through its accuracy, its truth, her character comes forward. Barthes's strong emotions toward this photograph are very apparent in the writing. The object is given almost a mystical meaning as it "brings forth" his mother from the dead. It is talismanic. Barthes's material story shows us how affect is an essential part of relating to an object.

He even goes a step further to say that his life narrative is what makes this photo important to him, asserting that the photo would not be at all important for readers. He does not share the photo with his readers in the text, heightening its importance and confidentiality. The explanation for the photo's omission is in parentheses, but to me, it speaks volumes for understanding what punctum means for Barthes (1980): "(I cannot reproduce the Winter Garden Photograph. It exists only for me. For you, it would be nothing but an indifferent picture, one of the thousand manifestations of the 'ordinary' . . . at most it would interest your *stadium*: period, clothes, photogeny; but in it, for you, no wound)" (73). When affect is attached to the object, it becomes meaningful; when it is not, the object only interests our intellectual curiosity, our studium—it holds no power for us as viewers. It does not move. The act of withholding the photograph is one I continue to consider. Why write so much about the photograph, an entire book-length meditation, and never show it? I keep returning to the idea that some parts of our character, ourselves, are too close to reveal—this wound perhaps too deep for Barthes. And, when I think even further, I decide we as viewers could not experience the joy of Barthes's find, the thrill of his possession, for pain seems too often to be juxtaposed with joy.

Upon even more consideration, I see this omission as a part of the extreme phenomenological bent of the book; the photograph transports him to a past with his mother, and for us—we are not moved. As Barthes (1980) writes, "I am the reference of every photograph, and this is what generates my astonishment in addressing myself to the fundamental question: why is it that I am alive *here and now*?" (84). This idea of the photograph in relation to a person's sense of time relates to the principle of kairos—Barthes's punctum is explicitly tied to time, and he views some photographs as collapsing the perceived chronological distance of the past, present, and future for the viewer. He calls the photograph a "bizarre *medium*" because it produces "a new form of hallucination"—one that is temporal, making present something that has been (115). Barthes believes that when a photograph has the power to strike its possessor, to make them feel a wound, the photo is "a mad image, chafed by reality" (115).

The ending passage of *Camera Lucida* (1980) begins with a question: "Mad or tame?" A "tame" photograph is one that operates as studium, but the "mad" image is related to the punctum. The madness inspired by the image is created because its "realism is absolute"; it forces the viewer to stop in their tracks and "return to the very letter of Time." This "revulsive moment," in which time is experienced as a disruption rather than chronologically, is a form of transportation (119). The photograph holds open a moment through which its viewer is taken hold of. Barthes was seeking a wound, a disruption in time, and he found it in the Winter Garden photograph. His material story shows us how affect—desire, mourning, and patience—is a part of our interaction with objects, and he also emphasizes that the subject's relation to the object can potentially thwart a sense of a linear progression in time.

CARRYING THE LESSONS OF ANCESTORS:
BELL HOOKS AND BABA'S QUILT

bell hooks holds fast to a feminist theory grounded in experience, and many of her works give the reader a description of her early life in segregated Kentucky as she explores the ways in which white supremacist dominator culture and the patriarchy can harm the psyche. For example, in her memoir *Bone Black* (1996), hooks reflects on the racism she experienced as she moved from all-Black to integrated schools, and she also talks about the struggles and punishments she faced in her early life with her family as she was a developing intellectual being raised in a patriarchal culture that didn't understand her early feminist ideas and ways of being. Like Paolo Freire, hooks sees theory as a liberatory practice: for her, theory is not an abstract separation from the self; rather, it is an exposure of the self and experience to reflect upon society. As she writes in *Teaching to Transgress* (1994), we must bear witness to "pain and struggle" in order to "expose wounds to give us their experience to teach and guide, as a means to chart new theoretical territory" (75), and thus her works model this idea of bearing witness. To me, her writing does the hard task of holding the mirror up to herself, reflecting it to us, and thus changing the way we think about ourselves and our society after reading her works.

Not every reader walks away from the experience of her work with the same interpretation because of our varying standpoints and positionalities; in other words, it seems to me hooks intends to speak to multiple audiences in her writing and to deliver certain messages to each. For me, a white woman, hooks holds up the mirror of historical and contemporary oppressions; she names the ways whiteness is a force of terror in the Black imagination and urges us—as white people—to do the antiracist work of demasking the fantasy of white supremacy through our personal lives and choices, as well as in our institutions. Hooks (2009) calls readers to investigate the past and present:

> To name that whiteness in the black imagination is often a representation of terror. One must face written histories that erase and deny, that reinvent the past to make the present vision of racial harmony and pluralism

more plausible. To bear the burden of memory one must willingly journey to places long uninhabited, searching the debris of history for traces of the unforgettable, all knowledge which has been suppressed. (98)

Through her writing and recounting her own and others' experiences of white supremacy, in giving us the history of that oppression, "the burden of memory" is laid out, and readers—particularly white people—must take up hooks's call to action for change and for building a more just future. The work relies on the reader to recognize that they are entangled in the trappings of an oppressive history and that their whiteness has led to a form of privilege; hooks warns readers not to feel personally guilty about it but rather to work to see their own instances of privilege, their own perpetuation of biases, and to confront the biases of others and in institutions. This is a vision of the future in which hooks shows us a way we all can flourish and belong; it's a call to decolonize our lives, and it's one more people—especially white people—must heed. While writing of decolonization, hooks simultaneously develops a thread of reclamation of the past.

At times, hooks seems to be addressing a Black/minoritized Other[12] audience in her work and seeking to show them a way to strive for alternative, sustainable ways of being—I think this is one of the most profound messages in her work, and it's one that directly ties itself to a valuing of place and objects as a reflection of self and cultural experience. Part of that way forward for hooks—away from white supremacy and dominator culture—is a look back to the lessons of the past, particularly to the ways of agrarian living her grandparents and great-grandparents modeled for her as a child.

In *Belonging: A Culture of Place*, hooks (2009) details her return to Kentucky after her academic career elsewhere and the ways this return was a part of decolonizing her life and bringing her back to a sense of values and self she so desperately needed in order to attain a sense of belonging. She reflects, "Living away from my native place exploring the past and writing about it critically was a constant ritual of reclamation. It was a ritual of remembering that not only evoked the past but made it a central part of the present. It was as though I had not really left Kentucky as it was always there in my imagination—the place I return to—the ground of my being" (220–21). Throughout the book, hooks identifies herself as a regional writer, citing the influence of the place and the culture she grew up in as integral to her writing and theorizing. Several passages in the book also indicate hooks felt a sense of geographic and emotional exile from the Kentucky hills and the freedom of expression the culture supported, and furthermore, this feeling of exile could be extrapolated from the personal to the public, commenting on the experience of the African diaspora as a result of colonization and slavery (13, 17, 58, 132).

When you examine the two previous passages cited from *Belonging*, the second on "reclamation" and the first on the "burden of memory," it becomes clear that all audiences are meant to participate in the project of decolonization together, through different means but with the same end toward justice. Reclaiming the contributions of Black cultural production and values may have the potential to end modern forms of segregation and white supremacy.

In the following analysis of bell hooks's material story, I focus on hooks's project of reclaiming and defining an aesthetics of Blackness through the homemaking and quilting practice of her maternal grandmother, Baba. In her writing, hooks seems to effortlessly move from the personal to the political, showing how the stories and legacy of the women in her family speak to the larger culture of the segregated South in postslavery America. Again, hooks (2009) ties this project to the idea of reclamation, naming the names of her ancestors and showing how telling their stories is an act of resistance to white supremacist and patriarchal dominator culture's ways of making anonymous, entirely forgetting, and/or reappropriating without retribution the culture and art of Black people, particularly Black women:

> Then I want to tell her name, Sarah Hooks Oldham, daughter of Bell Blair Hooks. They were both quiltmakers. I call their names in resistance, to oppose the erasure of black women—that historical mark of racist and sexist oppression. We have too often had no names, our history recorded without specificity, as though it's not important to know who—which one of us—the particulars. (154)

hooks's emphasis on the particulars, on the material objects of the quilts, and her bringing the past into the present show an intense focus on the material key word *time* and the importance of memory. Memory—particularly for colonized peoples—is an act of resistance, and as a rhetorician, hooks emphasizes how the past is always the present, as she refuses to let history be covered over or forgotten.

Although hooks connects her family narratives to a larger public memory, she focuses on the particulars of her grandmother's quilt-making and the affect this had on her life. One major narrative in *Belonging* is hooks's reflecting on her life away from Kentucky as she pursued her formal education and her career; despite her success, she admits she often feels lost in this other world of academia—mostly because she sees some academics as being devoid of values and integrity.

She brings with her a piece of home to remind her from where and whom she came: her grandmother's quilt. In this case, we can see how hooks relies on the key terms *narrative* and *affect* when she discusses the quilt. In several passages, hooks refers to a particular quilt her Baba started to make that contained a design of the Star of David. In fact, this quilt is the opening image in her memoir, *Bone Black* (1996). The quilting scraps were made from dresses that belonged to hooks's mother and aunts—thus showing a part of their family legacy. Hooks (2009) describes this quilt as a "totem," one thing that "stand[s] between me and the madness that exile makes, the brokenheartedness" (17). For hooks, her exile is one of distance in time and geography, coupled with a loss of values and culture. The emotional connection hooks has with this quilt is very real as she discusses carrying it from place to place, proudly showing it to others. We can see how the quilt is a surviving piece of her grandmother and the wonderful, bold life she lived.

Furthermore, hooks (2009) makes this connection between the quilt and her grandmother through narrative. She describes how her grandmother did not read or write and that the act of creating quilts was Baba's form of art and storytelling. Hooks explains that as her Baba aged, she could no longer make quilts but that they used to sit together and bring out her old quilts to talk about them. They studied them as written texts, deconstructing the intention, design, and story behind each scrap. There are many passages that refer to this act of close reading of quilts across generations, but one of my favorites centers around the Star of David quilt:

> Significantly, Baba would show her quilts and tell their stories, giving the history (the concept behind the quilt) and the relation of chosen fabrics to individual lives. Although she never completed it, she began a piece of quilt of little stars from scraps of cotton dresses worn by her daughters. Together we would examine this work and she would tell me about the particulars, about what my mother and her sisters were doing when they wore a particular dress. She would describe the clothing styles and choice of particular colors. To her mind these quilts were maps charting the course of our lives. (160)

To me, hooks's words paint a picture of her and Baba sitting together, and I can see the quilt in my mind; I can feel—albeit in a limited way—what this moment means to hooks. Also, she is showing the reader how an aesthetics of Blackness exists in the tradition of quilt-making and how the art of it isn't just a mindless activity but a craft with intention, like writing. Quilt makers put themselves and their histories together as they create; the quilts reflect their character (ethos), stories, and history.

In our academic world, we tend to overlook things and people not connected to some grand literary written tradition—which is, of course, related to our deep, deep ties to colonialism. hooks reminds us that aesthetics can be rooted in the particulars of everyday life, in the folk objects created by people who may be poor or illiterate.

Through her work, hooks tells the reader she is grounded by her ancestors because they lived with integrity and a self-knowledge and humility that helped them transcend the oppressions they experienced. The women in her family, through their homemaking, hunting, and quilt-making, were able to express their deep sense of self in a form of aesthetics, an aesthetic that was oppositional to white supremacy. To return to the opening idea of this section, hooks shares these narratives about her life and the lives of her ancestors for a liberatory purpose; she sees herself as theory making through her writing. She is telling the story of her ancestors through the medium she practices, through her form of aesthetics. And this theory making, she explains, is a way for scholars and feminists to bridge their work to the past and to the women who may have been forgotten or erased or who were never attributed. "We are deeply, passionately connected," Hooks (2009) exhorts, "to black women whose sense of aesthetics, whose commitment to ongoing creative work, inspires and sustains. We reclaim their history, call their names, state their particulars, to gather and remember, to share our inheritance" (161). This inheritance in thought, ethics, and material is a part of the character-building work of the present; for hooks, it is a part of building a sustainable, antiracist world that centers on everyone's right to belong.

SOME CONCLUDING THOUGHTS ON MATERIAL STORIES

There are many material stories—yours, your neighbors', and other more well-known people's—that have yet to be discovered or written, that have yet to be analyzed. These five stories I share here only scratch the surface of a rich pool that surrounds us. There are perhaps as many stories as there are objects. These stories teach us about our interactions with the material; they codify certain material key words that remind us of our and others' daily engagement with objects.

For example, when we read material stories, we can see how the principle of kairos plays a role in the finder and collector's understanding of being "struck" by objects, the object's ability to transport the subject through time and to experience time in a way that defies its perceived chronological ordinariness. Kairos transports Barthes to see the essence of his mother; Benjamin experiences kairotic jolts when he finds a new artifact in his collection, seeing through its ordinariness to form a history of past ownership; Corder searches for objects of his past to bring them into the present to archive them for the future; hooks reclaims the tradition of quilt-making by Black women to resist white supremacy and build a theory of Black aesthetics for the present; I, upon seeing the the my Ozzie's china set, traveled back to her kitchen over a decade ago. To see the material through rhetorical principles, such as kairos, is to enrich the vocabulary surrounding our interactions with objects, and it also gives us a place to start in rhetorical studies for theorizing these experiences.

We can also see commonalities among these writers through their experiences of loss, exile, and mourning. The material ties these authors to their past, which allows them to live in their present and to build their future. Although these authors come from diverse backgrounds, cultures, and times, these themes pervade their work.

Furthermore, one motive for sharing and analyzing material stories in the classroom and in our scholarship can be to recognize instances of commonality in the ways we each interact with objects. If we can see the things that matter to others and the reasons they matter, this awareness gives us a whole new way to identify with the Other. When we understand that inhabiting the world is a process others undertake through their objects, we begin to see others' values, and their characters emerge. We meet the Other at the fold through engagements with the material. Corder often discusses character in its written form, ethos as revealed in style, as I discuss in chapter 1. But, there is room in his theories to read for the expansion of the search for character in texts beyond writing, as in objects. In the unpublished essay "Little Sorrows," Corder writes:

> In remnant rhetoric, a provisional and tentative rhetoric, invention will be slowed, I think, and revealed. We'll not simply announce our arrivals, but will also reveal our routes. We must make time to open doors in whatever texts are before us, time to look at the evidences of the self left in the texts, so that we may glimpse the remnant author. (322)

If we view material stories as texts to be analyzed, or, as Corder suggests, as a type of remnant, we are invited to see how others invent themselves. It is through this process of invention, of interaction with objects, that some clues about identity construction are revealed. It is only through time, care, and a certain rhetorical vocabulary that we can begin to see and understand the evidence of another's character. This chapter offers one way of investigating the finder and collector's work with material objects. There is still much more to be said about how the material reveals character, but as Corder believed, with time and effort, we can "cut apertures" and "open doors"—create thresholds and folds—to new ways of thinking and analysis that will reveal the Other to us.

When we consider teaching material-object analysis and composition of material stories in our first-year or advanced-writing curriculums, we want to emphasize the importance of students learning a rhetorical vocabulary so they can reflect understandings of things like character (ethos), time (kairos), and affect in their own writing. In this vein, we are asking students to wade through questions like, How might the material reveal your character? What lessons and emotions do artifacts instill and reveal about your living? We want students—like these professional authors—to talk about how their grandmother's quilt ties them to the generations of women in their family, to talk about how their favorite books provide a place of solace in a time of need, to talk about the photographs they keep of loved ones long gone. We want our students' stories to have force and power in the world. Assignments with a narrative epistemology at their center offer students a way to compose themselves for readers (ethos) and to practice a rhetoric that may lead to identification across difference.[13]

In the following chapter, I aim to open another door to understanding ethos, examining how place is essential in developing our character and to identifying with others. The message of this chapter, connecting ethos to our engagement with things, works to show how the rhetorical term has a larger definition than the traditional understanding of character in text. To create a more spacious definition for *ethos*, I see the need, once again, to widen the boundaries of the term to encompass its connection to our places.

3

MOVEMENT
The Possibilities of Place and the Ethos Appeal

I have been making a case for a hermeneutics of residue that looks to understand the wake of performance. What is left? What remains? Ephemera remain.

—José Esteban Muñoz, *Cruising Utopia*

If I don't search for the once-familiar evidences of our ordinary lives, then they will be gone. If I don't get them out and study them, they will be gone. If I don't try to understand them and myself, we'll be gone. We can only understand the mystery by studying the ordinary evidences of our lives, the site of memory.

—Jim W. Corder, *On Living and Dying in West Texas: A Postmodern Scrapbook*

The train slows to a crawl. We're in the tunnel between Queensboro Plaza and Lexington Avenue Fifty-Ninth Street. From the windows, all that can be seen is concrete and pipes and darkness. The subway car is packed with people. I keep hoping we'll move but we don't. The operator mumbles something on the speaker no one can hear. I feel that familiar tightness in my chest. I close my eyes and remember places. Dream visions of my backyard in Tucson where I picked the round, ripe grapefruits in winter, or the smell of the pine trees on the trails I used to hike in my New England college town, or my grandma's senior-living apartment in New Haven where—as a child—I would gaze out from her eleventh-floor balcony and plot out a future life in which I would live in a tall apartment building like her, "in the city." I remember places in order to move beyond the subway car, to review the other spaces and times in my life, to anchor myself. It's hard to explain in words what all these locations mean to me, how they have folded themselves into my memory, how they demand my recall, how they have influenced the ways I tell the story of my life and how I continue to invent myself.

DOI: 10.7330/9781646420636.c003

When we think about places, as I did in the subway, we are immediately bound up in the discourses of time. Being in a place usually
involves a subject—though the agency of that subject is continually sus-
pect. For some, it may involve an epistemological lens of inquiry—how
the subject has come to know, to think through, their place. For many, it
may involve a phenomenological inquiry—how the sense experience of
place determines its presence for the subject. For others, it may involve
an ontological inquiry—how the place exists through an originary gen-
esis, which unfolds and creates being. Perhaps this all is to say place lays
a claim on us and calls us to further investigation.

In this chapter, I want to explore the traces of place, the evidences
and ephemera of how places persist for us and can contribute to our
sense of character. I want to look at the movements and performances
we make in places that allow us to become more attuned to them, to
integrate them into our sense of self. I want to think about how we
represent places and how that representation can never cover the true
possibilities of places or reveal to others what they mean to us. I want to
talk about the rhetorical terms we use to describe our relationship with
places, particularly the term *chôra* and its association with affect.

I want to talk about the writings of Corder and Muñoz and to show
how each writer brings us to places through their writing, through their
account of movements and performances. I want to show the ways affect
is bound to places for them and how their works aim to show readers the
future potentialities hovering on the horizon of place. I want to show
how they are both creating a "hermeneutics of residue" (Muñoz 2009)
through their analyses and recollections of place. Corder and Muñoz are
an odd pairing, perhaps forged through my own affinities (and feelings
of mourning) for each writer. Placing them together offers a rich juxta-
position of rural and urban, queerness and male Western masculinity,
whiteness and minoritarian identities. Corder invites readers to wander
rural West Texas and to think on the eroding environment, the depressed
economy and loss of farming culture, and Muñoz brings us to punk-rock
club scenes and drag-club stages where queers of color perform identities
of difference in opposition to white, heteronormative dominance.

In this essay—I think that is the most appropriate noun to describe
this piece of writing—I keep circling around the subject of place. My
prose walks and turns as in a labyrinth: How do we fold into place? How
does place fold into us? How do we meet others, too, in the chaos of
our collisions?

I want my writing to invite my readers to close their eyes and to
remember their own places. I also want readers to remember the social

dimension of places—that we experience and move in places together and that multiple narratives and times exist in places.

The multiplicity of movements and the multiplicity of narratives remind us that place is not a static container that holds us all. Place is lively and dynamic. As human geographer Doreen Massey reminds us in *For Space* (2005), the Western philosophical tradition has privileged time as the dynamic mover of life, not space. In her chapter "The Life of Space," Massey asks readers to see space as "an open ongoing production," and perhaps this is a call to see the performative aspects of space and our movements in it. When we open up our minds to this radical conception of space, to seeing it as a stage rather than a container, there is a mental making "room" that allows us to see the "multiplicity of trajectories, and thus potentially voices" (55). Massey means to show how the idea of a master narrative of space and time is undermined; she offers us a way to decolonize space and time. This view allows us to think about living in spaces and times together.

I understand place as something we are always in the process of attaining, as something we are continually getting situated into with others and with things. As the scholar Edward Casey argues in *Getting Back Into Place* (1993), place is a *"condition* of all existing things. This means that, far from being merely locatory or situational, place belongs to the very concept of existence. To be is to be bounded by place, limited by it" (15). Place is the horizon and boundary of our lives. It is how we come to know each other, all things, and ourselves. Getting into place is rhetorical, and not just in the sense of understanding the context of a rhetorical situation as a backdrop for speech acts—as many scholars have argued. Rather, we can see place as the originary of rhetorical action because it gives place to all the variables in the rhetorical situation. I follow Rickert's (2013) lead in *Ambient Rhetoric* where he posits that rhetorical scholars have primarily focused on the agency of humans in rhetorical activity, and he thus argues there is a need for scholars to shift their perspectives to consider the essential contributions of the ambient to rhetorical activity. Rickert believes rhetoric "must diffuse outward to include the material environment, things (including the technological), our own embodiment, and a complex understanding of ecological relationality as participating in rhetorical practices and their theorization" (3). The verb *diffuse* here suggests that rhetoric cannot and should not be contained, particularly to an agent's actions and even further to a system of linguistic or symbolic meaning that can only be perceived by human agents.

To clarify, when rhetoricians come to the topic of place, particularly when we conceive of place as *chôra*—a term I explicate later in this chapter—the line between the discursive and the nondiscursive begins to blur. The rhetoric of place resides in discursive representation—maps, paintings, photos, writings—but it also unfolds outward toward the point where expression about place ends and thus meaning becomes nebulous. Meaning no longer becomes tied to text or even to symbols. Being in place, then, is often associated with performance and movement and with feeling, with affect—not just in a subjective sense of the term *I feel* but also a mood created by the matter of the place itself, the networked relations of the landscape, the weather, the animals, the buildings, and so forth.[1] The idea of being speechless while taking in the view from atop a mountain after a long hike or when looking out from an ocean cliff walk—that sense of awe places inspire—continually reminds us of the limitations of language. We both know and don't know a place. We can't completely capture its essence and explain entirely what it means to us and how much it matters to us.

This withdrawal of places from us need not be viewed in a negative light; rather, scholars can begin to view it as the territory that remains unseen, the dwelling places that, little by little, reveal themselves to us and eventually find their way into some discursive form. This process of attuning ourselves to the meanings of places is a practice we must theorize and be more aware of in our own lives, as it is a part of how we create character; furthermore, in this chapter I forward that this character development is connected to movement, or how we wander—mentally and/or physically—through place.

Imagine what could be revealed about our being if we were continually in the process of searching for what withdraws, what traces are left behind. We try to grasp place, finding small parts of it, eventually knowing there is still more territory over yonder, the yet unseen and unknown. Indeed, the search for place never ceases.

This chapter extends the work of the previous one in which I focus on the material in relation to rhetorical study. I argue in chapter 2 that an engagement with the material—investigating our own and others' affective relationships to it—has the potential to further our understanding of rhetorical ethos. Furthermore, I assert that the work of studying the material could help us recognize other humans who live and work through their own materiality, thus creating a fold between the self and Other. The study of place continues to diffuse the meaning of rhetorical ethos even further outward, and by this I mean it brings the term from the written text to the spaces we live. Rhetoric, as I argue in the introduction and first chapter, must be concerned with the process of dwelling in the world, as this aim widens its domain from the written and spoken arts to questions of being-in-the-world and ethics. I keep return-ing to Hyde's introduction in *The Ethos of Rhetoric* (2004) and his claim that rhetoric must be seen as a "'hermeneutic' and 'situated' practice, an art that informs and is informed by the way human beings dwell on earth" (xxii). As this chapter works to show, dwelling[2]—or the process of getting into place—is essential to understanding the development of character. Dwelling is habitual, like character, and it is forever unfolding and becoming, like character.

The term *dwelling* is most often associated with Heidegger, who in one of his lectures, "Building, Dwelling, Thinking" (1993), discusses how dwelling is a condition for building and thinking. Dwelling, according to Heidegger, is a way of achieving a "primal oneness" in the universe, or what he refers to as the fourfold "earth and sky, divinities and mor-tals" (351). Dwelling does this because of its function to preserve and save—its imperative to build places and things for future use. There is peace for humans in the practice of creating dwellings, in finding places to be. Heidegger asserts that mortals must continue to "search anew for the essence of dwelling, that they must ever learn to dwell" (363). We are continually creating place and yet place's originary impulse of dwelling means place shapes us—the relationship is cyclical, a snake eating its tail. Perhaps Rickert's (2013) interpretation of dwelling as practice more clearly explains the relationship among place, people, and character, as he writes that dwelling is "how people come together to flourish (or try to flourish) in a place, or better, how they come together in the contin-ual making of a place; at the same time, that place is interwoven into the way they have come to be as they are—and as further disclosed through their dwelling places" (xiii). The words "making" and "disclosed" are the ones I keep returning to as I read Rickert's words and compose this chapter because they remind me of how place is made by humans and reveals their ethos and yet how it also withdraws from them—awaiting disclosure through continual movements and our makings.

In this chapter I argue three main points: first, that the continual process of getting into place is inescapably linked to rhetorical ethos; second, that the nondiscursive elements of place make their way to the discursive through the revealing of place to us, a process that requires a continual attunement to place through movement; third, that subject/object divisions between the self and the environment, through this lens of getting into place as an act of movements, is one way the subject and object may unite at the fold.[3] The line of the fold is a visual image that best describes the ongoing synthesis among place and objects and us, between us and other people.

I also work to define and explain why rhetoricians should begin to think of place through the Greek term *chôra* rather than *topoi*. *Chôra* is a term rich with spatial, discursive, and embodied meaning, and I argue it will push conversations in the field about the creation and significance of place forward. In some ways, our rich tradition of engagement with the Aristotelian topics has limited our vision as a field in understanding places and writing about places, and even more broadly in the ways we teach invention and arrangement in writing. The displacement of *chôra* from our rhetorical lexicon censured an expressive and creative tradition in talking about place.

In conclusion, I discuss the dialectics of the inside/outside and the closing of the gap, even the folding of the subject/object, through what I am calling *chôraphillic memory*—or the affective, bodily engagement we have with place and how it enfolds us. I analyze how continually working on discursive representations of place allows writers to recover more of the unseen, unrevealed aspects of place—the parts of place that withdraw.

ETHOS AS DWELLING

Movement is significant to the rhetorical tradition. In Plato's dialogue *Phaedrus*, Socrates convinces his young counterpart to walk beyond the limits of the city and to sit under the trees and listen to the cicadas' inspiring song; this was the ambience created for a dialogue set on defining rhetoric and its uses. Further, we can imagine the peripatetic philosophers as they circled the walkways of the city of Athens, meandering down familiar footpaths. The stroll as a sense of pleasure and as means of transportation created for Greek philosophers a community structure that supported a deep sense of place. There is something here, I think, in the act of repetition, of following familiar footpaths. Consider the form of the labyrinth and the way it winds in a known pattern; the walker engages their body in movements through its twists and turns. And yet, the experience of the walk is in the service of reflection, a deeper knowledge of the self in place. Though the classical tradition uses the idea of walking as a way of describing a relationship with place, I am trying to consciously use the word "movement" throughout this chapter to be more inclusive of other forms of mobility that do not rely on the normative body. Repetition and return through means of movement, then, can inspire a type of knowing that encourages an intimacy with place.

We can even fast forward to more contemporary landscapes and think about the act of movement in urban spaces as ritual, as in the case of Benjamin's *flâneur* (2002) and De Certeau's pedestrian (1988). Wandering is part of developing a self-knowledge and it aids in the act of self-transformation.

I want to believe movement is a form of practice for dwelling, which is all related to the process of placing oneself. Movement is essential in knowing the self and the world. Casey forwards the connection between wandering and dwelling etymologically in *Getting Back into Place* (1993): "We can find an important clue by tracing the word *dwell* back to two apparently antithetical roots: Old Norse, *dvelja*, linger, delay, tarry, and Old English *dawdle*, go astray, err, wander" (114). It is the second part of this definition that interests me. Casey, too, describes a time when wandering played a key role in his engagement with place when he writes of his return to an arcade he used to play in as a child; the arcade has this magnetic quality—the time spent there was significant to him. He walks the reader through this arcade now—we can imagine its flashing lights and warning bell sounds, its crowded atmosphere, and its mood of teeming euphoria as the tickets dispense out of the machines. It is a space alive with movement. Casey writes, "One may *dawdle* in that kind of world, drift with it, follow its lead. . . . Dwelling is accomplished not by residing but by wandering" (114). It is interesting how the arcade is positioned as a dwelling place rather than, say, a family home—a site most people associate with the idea of dwelling. I also like how Casey positions himself in this milieu. He is a part of the world of the arcade; it acts on him and with him. He is not claiming to be the superior agent in this environment but rather one piece in the drama that unfolds. Movement in and through world(s) makes them feel familiar to us, and yet this critical movement also makes the place seem strange—we feel the pull of place, allowing us to follow its lead.

Movement has been identified as essential to being, or perhaps more accurately to states of becoming with other people, places, and things, by Gilles Deleuze and Felix Guattari in *A Thousand Plateaus* (2005); I am thinking particularly of the chapter "Becoming-Intense, Becoming-Animal, Becoming-Imperceptible . . ." In the section "Memories of Haecceity," they discuss how the body—its relation to space and time through its movement across longitude and latitude—creates specificity, a way of knowing that can work to place oneself in and among environments (261). It is important to note that their metaphors of haecceity as fog and haecceity as rhizome (263) show the ways they understand the comingling of places, people, and things as a process that has no beginning, middle, or end, and also that the participants in these environments are not reliant on or driven by human agency. It is here, too, where they discuss the idea of "becoming (animal-human-plant)" as happening through the construction of assemblages that form through movements (speeds)—often this movement is impercep-tible to the human eye (266). In the following section of the chapter, analyzing molecular movements of becoming, Deleuze and Guattari opt for the metaphor of a transparency in trying to further the idea of there being no beginning, middle, or end—just marking and lay-ers that show the forming of assemblages. World-making, becoming with "everybody/everything," is a process of conjugation, a meeting with "other lines, other pieces" in an abstract puzzle "that makes a world that can overlay the first one, like a transparency" (280). The repetition in movement(s), one layer adding to another, shows us how activity is essential to being. The wanderer must, I think, be a part of this commotion/locomotion. The assemblage of people, places, and things is wrapped up in movement. People's orientation to the outside is a mode of critical engagement that attunes them to the process of dwelling.

It is true too that we develop a certain intimacy with the places we inhabit and consider our own. This affective relationship with place should be accounted for in our discussions and attempts to explain its meaning in relation to our character development. Meandering through a familiar cityscape, as Benjamin (2002) discusses in *The Arcades Project*, can make the streets feel like an extension of the bou-doir (417, 422). Walking, de Certeau (1988) further asserts, transforms a place and gives it character (95). In the act of wandering—such as Benjamin's (2012) flâneur following his whimsies—there is a poten-tial for becoming "lost," even in an intimate place; or perhaps more accurately, the walker recovers a sense of wonderment for that place (419). Indeed, circling a familiar place, paying close attention to its character—through walking and driving, through research, through photography and sketching, through reflective writing—has the poten-tial to make what is familiar to us strange, to reveal the remarkable aspects of place. I also mean to suggest that understanding that place takes form only through our everyday practices—like walking or riding in a wheelchair—and at the same time, it continues to influence and build our characters.

Casey reminds us place is constructed through the idea of boundary in *The Fate of Place* (1998)—in some ways, Corder's words I cite earlier concretely demonstrate this concept of boundary. Casey, in one chap-ter, is working from Aristotle's metaphor for place as container in the *Physics*. Casey insightfully complicates and expands that metaphor:

Not only is a place two-sided in the manner of a boundary—insofar as it is inclusive and exclusive at once—but it is also like a boundary in the special signification that Heidegger detects in the ancient Greek conception of *horismos*, "horizon," itself derived from *horos* (boundary): "that from which something *begins its prescencing*." For a place is indeed an active source of presencing: within its close embrace, things get located and begin to happen. (63)

Presence, as a concept, has been foundational to rhetoricians—in the sense of what serves as evidence for people in argumentation, the kinds of topics (topoi) that have traction with particular audiences; I am specifically thinking of Chaim Perelman and Lucy Olbrecht-Tyteca's *New Rhetoric* (1991) and the section on "Selection of Data and Presence" and Burke's notion of terministic screens in *Language as Symbolic Action* (1968). Of course, these scholars draw from Aristotle as a framework for understanding rhetoric, and that similar base connects their work and allows me to make this synthesis. Often, early scholars in the New Rhetoric worked to understand how, psychologically, some evidence affects a listener while other evidence does not. There are main themes that play out in these writings, such as material objects, places, and voice having force in acts of persuasion; the degree of presence—or perhaps we can say identification—for listeners or audience members is a part of this act of persuasion. Though my project is somewhat moving out of the realm of persuasion as the *telos* for rhetoric—and in the next section I also explain a shift toward thinking of place through the lens of chôra rather than topoi—I still think this earlier work is not outmoded. Place, its weather, vegetation, buildings, habitats, and so forth, affects us, and perhaps *presence* is the word to use when discussing these effects. Affect, of course, does not have to have intent—or maybe it is fair to say intent may be there in communicative acts—but the outcome, or how the message is received, is often chancy, given the complex ecological system human agents find themselves to be a part of always.

I further want to assert that presencing of place is a project that is always going to be bound up with the nondiscursive. We can feel lost because we have no means to recover what we think we experience and know about a place. There are many places I feel connected to that I cannot explain the whole of; there is almost a level of language play, of synecdoche, when we begin to write on place—a part always stands in for the whole. A trace may be the only meaning we have.

The theoretical frame I am attempting to build through this brief section may need some explicit untangling before I transition to the later section on Greek *chôra*, a generative term through which to understand place—one that shows us how place is spatial, embodied, and discursive. In more succinct language, through this section I argue that movement is a rhetorical practice important to creating a sense of dwelling. As such, movement, I believe, is essential to knowing the places we inhabit and ourselves; I suggest that perpetual wandering—within particular boundaries, that is, cosmoses or provinces—may reveal place to us and may make the nondiscursive aspects of place known to us discursively; and I forward that rhetorical ethos is essentially tied to these movements in space and time. Corder and Muñoz serve as case studies of authors who deliberately consider their relationship with and search for place. In what follows, I seek to shift the rhetorical vocabulary about place in the field of rhetoric and composition by situating my investigations into revealing place through acts of movement in the term *chôra* rather than the more often-discussed term for place, *topoi*.

INTERLUDE I: WANDERINGS WITH CORDER AND GESTURES WITH MUÑOZ

Sometimes, we're compelled to write to not forget, to not forget places and loved ones and cultures.

When I accepted my job offer, I called Theresa Enos to tell her the news. I was expecting a pat on the back, but I didn't get it. Instead, I got a push, an insistence, an imperative to remember.

Her first words were a question, "What are the tenure requirements?" Then she added, "You better get those in writing, Rosanne." Theresa was always concerned with the particulars, and having been denied tenure on her first attempt, she was sensitive and shrewd about the demands of academic life. She was always trying to mentor me, even if I didn't always quite see it at the time. I remember saying something to the effect of, "I think I can get tenure with a book or an equivalent number of articles. I'll probably just do the articles."

"You better write the book," Theresa responded. "How else are people in the field going to know Jim Corder?"

Around the time I graduated, Theresa gave me her copy of Corder's *Lost in West Texas* (1988). On the title page, in his handwriting, it reads "To Theresa Enos, with fondest best wishes Jim W. Corder 2/1/90." I remember she handed it to me and said, in her sort of matter-of-fact Theresa way, "When I die, my son will get all my books, and I want to make sure you have this one." It's the only thing I have of hers.

Lost in West Texas (1988) is my favorite book by Corder because it's the book that helped me understand how place is a part of our sense of who we are. The book is a collection of creative nonfiction essays about the author's memories of growing up in West Texas and his longing to return there, though he feels returning is impossible because most of what he knew and loved about the area is gone. When I consider the title, I don't believe he means he has lost his way through his territory; rather, he dramatizes being lost as a way of recovering place. In the opening of the chapter titled "Late Word from the Provinces," Corder offers the reader explicit directions for how to get to one of West Texas's landmarks, the Croton Breaks:

> If you could go from Fort Worth straight as the crow flies just a little to the north of west, you'd be there after about 180 miles, though I don't know, actually, that I've ever seen a crow fly straight. The way there by the wavering, bending route that people take is longer by a little, maybe 195 miles. The road, though a little crooked, is chiefly west, as most of the roads I take are. (5)

The excerpt here reveals Corder's need to share this place with his reader, to invite us, using an informal "you" address to explain to the reader how to find this place. He is an insider writing the place for outsiders. The territory and direction of West Texas seem to call to him. The opening even has a sort of fantastical quality, as he asks the reader to envision a crow flying above the landscape, to see the territory through the perspective of aviation. Throughout the book we can see Corder is playing with the traditional concept of being lost. He proposes the idea that one can become lost in a familiar place because of continual interactions with it. He wanders this territory in West Texas, which he continually refers to as his "province" and "cosmos," because in the act of wandering he hopes to get lost. He wants to make the familiar strange. By becoming lost in a familiar place, Corder wishes to reveal something he doesn't already know about the place. I think in wandering, Corder hoped to make the nondiscursive discursive; he wanted the place to reveal itself to him.

Corder's writings on place have a fantastical quality—one might even venture to call it *mythic*. It is the type of discourse written when the whole truth cannot be apprehended, when place withdraws from us. For we must tell and write myths when the truth is not sensible to us.[4] Roberta, his widow, told me Corder wanted to write "an epic for the common man." I take this to mean he wanted to represent the stories of white working-class people from the West—like his grandparents and parents.[5] He views these stories in opposition to the Western Canon, at least the one he studied as a graduate student of English literature in the 1970s. Those stories, from Europe and Greece and old New England, were not from his land or about his people.

For him, West Texas as territory becomes a world unto itself—the set-ting for these narratives. Corder (1988), I argue, is writing a cosmology for West Texas. He describes the territory through specific geographical markers, which serve as boundaries of his cosmos: "The cosmos, as I am able to apprehend it, stretches from the Double Mountains northwest-ward some forty miles to the Big Rock Candy Mountain. On up that road from Aspermont, through Swenson, through Jayton, where my family lived, past Girard, I'd see it after a while off to the left." The center of the cosmos, for Corder, is the Double Mountains; he claims they are "the dwelling place of God" and "the markers of [his] province, they are the first boundary of the cosmos" (7).[6] For the purpose of *Lost in West Texas,* Corder claims this territory in West Texas as his cosmos; in some ways it feels like the site of origin for him, a site he feels compelled to con-tinue to return to, to wander around, and to think through. Place helps locate Corder, his understanding of himself; he sees place as integral to ethos development.

We, like Corder, can feel lost because we have no means to recover what we think we experience and know about a place. We may have no means to recover and describe the people we have lost. We may have no words. We may have no images. We may have nothing. Corder (1988) captures this moment in which knowledge and discourse end for him in his search for West Texas:

> And I am lost. I always find myself trying to think through West Texas, out of West Texas, back into West Texas. Scarcely any work proceeds long without angling somehow through, into, or out of West Texas. I'm always looking for West Texas or my part of it, and not finding it. My part of West Texas doesn't show up much in books. Can I get a witness? Why is it never there? Can I get a witness? (90)

I excerpt this passage for several reasons. Interestingly, it emphasizes the connection between movement and the discursive. The preposi-tions Corder uses, "through," "out," "into," and "back," remind the reader that revealing place is a process—whether it be through writing or wandering, or more accurately, though both writing and wandering. The process involves labor, as expressed through the key verbs "trying," "looking," and "finding." Corder does mean to suggest his mind wan-ders while writing—which is a form of labor—but because *Lost in West Texas* also chronicles a road trip through the territory, he also means to talk about his wandering in a physical way. We are invited to read Corder as practicing an embodied form of wandering, like the peripa-tetic philosophers. He labors in a material sense of walking and driving through West Texas. At the end of the passage, Corder admits that, in some ways, the discursive has failed him, that he cannot find the West Texas he imagines.

His call for a witness to corroborate his version of West Texas also strikes me as searching for a discursive representation that captures the affective feeling of his experience of place, and even in some ways of time. Corder never gave up the search for his version of West Texas; he continued looking and searching, and he kept trying to make the nondiscursive discursive. That search is probably why I became a witness for his work, why I wanted to write about him. I keep thinking if I get Corder down, if I heed Theresa's imperative to write the book, he won't be lost, and neither will she.

Sometimes, we're compelled to write to not forget, to not forget places and loved ones and cultures.

My friend Jess and I packed the Mexican Coke bottles in a reusable bag. I can't remember how many bottles there were, but for some reason they weren't in a pack, so they slightly clanked as we took turns holding the bag while walking the mile from my house to the event.

We were on our way to meet José Esteban Muñoz. His book, *Cruising Utopia: The Then and There of Queer Futurity* (2009), had been published a few years before. He was at the University of Arizona to give a lecture as part of the Miranda Joseph Endowed Lecture Series. We were attending an invitation-only workshop with Muñoz where graduate students who were publishing in the area of queer studies could share their works in progress with him and receive feedback.

I wasn't a queer studies scholar, and I also wasn't very far into my graduate studies, but I remember Caryl Flinn and Adela Licona interceded somehow to get me on the VIP list. I so wanted to be there. I so wanted to meet this person who wrote about identification in ways that forwarded my thinking, whose prose electrified my mind and drew me into a world of performance of queer identities, describing the stage performances of artists like Vaginal Davis, Carmelita Tropicana, and Kevin Aviance. In *Cruising Utopia*, Muñoz (2009) looks to the theories of Ernst Bloch to lay out what he calls an "oddball endeavor" in thinking about the queer, utopian possibilities afforded by works of art, text, and performance (26). Muñoz insists life should not be dictated "by the spatial/temporal coordinates of straight time" and that when we experience and analyze a performance, particularly by queers of color, we see a refusal of the hegemonic present and an opening toward a future of queer potentialities, or ways of being (31).

Muñoz plots out a future that doesn't rely on reproduction and heteronormative visions for a good life. Instead, he invites readers to take the drug ecstasy with him in the conclusion of *Cruising Utopia* (2009); he insists we step out of straight, chronological, and ordinary time and into "ecstatic time," or "the moment one feels ecstasy, announced perhaps in a scream or grunt of pleasure, and more importantly during moments of contemplation when one looks back at a scene from one's past, present, or future" (32). This orientation to time is similar to discussions on kairos I was just beginning to encounter in my own reading. Muñoz, too, gives readers a language in which to be hopeful and excited for the future, without the drive for reproduction and having babies—which I am all about. Also, both his books, though academic in nature, helped me see an example of how to write and publish in a way that relies on narrative and case studies and descriptions of places and people that matter to the author.

Furthermore, in chapter 4, "Gesture, Ephemera, and Queer Feeling Approaching Kevin Aviance," Muñoz (2009) does the work of describing how movement—in this case Aviance's voguing—is a form of expression of queer identity that resists heteronormative presentation of the male, Black body and allows for different ways of being and becoming. Muñoz continues to say queerness operates outside straight space and time and thus cannot be mapped or recognized by those codes. He proposes that researchers develop a hermeneutic of looking at the performance of queerness as fleeting and "lost;" the researcher is then led to think of the study of queerness as "ephemera," trying to track down the "trace, the remains, the things that are left, hanging in the air like a rumor" (65). Muñoz mentions *Paris is Burning* (Livingston 1990), the documentary that features drag artists, like Willi Ninja and Angie Extravaganza, as a part of this queer archive of feeling in which the audience sees the spaces of the drag balls in New York City and the performance of queer identities in motion. The director Jennie Livingston, through her interviews with the drag "houses" and their "mothers" and "children," as well as coverage of the performances in the film, coupled with defining terms like "realness," offers a window into this world and its participants. In several scenes, we see the categories the queens compete in, like "executive" and "military" and "schoolboy," and "realness" is the ability to be the essence of that category; in other words, for that performance, you are an "executive," you "pass," even if the homophobic and racist barriers in the outside world prevent it in everyday life.

Muñoz (2009) frames this chapter with a personal narrative, discussing his Cuban background and a moment from his childhood when the male members of his family made fun of the way he walked because he swayed like a woman. He became sensitive to his movements and their excess, controlling his walk and projecting what he perceived in the movements of other men. He didn't want to be read as queer and desired to pass in order to be safe (68). This recollection relates to Aviance's dancing, as Muñoz observes a kind of gender play in his movements; however, in the moment, Aviance is able to express his inner realities out of joy and not fear: "His gestures are *unapologetically* femme. His fingers swiftly minister to his face, as though applying makeup. His movements are coded as masculine (strong abrupt movements), feminine (smooth flowing moves), and, above all, robotic (precise mechanical movements)" (76; emphasis mine). Aviance's gender is not to be mapped by some binary code; he is even described as posthuman. Muñoz argues that the audience appreciates Aviance because his performance evokes "the pleasures of being swish and queeny that they cannot admit to in their quotidian lives" (79). There is a process of identification happening in these performance spaces. The spectators "show love" for the queens and dancers because they are let into the queens' worlds and can be themselves through them—the spectators think, in some way, that the queens and dancers move how the spectators want to move. The dance floor is a haven because when these performers and spectators leave the balls, they face prejudices, oppression, and violence from a world that doesn't show them love but rather polices their movements and thus makes them police themselves in their expressions, as Muñoz describes having to do as a child. Muñoz asks us to think critically about the way performance queers space and time to offer potentialities for nonnormative subjects, as Aviance embodies "a message of fabulousness and fantastical becoming" (80).

I don't remember much of the details of the afternoon with Muñoz. I remember the feeling of that moment more than the conversations themselves. Muñoz created a space for graduate students to share their work that allowed us to imagine a future where this work would live. He modeled a form of generosity I hoped to enact myself someday. He plotted out what a future in the academy could look like if you were lucky enough to make it, and I did think that perhaps I could make it after talking with Muñoz. He helped me see there was a space for me. I'm sure he did that for a lot of people, and for scholars of color, that moment might have been even more transformative.

At the end of the talk, Jess and I presented the bag of Mexican Coke bottles to him. These referred to an image by Andy Warhol Muñoz references in the beginning of his book. Muñoz (2009) writes that the Coke bottle in Warhol's art allows us "to see the past and the potentiality imbued within an object, the ways it might represent a mode of being and feeling that was not quite there but nonetheless an opening," and the focus on everyday, commercial things as a part of art may signal the utopian possibilities ahead (9). I don't remember Muñoz's reaction to the bottles of Mexican Coke, but Jess says he made a joke about it, thanking us for the "dirty capitalist water." Surprisingly, I only remember what I felt, which was a sense of calm and acceptance. I felt Muñoz saw me not just for who I was at the moment but what I could become. He signed my book, "April 3, 2012 / To Rosanne / Best of Luck with your Queer Futurity / José."

They're gone now—Jim, José, Theresa. There's a form of mourning for the works they never wrote or published, for the words they didn't get to speak. It's hard to explain what I feel, except to maybe say I'm trying to recover what's lost. I circle back to Corder's and Muñoz's writings to trace the connections they make among movement, place, and affect, to see the ways character (ethos) is understood and expressed.

Sometimes, we're compelled to write to not forget, to not forget places and loved ones and cultures.

BEYOND *TOPOI*: THE GENERATIVE POSSIBILITIES OF *CHÔRA*

> And yet, "khora" seems never to let itself be reached or touched, much less broached, and above all not yet exhausted by these types of tropological or interpretive translation.
>
> –Jacques Derrida, *On the Name*

When scholars in rhetoric and composition discuss place—either through the act of writing or through the physical—they traditionally turn to the word *topoi* because it is a rich term in its own right, as it relates to geographical places and to the place of ideas (topics) in argumentation. There are noted exceptions to this invocation of *topoi* (Rice 2007; Rickert 2013; Ulmer 2002); however, place-based analyses—and other writings on rhetorical invention in argument—have focused on *topoi* as the central term.[7] I see this focus as a result, perhaps, of the field's early reliance on Aristotelian notions of rhetoric—particularly those scholars who were reviving rhetoric in English departments in the service of teaching composition. However, understanding and speaking of place was more complex in ancient Greece, and of course even now, than the writings of Aristotle indicate. The Greek term *chôra* also was a part of representing place. *Chôra*, to me, has rich connotations, as it is associated with spatial, discursive, and embodied meanings; in this section attempt to draw out these threads of the definition for the term.

Chôra covers more ground than *topoi* quite literally because it is often translated as "region" or "countryside"—the space beyond place (*polis*)—but also because *chôra* predates *topoi* as a term in the Greek lexicon (Walter 1988, 120). It is often said to explain the creation of place—it is a generative place for the creation of places. *Chôra*—because of its translation as "receptacle," or "site," for creation—takes on the qualities of the places and things it holds, and thus it is a hard term to be "reached" or "touched," as Jacques Derrida (1995) notes in the epigraph at the beginning of this section. At times, it eludes a clear discursive description. For this reason, I desire to shift the thinking of place as topoi to place as chôra in order to see place as a thing that withdraws from speakers and wanderers.

I want to briefly discuss the term *topoi* and its usefulness to rhetorical study and composition teaching before moving on to *chôra*. Invention, in the Aristotelian system, is of supreme importance, as it is the way of discovering the means of persuasion. Aristotle speaks of invention through the use of topoi (topics), with which the speaker searches out the values and beliefs of the culture and how to present them to their audience in meaningful ways. As George Kennedy, translator of Aristotle's *Rhetoric* (1991), explains, "*Topos* literally means 'place,' metaphorically that location or space in art where a speaker can look for 'available means of persuasion'" (45). We communicate the proofs of our argument through the form of the syllogism in logic, the enthymeme in rhetoric. The enthymeme is like a syllogism, only it is missing the minor premise and is best used on an audience that does not require lengthy chains of argumentative reasoning to be persuaded of a truth. As Aristotle (1991) notes, to be enthymematic is "to see the true and [to see] what resembles the true, and at the same time humans have a natural disposition for the true and to a large extent hit on the truth; thus an ability to aim at commonly held opinions [*endoxa*] is a characteristic of one who also has a similar ability to regard the truth" (33). Rhetoric's reliance on opinion to inspire belief is emphasized in the treatise. The topics (commonplaces) are sometimes in opposition to each other (of course, there are several opinions on a given subject). Furthermore, the speaker must rely on their knowledge of the situation, the subject, and the audience to guide their selection of topics. The topics a speaker chooses to present and the way they arrange the evidence communicate to the audience whether or not the speaker is a person of their time, and one who knows the feelings and values of their listeners. The topics remind us rhetoric is for life; it is about communicating with people for certain ends. It is no wonder the topics appeared useful to those rhetoricians in the twentieth century who revived their study, and one of the most prominent scholars of neoclassicism in rhetoric and composition was Edward P. J. Corbett. His famous textbook, *Classical Rhetoric for the Modern Student* (1965), presents the Aristotelian topics as a system for invention in the composition classroom.

However, this rich tradition of engagement with the Aristotelian topics has, in some ways, limited our vision as a field in understanding places, writing about places, and, even more broadly, teaching invention and arrangement in writing. Aristotle may have displaced an expressive and creative tradition in choosing to use the term *topoi* in his treatise. The erasure of *chôra*, through Aristotle, has certainly contributed to what I call the *false divide* between rhetoric and poetics. As E. V. Walter (1988) notes in his detailed discussion on the differences between *topos* and *chôra* in *Placeways*:

> In the classical language, *topos* tended to suggest mere location of the objective features of a place, and Aristotle made it into an abstract term signifying pure position. The older word, *chora*, retained subjective meaning in the classical period. It appeared in emotional statements about places, and writers were inclined to call a sacred place a *chora* instead of a *topos*. (120)

This older, metaphysical meaning of place is erased in the Aristotelian tradition. Affect was a part of this older conception of place. Place was even given its own character, was named "sacred" rather than just serving as a mere container for things, people, and ideas. *Chôra*, as a term with many meanings—some of them connected with emotion—was too elusive and expressive for Aristotle's liking; it could not be contained, systematized, or explained.

However, Plato was more invested in *chôra* as a term and worked to explain its function and properties in his dialogue *Timaeus* (2013). Many contemporary scholars (Casey 1998; Derrida 1995; Rickert 2013; Ulmer 2002; Walter 1988) look to this text in their discussions of the term. Plato seemed more willing to explore the metaphysical and the sensuous than did Aristotle. *Timaeus*, in fact, has the potential to be read as a creation story in which the demiurge, out of necessity—another interesting translation of *chôra*—creates places from the elements (earth, wind, fire, water) through a process of geometrical proportioning. It is important to note that the character of *Timaeus* is a Pythagorean; it is not Socrates, the philosopher, who speaks of creation, but a mathematician and an atomist. *Chôra* is the receptacle for creation in *Timaeus*, the prerequisite for the development of places (*topos*). As Derrida (1993) writes on Plato, "It [*chôra*] is what you open to 'give' place to things, or when you open something for things to take place" (9). Walter (1988) adds to this by explaining that Plato thought of chôra as "a matrix of energies, the active receptacle, in contrast to Aristotle's later idea of the neutral container" (121). Chôra has generative possibilities, the kinds that suggest a live process of invention. It can also be seen as the interval between chaos and order, the coming together of a form before it is a form. More broadly, this interpretation is getting closer to my earlier assertion that place has nondiscursive aspects.

When I think about chôra in terms of writing, it seems like an invitation to write prose that wanders, prose that is continuing to invent itself. Writing on place, by extension, can feel like an attempt that comes closer to the ideal form of expression of the affective feelings place gives us. Gregory Ulmer (2002) asks a good question to scholar-teachers, "How [do we] practice choral writing?," and he later suggests that "it [the writing] must be in the order neither of the sensible or the intelligible but in the order of making, of generating" (67). The wanderer continues to make place for themselves. *Chôra* serves as a term that can explain this practice of movement (embodied and written). The next three subsections attempt to define chôra (spatially, discursively, and bodily) for the purposes of showing the theoretical underpinning for understanding place in regard to one of my main assertions in this chapter: that place withdraws from us discursively and must be revealed to us in a process that requires a continual attunement to place—the main practice of this process being movement.

Chôra as *Spatial*

In this section I illustrate the ways *chôra* is understood spatially. It is a term beyond *topoi*, signaling region or horizon. The sheer vastness of chôra—beyond the human eye and toward the horizon—led ancient thinkers to see it as a place prior to the creation of places. Indeed, chôra is seen as the receptacle for places and things. This idea of chôra as receptacle comes from Plato's *Timaeus*, but I am interested in how modern thinkers translate and discuss this aspect of its definition, as it reveals place as dynamic, even alive.

Derrida and Casey insist *chôra* is to be seen as its own term for place, separate from *topos*—Casey (1998) even asserts that *chôra* precedes *topoi*: "It [chôra] is what the Demiurge [Plato's divine character in *Timaeus*] encounters upon his intervention into the scene of things: hence its Necessity—so particular *topoi* ensue from creation. *Demiurgic creation consists in the configuration and specification of things in particular places within a pregiven (and already regionalized) Space*" (35; emphasis in original). This interpretation highlights the idea of chôra as related to necessity for creation, to make order of the things. Casey's description is hierarchical in a way, with chôra at the top and then *topoi* and then things. What strikes me in this description too is the attention to the interval through his use of the word "pregiven." In fact, in a later passage, he clearly says topos "is a derivative and comparatively late moment in a sequence of three stages [of creation] whose first two moments are concerned with *chôra*" (41). I think it is important to note chôra is the place for topoi; topoi can follow creation of place.

The region must be shaped first, from the chaos, before place(s) emerges. *Chôra* is also translated as the act of making room, as Derrida (1993) describes: "Chora is the spacing which is the condition for everything to take place, for everything to be inscribed" (10). The act of creating space, the idea of expansion, of making the region (receptacle), is what he is after here. The use of "condition" is revealing, as it again alludes to the idea of time. The right time—and here I am specifically referencing kairos—will lead to the condition for things and places to "take place." His use of the verb "inscribed" is also striking, with its obvious reference to writing. The receptacle maintains its own properties as container, yet it also gives space for all things to be held within it. And it keeps changing, with time. Place is not a static thing.

It is this generative capacity *chôra* highlights that makes me want to embrace the term in relation to my argument that place withdraws from us and must be continually discovered through movement. Rickert's (2013) words justify this synthesis between place and movement: "A chôra is not just the outlying territory on which the city depends. Rather, it becomes a fundamental cosmological principle, the receptacle (*hypodochen*), the matrix (or womb, *metra*), for all that comes to be" (49). This explicit connection between chôra and cosmology reaffirms the idea that places are always becoming; their dynamism obscures them from being completely known to us. Again, the cosmos is finite—it has a container, and there can be several cosmoses—but cosmos is not the universe, is not universal. The cosmos of West Texas is not associated with the term *topoi* for Corder but rather is a part of a locatory matrix for the people, places, and things he had come to know as a child and that he had come to rediscover as an adult—West Texas is the receptacle, the chôra.

Again, I find more connection to cosmos and wandering and chôra in Casey's (1998) writing: "Room translates *chora*, one of whose affiliated verbs in *chorein*, 'to go,' especially in the sense of 'to roam.' . . .

All the Atomists believe the primary bodies are in constant motion, a motion that requires room in which to move" (83). Chôra allows things to become and to be because it gives everything room to move, even if we are only talking about movement on the atomic level. But for my project, I mean to think about movement in the visible sense of locomotion through walking, or riding in a wheelchair, or taking a train. Chôra gives us room to explore, to see the open country; it is spatial in definition. Yet it still remains intangible in some respect; for example, we may sensuously experience the cosmos making room for us (and even this is a great act of attunement toward place), but we may be unable to discursively describe such phenomena. Place gives us place, if that makes any sense; we must admit there is some force in play that anchors us to the land, a connective capacity that "furnishes an ongoing ambience" (48) for us and our places and our things—perhaps that force is chôra?

And, most important, we must not see the chôric receptacle as a neutral one; the ambience chôra creates is affective. I use the word *affect* in a distributive sense to reinforce the idea that place has character, mood, and feeling. Walter (1988) explains place as having affect in *Placeways*:

> It [chôra] is not only physical space but expressive space as well—a container of feelings. According to the myth of creation that Plato tells in the *Timaeus*, the powers and feelings in *chora* made the receptacle vibrate, shake, and rock wildly, until the demiurge created a cosmos by shaping the *morphai* into regular geometric forms. Nevertheless, after creation, space remains expressive—a container of feelings. (123)

Chôra literally shakes things up—perhaps that is why I gravitate toward this term; it is not safe. *Topos* does not evoke such feeling, particularly as Aristotle constructed it; it was meant to describe, it was meant to be exact, it was meant to be a neutral container. *Chôra* is too wild to be tamed like *topoi*—and, additionally, chôral writing is hard to tame in the sense of its submitting to the conventions of arrangement as outlined in Aristotle's *Rhetoric*. *Chôra* allows for physical and written wandering; it is pure invention. And to me, it is a better term than *topoi* for understanding place for the specifics of my analysis.

Chôra as (Non)Discursive

Although *chôra* is most readily thought of as a term connoting physical space, like a container, it also must be approached for its relation to discourse. Derrida (1995), in fact, draws upon Plato's discussion in *Timaeus* to propose that chôra is neither "'sensible' nor 'intelligible,' belongs to a 'third genus' (*triton genos*, 48a, 52a)" (89). This idea of *chôra* as a middle term of this dialectic shows how it is not related to *logos* proper—if we think of *logos*'s translation as "the word," we can see how *chôra* might not be something communicable—hence the difficulties in defining the term. Plato, and by extension Derrida, does not wish to say place as chôra can never be understood entirely; rather, the discourse that surrounds chôra is not to be legitimate logos "but . . . a hybrid, bastard, or even corrupted reasoning (*logosimo notho*). It comes 'as in a dream' ([*Timaeus*] 52b)" (90). Writing the chôra need not be wrapped up in logical proofs, *doxa*, and enthymemes; it is not like topoi in that way.

Chôra is a dream discourse, an imaginative and perhaps sometimes illogical and sensuous way of expression and knowing.

Writing the chôra is beyond categorical thinking, the submission to the either/or; it is a discourse (and place) that "trouble[s] the very order of polarity, of polarity in general, whether dialectical or not. Giving place to oppositions, it would itself not submit to any reversal" (Derrida 1993, 92). Representing chôra in a written or physical form is a challenge; it is discursive and nondiscursive; it is both present and absent because it withdraws from our logical and sensible ways of knowing. As container, chôra also takes on the properties within it, leaving none for itself.

Derrida spent much time with this concept of chôra in a material sense when he tried to create an architectural representation of the term with a famous architect Peter Eisenman. Although their *Chora L Works* (Derrida and Eisenman 1997) project never came to fruition in physical form, as a public garden, their discussions and plans for the project are documented in a book by the same title. In one conversation, Derrida insists chôra is an idea that is opposite of how traditional architecture has been imagined: "Everything inscribed in it [chôra] erases itself immediately, while remaining in it. It is thus an impossible surface—it is not even a surface, because it has no depth" (10). Many of the statements made by Derrida in the book are in the service of defining chôra and also in trying to think through how it can be represented in some sort of discursive (material) form. To me, though, throughout their dialogue, Eisenman seems more optimistic that the two will find a representation for chôra. He responds to Derrida's challenge of the "impossible surface" with this conjecture: "We should try to find a program for the presence of the absence of chora and concentrate on making that sensible [to someone experiencing their exhibit]" (10). The paradox of presence and absence is one this book helped me see and experience—literally. When checking out *Chora L Works* from the library, I noted that the book had what looked to me to be holes drilled through its pages. The holes made a design, but when I confronted the written text, the holes seemed random, and it became difficult to read at several points. I kept thinking—Why the holes, Derrida? At first, I thought it was some artistic gesture, but then I realized the book—in some ways—is deconstructed. And the holes, I would say, represent a moment of presence and absence in the reading of the text. Disruption. Sometimes, the words can be filled in by the reader, given the context of the sentence, but other times, there is a withdrawal of the text—there is no discourse. The holes are representative of the very paradox of presence and absence Derrida and Eisenman were working to create in their architectural project—chôra.

Chôra's description as a middle term (a hybrid or bastard reasoning), and its property of being both present and absent, makes it essential to discourse on place because we cannot only rely on the factual or the purely imaginative for our understandings. As Rickert (2013) notes, "Life cannot be reduced to the idea, to logics, to the salient" (59). This is a call for affect, to see the emotions the container of place holds and how these emotions act on us and with us. A rhetorician who studies place must operate in a discourse not just of logos: "A choric rhetorician will attend to memory, networks, technologies, intuitions, and environments (places), because these things all touch on place as something generated, not statically present and hence prereceived" (67). The focus on an inventive discourse for place is essential to the wanderer, who keeps searching for the parts of place that withdraw from them. Place's dynamism leads to this withdrawal, so we too must continue to be in constant motion with place—looking for where it reveals itself to us, finding the inventive matrix that creates all people, places, and things.

Chôra *as Embodied*

Place is often used, too, in the description of someone's station or rank in society and when we discuss a reservation or a held place for someone to occupy. When place was used in that way in ancient Greece, the term *chôra* was preferred. People are in the locatory matrix chôra provides. As Derrida (1993) writes, a place can be "occupied by someone" (109). Casey (1998) spends several passages in *The Fate of Place* arguing that embodiment sets the condition for being in a place (233) and also that the body itself is a place: "Its very movement, instead of effecting a mere change of position, *constitutes place*, brings it into being" (235). *Topoi* does not have an embodied meaning; it operates in the realm of ideas, especially when we consider its role in argumentation—*topoi* is disembodied. Given my interest in movement as an act of practice for dwelling in this chapter, *chôra* again makes more sense as a term for place. We can only experience place through our bodies, the emplacement of our bodies in place, our bodies as place. This supports the idea of chôra as a hybrid form, as an embodied knowing of place; it is not sensible completely—yet sense must play a role in our hybrid reasoning to ascertain the affect of place.

Our knowledge of place is—again—not a form of truth, a logical discourse, or a sensible one either. Place knowledge does not operate on the level of the universal; place, and our knowledge of it, is tentative and changing. The use of cosmos to describe the place we wander alludes to that dynamism, place's constant cycle of invention. Casey explains in the *Fate of Place* (1998) how the cosmos, and our knowledge of it, must be embodied:

> The cosmos is sensed in concrete landscapes as lived, remembered, or painted: it is the immanent scene of finite place as felt by an equally finite body. Where the universe calls for objective knowledge in the manner of a unified physics or theology, the cosmos calls for the experience of the individuated subject in its midst—with all the limitations and foreclosures this experience brings with it. (78)

The idea of our knowledge of place as finite and embodied, as having a stopping point with limitations and foreclosures, points to the fact that the universal knowledge of place—if there indeed is such a thing—withdraws from us. Memory, writings, and paintings can only go so far in their discursive understanding of place. The individual subject is flawed; there are limitations to agency, and recognition of that limitation is important to any project undertaken in our postmodern time. I don't think we can altogether foreclose on the usefulness of discursive productions on place—writings, drawings, maps—as they come from a significant amount of time moving in place. There is something tangible and yet imaginative in those reflections on place—they are chôric.

Walter (1988) describes the reflections of the wanderers of place (as chôra, as cosmos) best when he says their discursive productions are "sensuous cognitions born in the dark [that] illuminate topistic experience" and that wanderers use a "mode of perception" that requires "dreaming with [their] eyes open" (122–23). The wanderer is a somnambulist. This metaphor is a powerful one. It suggests that our relationship to place is not logical but is indeed embodied—and even affective—and also that we are always half conscious in all respects of the full meanings of place.

West Texas is a dreamscape for Corder (1988); he is there—present with the chôra, walking and driving through the chôra—but not fully awake, never fully attaining all the evidence of West Texas or getting West Texas all down right. He describes his wanderings: "I can't find Jayton [a town in West Texas]. I go looking, looking. I go looking to find faces and ways and places, but map and memory fail, and what I have is all there is, my little memory text" (90). Recollections are hazy and fuzzy—dreamlike; memory too is hybrid reasoning—it is not logos and it is not sensible and it is not completely imaginative. Memory, too, can be flawed.

There is a continual dialectic happening with the chôra: the dialectic of the inside and outside. There is a withdrawal of our places from us: one that causes us to be in a perpetual state of wandering to get back into place. As Walter (1988) remarks, "Human experience makes a place, but a place lives in its own way. Its form of experience occupies persons—the place locates experience in people. A place is a matrix of energies, generating representations and causing changes in awareness" (131). To unpack, we are in place as bodies in motion, but we are moving through places (chôra) that contain us—and not just us, but other bodies, emotions, places, things. Place as chôra has its own inventive capacities and its own dynamic life, so we must continually be in motion too in order to work through this dialectic between us and place, for motion helps us make the nondiscursive aspects of place discursive. In the next section, I hope to further explain the outdated metaphor of the inside/outside and, by extension, try to posit a theory in which the gap between us and the environment is bridged through passageways created by acts of wandering place. Movement creates what I am calling *chôraphilic memory* with place; in other words, we are able to fold the inside out and create a synthesis between us and place—discursive representations of place, I additionally argue, are the result of this synthesis.

INTERLUDE 2: THERESA, ARIZONA SUNLIGHT, AND SWEET TEA

The fondest memories I have of Theresa are our visits at her home. We used to sit in her living room—I on her purple leather couch, and she across from me in her high-backed chair, propping her feet up on an ottoman, the Arizona sun blazing through her bay window against my back. There, we'd drink sweet tea, play fetch with her dog and cat, and talk the hours away.

She told me all manner of stories about famous people in the field and about her kids and grandkids and Texas and what is was like being

Jim Corder's student and her days in competitive ballroom dance. And I told her about my family and friends in Connecticut and how much I missed them and my aspirations for the future (to return to the East Coast) and the new recipes I was trying at home and the latest themed party we hosted. We talked about her health. We talked about what would happen if she couldn't continue to direct my dissertation.

She'd always start out these meetings with business, though, taking out the paper copy of my latest draft of my dissertation. She'd turn on the floor lamp beside her and put on her reading glasses. We'd sit in silence as she scanned the words on the paper in front of her, rerembering the written comments she had meticulously taken the time to write on the draft she would later hand to me. I can hear her critiques of my writing, things I still say to myself even now as I compose: "Rosanne, this chapter needs a transition. How does what you said here build on to the next idea?" "Where are your Swales moves, Rosanne?" Or, my personal favorite: "Well, there were a lot of infelicities of sentence structure here."

Though Theresa was fierce in her critique and in her mentoring, there were always equal moments of praise and admiration for the work: "This is wonderful." "People are going to read this in print someday, Rosanne." "You've not just historicized Corder in your work, but you've taken his theories and made them applicable for today's field." She never judged me and she respected me for who I was and she believed in me and my work, which is what I really needed at the time.

It was the hardest work. At times the list of edits seemed endless. Sometimes, I'd go home and cry afterwards. But I couldn't imagine doing the work with anyone else. Theresa was my best editor, the person I wrote for and with.

When she died, I put the book project aside; I put these theories of ethos aside and Corder aside. It was too painful to read Corder. I convinced myself it would be okay if I didn't write a book. I thought there wasn't an audience for the work. My audience died when she died.

Little by little, I gained momentum to write again. I kept thinking about how much labor went into my dissertation, of all the hours in the living room and all the sweet tea we drank. Though this isn't the same written product by a mile, there are hints of that original dissertation work, there are still sentences and ideas here Theresa poured over and loved.

I began mentioning the book project at conferences. I started talking to my colleague Harry in free moments at work. I talked to my graduate school friends about my ideas. I participated in a junior-faculty writing group at CUNY. People seemed interested. I began to believe there was an audience to write for and that now was the time for a book like this, a book that—as my dissertation dedication described—was intended for scholars who, like Corder (1993b), desire to do a "scholarly sort of work but to write in a personal sort of way" (281).

After Theresa's death, it became important to write about these memories, the people I loved, the places and the things that reminded me of them. It became important to show that this kind of memory work—this kind of loving work, this chôraphilia—belongs in scholarship, is the driving force of it all. How do you write a book about ethos without giving up the origins of your character? Would I have become a scholar without Theresa and the living room, the purple couch and the Arizona sunlight, and the scrawled-on paper copies of my drafts and the sweet tea? Shouldn't our students be invited to trace their places and to write of their people and their things?

Sometimes, we're compelled to write to not forget, to not forget places and loved ones and cultures.

FOLDING AND UNFOLDING: THE CASE
FOR CHÔRAPHILIA AND MEMORY

Topoi, spatially and in argument, are used to separate and make categories; they create boundaries and divide one idea or region from the other. The dialectic of the inside/outside functions this way too—when we see place as topoi, we create separations among places and people and things. Place as chôra allows us to see synthesis of what was once thought of as separate and discreet. Furthermore, the subject/object dichotomy is called into question through this critical orientation; we can see the possibility of its being bridged, or even—as a scholar like Rickert (2013) would argue—that there is now no such thing as the subject/object binary, at least when we see existence from an ontological perspective (43). I don't think that I can make the claim that there is no separation between subject and object, but I do think there are practices and ways of being that allow us to be in a state in which the subject and object fold in on each other—in which there is a coexistence of ourselves and the places where we dwell. I want to say that movement—both embodied and in mind—is one of the vehicles that create passages in order to fold the inside out.

Muñoz's invitation to take ecstasy in *Cruising Utopia*, to live outside of straight time and in an altered present state, is a utopian discourse that scrutinizes the movements in performance that may lead the viewer to see the potentialities of a more just world.

Benjamin was also given to writing about practices of cruising the city, high on hashish. In *The Arcades Project* (2002), he particularly focuses his discussions on the image of the flâneur and his practice of roaming the streets of Paris. This person, this wanderer, described as a daydreamer, fascinates me (423). He, like the traveler Walter describes, "dreams with his eyes open" (123). I assert that the flâneur experiences and knows place as chôra because the outside becomes the inside for them. The exterior, spatially, becomes interior as "[a]rcades are [seen as] . . . passages having no outside" (406); furthermore, Paris is seen as "one great interior. . . . the city can appear to someone walking through it to be without thresholds: a landscape in the round" (422). This idea of a space without threshold, without restraint, is reminiscent of chôra, beyond the boundaries of topoi. The flâneur roams through this landscape as in a dream; for it is only in a dream state that the "rhythm of perception and experience is altered in such a way that everything—even the seemingly neutral—comes to strike us; everything concerns us" (206). Benjamin's use of *concerns* here is important to me, as place no longer becomes a neutral container, a backdrop for subjective experience; rather it concerns us, and—to go even further—becomes folded into us. Dream consciousness, too, is a persistent concept for me when considering place and our experience of it. In fact, in this section, I want to further the idea that memory—both in body and mind—is an integral part of experiencing place.

Memory, when we talk about it in the subjective sense, is dreamlike. I am reminded of Tennessee Williams's *Glass Menagerie* (2011); in the opening, Tom, the narrator, tells the audience, "The play is memory. Being a memory play, it is dimly lighted, it is sentimental, it is not realistic" (59). The soft lighting and the dimness of memory filter the ways we know place. Forgetting is the darkness of memory; it is where experience withdraws from us. Place, too, has its unseen and unknown—and if we want to be Platonic, unremembered—aspects. Grasping place as chôra involves an exploration of memory and its dreamlike qualities.

Many scholars have linked attachment, or love, *philia* in Greek, with topos—topophilia, which means love of place. Corder (1988) even invokes this word in describing his nostalgia for West Texas (88). However, I am advocating a change in thinking about attachment to place as chôric, and thus it makes sense to create the term *chôraphilia*. Love of place (chôra) involves a recognition of its simultaneous folding and unfolding—its synthesis and withdrawal from us. Chôra, like memories, is ever present and absent in our conceptions. And, thus, I find *chôraphilia* to be a more complex term to use in describing our constant embodied, emotional, and mindful experience of place.

I turn to the concept of the fold in my understanding as to how place can be seen as a part of us and us of it. Rickert (2013) tries to show his readers how a shift in seeing place as chôra encourages scholars to believe humans are not autonomous and separate from their environment: "From the choric perspective I seek to explain here, minds are at once *embodied*, and hence grounded in emotion and sensation, and *dispersed* into the environment itself, and hence no longer autonomous actants but composites of intellect, body, information, and scaffoldings of material artifacts" (43). The key words in this sentence are highlighted by Rickert to emphasize a condition of human simultaneity—we are at once embodied and folded into our surroundings. It is important to note the use of the word "composite," as it suggests a combining of all these elements. And further, Rickert does not merely mean these things are *linked*—like the metaphor of the network—but that we see place [topoi] and person as "coadaptive, as they are enmeshed and enfolded, making them mutually conditioning entities that have already emerged from a larger, worldly whole" (106). The verb "conditioning" here signals to me a mutual movement. Although conditioning may only be used here in the sense of microscopic movement in reference to the vitality of things, I think we can also interpret it to mean movement in a visible sense, such as locomotion. The larger place of emergence, for place and person and language, is the receptacle itself, the chôra. To add to the words describing this synthesis, we get Casey's (1993) description of place creation: "The body and other items in the scene—whether they be other human beings, pieces of furniture, paintings on the walls, the walls themselves, or whole buildings—co-participate in creating a place" (141). Again, "participate" is a lively verb, yet it is applied to all things—human and nonhuman—that inhabit this scene. When there is an even distribution of agency across all things in a place, we can begin to see it as a "larger, worldly whole," and we can additionally understand how the fold can be a useful metaphor to describe the ways all things are "mutually conditioning entities."

Deleuze is often associated with the revival of the fold in twentieth-century philosophy—of course the fold is a concept that can be traced back to the baroque period[8]—but it is important to see how the metaphor can be a useful image for relations between our environments and us. Deleuze, of course, follows Michel Foucault's lead in talking about how institutions create the modern subject as this subject folds the values of the outside in—one need only to read Foucault's *The History of Sexuality* to understand how power circulates from institutions and suppresses the individual. Foucault, Deleuze (1986) asserts, did not seek to encounter the self on the outside but rather to find how the other is folded into the subject (98). There is a lessening of the distance between self and other, far and near, to the point that the "*inside-space* . . . will be completely co-present with the outside space on the line of the fold" (118). Yet, how does the fold occur? What are the conditions that anticipate the creation of the fold? I think the answer lies in Deleuze's description of movements across the outside and the inside. He writes, "The outside is not a fixed limit but a moving matter animated by peristaltic movements, folds and foldings that together make up an inside: they are not something other than the outside, but precisely the inside *of* the outside" (96–97). This description is perhaps confusing because there is very little distinction as to what constitutes the inside—but we can interpret it to mean movement precedes the fold and the fold creates the enmeshed condition of the inside-out. This is the site of copresencing or coparticipation, or whatever word one wishes to attach to the phenomenon.

When we want to think of the human role in this process of the fold, and again we must see the human as one actor among a series of coparticipants of distributive value, we must turn to analyzing how humans create movement across and among their environments. These acts of wandering—both embodied and mental—must in some way create the line of the fold. We are always participating with the outside—it is a given—but the outside too participates with us, precedes us and creates us. But don't we also work to create it (the chôra)? Embodiment, for us, is the key to our understanding of the fold and our participation in movements. As Casey (1993) describes, place (chôra) is the receptacle for our wandering and daydreaming:

Place ushers us into what *already is*: namely, the environing subsoil of our embodiment, the bedrock of our being-in-the-world. If imagination projects us out *beyond* ourselves while memory takes us back *behind* ourselves, place subtends and enfolds us, lying perpetually *under* and *around* us. In imagining and remembering, we go into the ethereal and the thick respectively. By being in place, we find ourselves in what is subsistent and enveloping. (xvii)

One thing Casey brings forth is that embodiment is only known through our relation to place—we can only understand our being by being in place. And, place is also the receptacle for our movement—both bodily and in mind. In the next subsections, I hope to elucidate how memory plays a role in our experience of place and the ways we are folded with it.

Embodiment and Memory as Fold

Subjective memory cannot exist without the sensuous perceptions of the body. Just from a logical perspective, we are transported into our memory sometimes through sensation—a familiar smell, the way something feels in our hands, the music that played during this or that event. Memory has a way of transporting us through time to other places. Gaston Bachelard (1994), in fact, speaks to the capacity for people to become enamored with their first home—their childhood home—in the *Poetics of Space*. This *chôraphilia* with the home is only made possible, he asserts, through the "passionate liaison of our bodies, which do not forget, with an unforgettable house" (15). The body is indeed the site of being in a place, of dwelling as movement through the house; and thus the body instantiates memory. Bachelard continues in this same passage to describe the strong connection chôraphilia has with the body: "The house's entire being would open up, faithful to our own being. We would push the door that creaks with the same gesture, we would find our way in the dark to the distant attic. The feel of the tiniest latch has remained in our hands" (15). What Bachelard is describing is muscle memory and the ways we gain access to places through our bodies. Many of us can remember a specific door or window that had to be opened a certain way in a house we once inhabited. The tactility of our bodies moving through space must create a connection with place that allows for a fold to occur. Our being and the house's being are not separate things, I think. How can we not account for the body in considering our attachment to a home, even if we have not been there for a long time? Nostalgia for a place, perhaps, is not an ache originated in the mind for a time past but in the body, in the flesh. Our body knows the places we have been, too. It makes us feel a kind of copresence with a house or another sacred site, yet we are sometimes displaced or absent from this place.

We must delve further into Bachelard's (1994) notion of the house in relation with our being. Bachelard does not mean to say perceptions create memory; this view of the relation between body and place is too simple. Rather, he means to communicate that bodies "enter, and are taken up, into places" (Casey 1993, 102). Bodies are folded into places. And Bachelard is trying to account for "the phenomenon of body memory . . . how bodies remember certain places to have been and how to orient and reorient themselves in regard to these same (and like) places" (Casey 1993, 102). Bodies belong to places, and indeed places belong to bodies; they are copresent through the phenomena of movement and muscle memory.

Casey, in fact, goes a step further in connecting body to place through the idea of the universal flesh. Of course, he is looking to the phenomenologist Maurice Merleau-Ponty and his book *The Visible and the Invisible* (1968), and I want to return to Merleau-Ponty for a moment to discuss his conception of flesh. He defies our understanding of flesh as just part of the body; for him, it is part of the body and yet beyond the body. Flesh is also in the environment. He defines flesh, at first, by what it is not:

> The flesh is not matter, is not mind, is not substance. To designate it, we should need the old term "element," in the sense it was used to speak of water, air, earth, and fire, that is, in the sense of a *general thing*, midway between the spatio-temporal individual and the idea, a sort of incarnate principle that brings a style of being wherever there is a fragment of being. (139)

Merleau-Ponty's discourse is that of the elemental; he is thus in the discourse between logos (the real) and the imaginative. I think he is in the territory of chôra here in this definition because flesh seems to be acting as receptacle for being, or a style of being. To see flesh as embodiment and yet beyond embodiment is to recognize it as a fold of all things. Casey (1993) describes how flesh as body and flesh as environment fold together:

> The two porous surfaces, one belonging to the circumambient world and the other to my *corps propre*, intertwine and become at once co-experiential and co-essential. My lived body rejoins a wild place—this free-standing grove of trees, that unruly patch of sea—as the flesh of one takes in the flesh of the other. As I come to know it from within such a place, despite its wildness (or rather, just because of it) becomes "flesh of my flesh." (10)

This passage highlights how our bodily flesh, as substance, is porous, and the environment, in some degree, must pass through us. Again, the adjectives used to point to a synthesis of place and person, "co-experiential" and "co-essential," show a lively connection between the two. The fold, as described here, is one flesh to another flesh. The end of the passage refers to the communion of followers with Christ, as they consume—perhaps one can say fold—the body of Jesus into themselves. Depending on the denomination of Christianity being practiced, the body and blood of Christ can mean communion or consubstantiation with God. Either way, though, taking communion is a symbolic act of being with Christ. There is something about this action of one flesh taking on the other—even when we consider it only in the form of self and environment—that is ritualistic, spiritual even. In some ways, Casey's description of the intertwining of the flesh is poetic and relates to a discourse beyond the logos of knowing a place. For this reason, the comingling of the flesh—person and place—is not an act of topophilia but of chôraphilia. In the next subsection, I move beyond embodiment to the act of mental wandering as part of the process of the fold that leads one to experience chôraphilia.

Dreaming and Memory as Fold

Memory not only exists in the body but also requires the mind to wander from the present, to skip through space and time. This mental wandering helps us "abide within ourselves" (Bachelard 1994, xxxvii), and it is essential to how we came to dwell in our current and past places. We are compelled to seek out the places (and times) that matter to us, whether we go to these sites in a physical sense or we travel to them through our memories: "As Freud, Bachelard, and Proust all suggest, to find place—a place we have always already been losing—we may need to return, if not in actual fact then in memory or imagination, to the very places we have once known" (Casey 1993, x). Places withdraw from us—we lose them—but to return to them is to renew the connection, the fold we have with our sacred places.

I am concerned here with our ability to dream about places, to call them forth and make them present to us, as I am in the opening of the chapter when I describe invoking places while stuck in the subway car. However, I don't think this making present is always a unilateral directionality in the sense that the human subject wills the place to return. I wonder if, too, the place itself—as fold—somehow wills itself into presence. The pull of place cannot be denied. West Texas, I think, called to Corder—was enfolded in his flesh. Muñoz feels the pull of punk-rock stages and the spaces of drag shows, asking his audience to relive the performances that matter to him. Place is persistent, I want to assert. Even Bachelard (1994) thinks place's agency is strong: "It is a strange situation. The space we love is unwilling to remain permanently enclosed. It deploys and appears to move elsewhere without difficulty; into other times, and on different planes of dream and memory" (53). His second sentence is important here because space is the subject, it has agency—it is "unwilling" to yield to a state of not being present. The fold of place, as Bachelard describes, also relies on a nonlinear sense of time—or the linear is disrupted as the past interrupts the present. Chôraphilia is then a state in which place claims us and folds itself into us through the vehicle of memories and dreams.

It is not unreasonable, I think, to say that place—even when we are not in it physically—plays a role in how we see ourselves and in shaping our characters. I think the fold of place—created through embodied and mental memory—literally makes the outside part of our interior life. Dwelling through movement must be connected, then, to rhetorical ethos. Although Casey (1993) doesn't say the word *ethos* in his descriptions of our relationship with place, I think he captures well the idea that place is folded into us and must be a part of our characters:

> Part of becoming intimately acquainted with a particular place is seeing it as with me at all times, not only physically in the manner of something present-at-hand or instrumentally like a ready-to-hand entity but as something I remember stays with me over time and in different places. In memory as in architecture, the things *I am with* help to constitute an ongoing "aura," an enveloping atmosphere, which surrounds me. (129)

Could Casey's "ongoing 'aura'" be thought about in the sense of place as having a type of character? And, if we believe in the fold as a possibility, could we also say a place's character influences our own? I want to believe this is true. I want to believe ethos is not just connected to abstract ideas or values (*doxa*) a culture creates, or is only connected to textual style; I also want to see ethos as connected to material things and worlds. Ethos is not abstract, but concrete; we can point to this park, that school building, this canyon as a source of how we came to know who we are. And even if these places ultimately withdraw from us, we still yearn to feel communion with them through the fold.

In the next section, I specifically delve into Corder's writings on place in order to demonstrate that place is a part of our conceptions of rhetorical ethos. Understanding ethos is only accomplished through establishing a connection to place in terms of movement, shifting our conception of place from topoi to chôra, and seeing place as a part of us through the concept of the fold. I focus on Muñoz's writing on queer performance as leaving a trace, like an aura, that opens up a world of potentialities for queer subjects. Both Corder and Muñoz are chôric composers, writing a discourse of dreams, a discourse that looks back at the present and past in order to project the subject into the future.

WANDERING ACROSS WEST TEXAS: JIM W. CORDER'S REPRESENTATIONS AND WITHDRAWALS OF LANDSCAPE

Nostalgics—most of us some of the time, some of us all the time—can't have what they ache for. Neither can I. I have wanted to find sources, origins, forces, and track them all the

way to here [West Texas]. I can't. There aren't enough words and
pictures. I can't find the rest, or I'm unwilling to make the rest
                            —Jim W. Corder, *Little Sorrows*

I continue to be a witness to Corder's search for the origins of his ethos in the places he once was and in the things he once owned. These searches reveal a type of nostalgia that originates from the power of embodied and mental memories, as well as from a strong sense of displacement from his places and times in the past. As Casey (1993) writes, we cannot think of nostalgia as only connected to lost times, but rather it is also "a pining for *lost places*, for places we have once been in yet can no longer reenter" (37). It is important to understand how places are things we can both enter and be separate from, how they are present and absent from us at the same time, and how they withdraw from us wholly and discursively. This understanding of place is a part of seeing it as chôra. Although Corder did not use this term explicitly, I believe he experienced the chôra of West Texas and worked to articulate his experience as best he could through his representations of the search for that place.

Corder connected his love of place to the notion of topophilia, but I think, because of how he describes his relationship to place as one of presence and withdrawal, that it is more accurate to say he was afflicted with a case of chôraphilia. The images of the fragment, the remnant, the scrap, the piece, the trace, are strewn throughout his writings; he believed in place as synecdoche—it was both folded in him and unfolded away from him. In *Lost in West Texas* (1988), he writes that he cannot reenter his places as he did once:

> It's all fragmented, but only partially indexed. I can call up pieces: a lost birthplace here, a map of the territory yonder; a mill here, an outhouse there, ruined house and schoolteacherly aunt over the way; a weed, a snake, a longing for food; the shadowy indeterminacy of it all; a drought; a hope for poetry; yonder, a little evidence that the world exists, and over there, some notion of what changes; here a little notice of what fall will bring, there a little account of going back. I can call up pieces, but I can't get it all back, for I never had it all. (101)

The prose reads like a list: some of the items are places, some are people, some are events, and some are feelings. Indeed, the prose itself mirrors Corder's feelings of fragmentation, as he strings together sentence fragments to make a whole. What also draws me to this passage is its reference to time—his past, present, and future relationship to West Texas. His admission at the end of the excerpt that he never fully knew West Texas reminds us of how this condition of fragmentation was always the case for Corder, even in the past—though, I assume, Corder may have felt he knew West Texas, had it all down and accounted for, in the past. Yet, as he gets older, perhaps he sees that assuredness as a falsity? Or, maybe he is starting to embrace the postmodern condition of fragmentation and deconstruction? Isn't it also true that there is a limitation to discourse; are we ever able to communicate the whole of place through our words, pictures, and drawings? Whatever the explanation for place's withdrawal, Corder felt its absence through fragmentation.

Yet he was compelled still to seek out these fragments. Reading Corder's creative nonfiction captures the ups and downs in his search for West Texas: the sadness of its withdrawal, the hope in its recovery, the excitement of its return when an artifact or memory is recovered. He explains the motive for his continued search in his book *Living and Dying in West Texas: A Postmodern Scrapbook* (2009):

> If I don't search for the once-familiar evidences of our ordinary lives, then they will be gone. If I don't get them out and study them, they will be gone. If I don't try to understand them and myself, we'll be gone. We can only understand the mystery by studying the ordinary evidences of our lives, the site of memory. (157)

Ordinary evidence, I believe, is recovering the places and things of his past. These concrete things are spatial representations of memory. Corder was embarking on this process of recovering memories through wandering in West Texas, both physically and mentally. Memory was the vehicle that allowed the fold of place and self to occur—explicating memory was the only way to make the nondiscursive discursive.

Getting lost in West Texas was the only way these memories, and then later, discursive representations, could be recovered and created for Corder. His is a project that reminds us of the importance of describing our places for each other as an act of emergence. In order for people to understand one another, their places must be focal points in stories about themselves—for most of us can understand the emotion of chôraphilia and relate to its expression. As Bachelard (1994) urges readers in *The Poetics of Space*, "Each one of us, then, should speak of his roads, his crossroads, his roadside benches; each one of us should make a surveyor's map of his lost fields and meadows" (11). This project of representation of landscape allows readers to, in a second-hand way, understand the writer's process of dwelling. Representation also allows the writer to return for another look. This impulse toward return to place inspires movement—whether in mind or in body; I have been calling this form of movement *wandering*. Wandering, as mentioned before, is a repetitive process. This is especially true for Corder as he continually drove out to

West Texas and surveyed the land. In *Chronicle of a Small Town* (1989a), he describes his search for West Texas almost in terms of a dream, a search that was not guaranteed to yield factual evidence or data:

> It's at any rate a search for what is not, for the thing that never happened, for the place that never was. That doesn't mean there is no reason to look. I'm also there, and the others are, and the places are, and there are always reasons to look, to get into as many situations for seeing as possible. We ache for home even if it never was; we always know better and don't, and love a place—or don't love it—even if it never was. (167)

There is a form of contradiction in this excerpt that makes a reader pause at the end of his last sentence—the idea that the place may not really exist. Perhaps it exists only in his mind. But, things do indeed exist—he exists, other people who lived there exist or existed, and the places can be found on the map. Being, though, doesn't confirm a sense of logos—nothing about West Texas, for him, can truly be verified, which might ultimately drive his reasoning for looking through different angles at the same territory—for writing several different books and articles about West Texas, for drawing several images of West Texas, and for collecting several objects from West Texas.

The point, I think, was never to find affirmative answers about West Texas but to keep up the search, to keep getting lost. There is fallibility in the human agent that makes them unable to ascertain the whole of place. We reach a limit in our understanding of the chôra; we fail to grasp it discursively. Corder (1989) expresses this point at which there is no knowledge:

> When you look everywhere, look back or out or sideways or in or down or up, wherever that is, you come at last, in any direction, to the place of which there is no knowledge, of which there can be no knowledge, come to that place but not into it, come only to abut it. But I don't know how to look everywhere and can't see everywhere, were I to come close. I have looked, hoping maybe to find myself or others, failing. (167)

The first phrases speak of active movement—both physical and mental—that is required in exploring every facet of a place. When we come to the place where we "abut" knowledge, it is the place, I believe, where place withdraws. We cannot fold this part into ourselves. But if we keep circling, repeating our movements, the fold must expand; our knowledge of place must become larger, until—once again—we are reminded of the limitations of discursive knowledge, the word, and logos.

On this journey, though, I think Corder recovered a sense of who he was, though not the whole of it. There were discoveries of pieces that made up the fold between self and place. These blessed particulars were found only through wandering landscapes and memoryscapes. As he writes in *Little Sorrows*, an unpublished piece, "I want to hold the ordinary, to keep it, to remember it. Perhaps it's just nostalgia. Perhaps it's my age. I don't think so. We become remnants, and then we go away. We ought to remember each other, our appurtenances, our places, we're likely to disappear" (144). This impulse to remember and to return to the land is strong in his work because, I believe, he saw the recovery of a past self, things, and places as explicitly connected to rhetorical ethos.

Ethos is not just a textual project for him, and by extension for many other people; rhetoricians must start seeing it as material. Ethos is explicitly connected to our process of dwelling. Though ethos may never be fully recovered or fully spoken, there is still a pull to search for it, as Corder writes in *Little Sorrows*: "And yet words and pictures are real. I am real. You are real. We are our time, already here, present, yet also waiting to be found. Scraps are what there is. Remnants" (303). I wonder whether these scraps and remnants can only be found through wandering? I believe, through his creative nonfiction, that Corder describes a practice for how to recover and understand ethos beyond its written manifestations.

PERFORMANCE(S) THAT BRIDGE SPACE AND TIME: STAGES WITH JOSÉ ESTEBAN MUÑOZ

> It [potentiality] is something like a trace or potential that exists or lingers after a performance. At performance's end, if it is situated historically and materially, it is never just the duration of the event. Reading for potentiality is scouting for a "not here" or "not now" in the performance that suggests a futurity.
>
> –José Esteban Muñoz, *Cruising Utopia*

In chapter 6 of *Cruising Utopia*, "Stages: Queers, Punks, and the Utopian Performative," Muñoz (2009) includes black-and-white images of punk and queer club stages—La Plaza, the Silver Lake Lounge, the Parlor Club, Spaceland, and Catch One—by the photographer Kevin McCarty. The images break up the text and remind the reader that Muñoz is writing about the performative as not only temporal but also spatial. The spatial aspect is important because he is arguing that queer feeling, the feelings of queer youth in particular, can be dismissed by heterosexuals as a "stage" in time, a "phase," but not a life reality (99). Again, this chapter reflects Muñoz's larger project, which is to step out of hegemony—particularly heteronormativity, but also white supremacy and late capitalism—and step into the queer performative, which holds the promise of a better future for those subjects who do not fit the norm.

Muñoz's writings rely on embodied memory of place, and as such relate to the idea of place as having affective meaning; we may even venture to say these McCarty images inspire a type of chôraphilia in the audience as they remember the space and time of the performances they witnessed. Muñoz (2009) remarks how these photographs are just of the stages with their lights on—they do not contain people or equipment; rather, they display "that moment of possibility right before an amazing band or performance manifests itself on stage." The photographs, he continues, are a form of "anticipatory illumination," and they show how a performance space can be imbued with meaning even after the performance is over; he writes how "the best performances do not disappear but instead linger in our memory, haunt our present, and illuminate our future" (104). The photographs offer a form a play for the viewer' sense of time. The material existence of the rooms is pictured for viewers as an inviting way into memory, as they feel their connection to the past, how it lingers today and then can shape a future self.

Though Muñoz's book is academic in nature, and not in the vein of the creative nonfiction genre of Corder's writings, we can still feel the intensely personal relationship Muñoz had with these stages, the performing artists he discusses seeing on them, and the ways McCarty's photographs inspire a sense of chôraphilia for what continues to withdraw after the performance, a hope for what is not yet here.

In one section, Muñoz (2009) describes his experiences of seeing the performer Vaginal Davis at a club called the Parlor. McCarty's image of the Parlor stage shows how the decoration is reminiscent of a Victorian parlor scene with red heavy drapes and golden tassels, a chandelier, and framed artwork on the walls. Vaginal Davis—her large, black frame taking up the whole of the small space—wears her queer punk outfits and performs "a delicate flapper dance" (110). Muñoz's adjectives to describe this scene are fantastical, as if stepping into the parlor and its performances allowed for an escape from the world outside; the ethos of the parlor used "past decadence to critique the banality of our presentness for the purpose of imagining and enacting an enabling queer futurity" (111). Muñoz emphasizes how queer performance—when read through the lens of finding what lingers after—opens the door for understanding the self in the past, present, and future; it's a theory of subject development—in Muñoz's case, the development of the queer subject in difference.

The space of the Parlor—and others discussed in the chapter—seem to be enfolded into Muñoz's sense of self. It feels as if he needs to recall these spaces to show their hold on him and others. Muñoz (2009) writes of his affective relationship to the queer punk scene:

> I dwell on and in this stage because I understand it as one brimming with a utopian performativity that is linked to the ideality that is potentiality. This potentiality is always in the horizon and, like performance, never completely disappears but, instead, lingers and serves as a conduit or knowing and feeling other people. (113)

Muñoz's use of "dwell" here is important because I think he means it in a sense of being able to flourish, as I describe in the opening of this chapter. He sees these spaces as a way of understanding himself, of understanding the emergence of his queer identity in difference—not only the emergence of his own identity, but in others too. He sees place in the ways I have been trying to set out in this chapter, as something folded into us, into others, that helps us know and be with each other. His writings show how we must attune ourselves to the material and place in our everyday in order to think on and create the future.

SOME CONCLUDING THOUGHTS ON PLACE AS CHÔRA

When you close your eyes and think on the places that matter to you, what do you see? How do you feel? How do you move through these places? What do you know about yourself and others? What has yet to be revealed and known? Learning these methods of tracing the self and others through place—practicing a hermeneutics through movement that interrogates the chôra, or what withdraws—can lead to a discourse that is rich in possibility and holds an inventive stance toward the self, others, and the future.

To summarize, I've been trying to show how rhetorical scholars should value movement as a practice because (1) it shows us a way for doing rhetorical work—particularly connected to ethos—as a form of spatial analysis; (2) it helps us rethink our conceptions of place, shifting from topoi to chôra; (3) it encourages us to see the ways place is both present and absent from us, and how this relates to our ability to represent (or not represent) our attachment to place discursively; and (4) it creates a synthesis—or fold—between place and embodied and mental memory; this too may lead us to think about our relationship to others in place.

This study also encourages scholars to see place as essential to rhetorical activity. It is not just a backdrop for human action but greatly influences and even coparticipates in communication acts and world creation. This book tries to show that rhetoric is not just the word. Place contributes to the pathos and ethos of rhetoric. Scholars must continue to acknowledge the material dimension of rhetoric, to see it as "an embodied and embedded practice," as something that emerges from an environment and situation; rhetoric is comprised of "interactive engagements, redolent of a world that affects us" (Rickert 2013, 34). This study of the practice of wandering and movements in the chôra works to draw attention to the material dimensions of rhetorical ethos specifically, to see how place is folded with us and how we share place with others.

My intention in chapters 2 and 3 is to build a sense of understanding ethos as it applies to the material and place—I am looking to scholars and professional writers as case studies to speak alongside and with these theories from rhetoric and philosophy. I want to ground these theories in narrative. I also include my own narrative, my own stories, that reveal my affective relationship to the topics and to the writers cited. One of my motives is to trace reasons for writing outside the concept of transfer. Sometimes, we're compelled to write to not forget, to not forget places and loved ones and cultures.

Mainly, I want to show how writers write to discover and make sense of themselves in the world. I argue that writers trace their affective relationships to the material and to place and to time to reveal their characters, to be with their audiences, and perhaps—in some ways—to see their writings as a way to transform themselves and readers. When we foreground *ethos* and *identification* as key terms in the practice of rhetoric and its pedagogy, how does emphasis this change our orientation to curriculum development in first-year writing? What would a first-year writing curriculum look like if it privileged the self in community and looked to local issues in place as a subject?

There are many ways to practice a pedagogy with ethos and identification at its center—I myself have experimented with several place-based and material assignments throughout my tenure as a composition instructor. What I offer in the next section is not a definitive guide for teaching this kind of writing, but I do hope to begin a dialogue for a different goal for composition—one for which we put aside issues of transfer and thinking through our own disciplinarity and take up subjects that remind us of rhetoric's ethical potentialities for being with and working to understand others.

4

FOR AN AFFECTIVE, EMBODIED, PLACE-BASED WRITING CURRICULUM

Student Reflections on Gentrifying Neighborhoods in New York City

MOVEMENT / PLACE / PEDAGOGY

"You've given your pound of flesh to New York City, kid. It's a meat grinder," my roommate says as I limp into the house, hands and knees skinned and bloodied. I had fallen in the street. In a matter of moments there had been uneven ground, the shuffling of feet and forward momentum, the force of the earth pulling me into the black concrete, and I helplessly slid across it. It is interesting how pain, as Sara Ahmed discusses in the *Cultural Politics of Emotion* (2014), makes us aware of the surfaces of our bodies and the potential for making and unmaking boundaries (25). For a moment, the street and my body and the passing cars and the onlookers were an assemblage. This flesh of New York City, which my body had now been "given to," was a plain of possibilities, the realization of Deleuze and Guattari's (2005) concept of the fold. In this episode of "Becoming New York," movement was essential to being, or perhaps more accurately to states of becoming with other people, places, and things.

This becoming is a fold, one flesh (my own) joining to another flesh (the city of New York). There is something about this action of one flesh taking on the other that is ritualistic, spiritual even. Perhaps my giving of flesh to New York City is a rite of passage to claim the status of New Yorker? I am being somewhat facetious here, but I do believe the intertwining of the flesh is a poetic act—we could even venture to say this idea inspires a discourse of wonder in relation to place. Writing about the flesh and the emotions brings us beyond the logos of knowing a place, beyond identifying it on a map and marking its boundaries. This knowledge brings us to the metaphor of place as fold and reminds us that we live in it alongside others in community—it reminds us that the end of place knowledge is self-knowledge and is part of rhetorical identification(s).

DOI: 10.7330/9781646420636.c004

Composition instructors must ask students to think beyond logos in writing, to turn toward the embodied and affective modes that center on the ethos and pathos appeals, as place-based writing in the curriculum inspires. The field's turn toward god terms, like *cognition* and *academic transfer*, take us away from the body, away from the emotions, away from the neighborhoods and communities that surround our schools, away from the material as a whole. Writing, instead, focuses on advancement in the academy as students consider the discourse communities they belong to inside our walls and then work ever so hard to reproduce them.

As outlined in the introduction, key texts in the field, such as the WPA Outcomes Statement, *Naming What We Know* (Adler-Kassner and Wardle 2015), and *Writing across Contexts* (Yancey, Roberts, and Taczak 2014) frame rhetoric as a mere set of strategies to employ in writing— "negotiating purpose, audience, context, and conventions" for the purpose of teaching students how to achieve personal advancement in their disciplinary fields and eventually in their workplaces (Council on Writing Program Administration 2019). These texts cast the applications for the study of rhetoric in a narrow way—as tools for professionalization.

In my view, writing studies has become too focused on its own disciplinarity and its position within the academy.

Acceptance in the academy shouldn't be the end of the discipline; it's an admirable goal, but not the ultimate. In my view, we must bring students into inquiry that allows them to investigate their places in the world and to see how their educations can be applied to analyzing their local contexts, writing from their standpoints, and eventually acting within their communities. We must teach how writing is a process of transformation for the writer and their audience. In this era of Trump, we cannot subscribe to a professionalization model that undermines the importance of critical analysis that leads to the work of social justice.

Furthermore, writing is not always a cognitive, logos-driven process (á la threshold concept 5, Adler-Kassner and Wardle 2015, 71). Writing can be about economic survival, reckoning with demons, escaping our realities, praise and blame and prayer. I need not reiterate the many instances we use writing to continue living.

The place-based, embodied, and affective pedagogy I am calling for throughout this chapter asks students to consider the following questions: How do we know place? How do we become a part of place, and how does it become part of us? How is writing about our places an expression of self to others? Place-based writing, at its heart, is about learning to live together. Heidegger (2013a) asserts that we must "ever learn to dwell . . . to search anew for the essence of dwelling" (363); because dwelling is the condition for building and thinking, we and our students must inquire as to what the conditions for dwelling in community are and how we learn to dwell with one another. These, of course, are questions of identification, and they privilege pathos and ethos over logos-driven epistemologies.

The above questions frame rhetoric as a discipline for the purpose of learning to live and inquire together, and this—in my view—should be the focus of the FYW curriculum. As a scholar-teacher, I perform a place-based epistemology. I am wandering —in my neighborhood in New York, on my campus, in my mind—as I write. These movements, I'm convinced, are a part of dwelling, the situating of the self and making of worlds. Dwelling is the foundation of rhetoric. The belief that wandering is a rhetorical practice is undeniable to me, as I discuss in the previous chapter, but I want to say more, I want to explain how acts of wandering create a sense of wonder in us as we work to uncover and create knowledge about places and ourselves. Place knowledge also allows us to form new lines of inquiry and research through the spaces we inhabit and to address local issues with solutions. Knowledge of place is not merely logos (the mind, the word, logic), but it is felt, embodied. Place-based writing requires us to think about epistemology differently, to indeed see movement as a form of knowledge production. Writing about these revelations can work to transform writers and readers.

I argue that placed-based inquiry and writing should play a larger role in our first-year writing curriculums because it allows students to analyze their place in the world, express their experiences to audiences, and respond to challenges they see within their communities. Since the publication of Nedra Reynolds's *Geographies of Writing* (2004), we have seen many books and articles discussing the importance of place-based writing in the field of rhetoric and composition. These works fall under distinctive categories, such as ecocomposition (Weisser and Dobrin 2001; Owens 2001; Walker 2010), urban and rural literacies (Brooke 2003; Eppley 2011; Kinloch 2010; Tolbert and Theobald 2006), and critical pedagogy/service learning (Flower 2008; Goldblatt 2007; Mathieu 2005; Parks 2010; Shor 1999). There are even some recent articles on mobile technology's role in understanding place in the classroom (Holmes 2016; Rivers 2016). We have also seen the release of textbooks that focus on place-based writing pedagogies in first-year writing (Gaillet and Eble 2015; Mattieu et al. 2013). This work, I believe, is a response to the ways education (particularly on the secondary level) has become a disembodied, logos-based corporation. Place-based scholarship asks educators, and by extension students, to examine their local contexts, to ask existential and social questions in regard to their surroundings, and, in many ways, to physically explore those surroundings. As Robert Brooke (2015) passionately describes at the end of his most recent edited collection on place-based education, it is the standardization of education we must push back against: "National standards and a core curriculum serve a migratory, placeless model of education serving a largely migratory business sector. By contrast, a place-conscious education system serves an educational model of an active citizenry" (235). This "active citizenry" Brooke describes imagines students as being more aware of issues in their local communities and as involved more in processes of decision-making in those communities. Education, then, is one way to create further opportunities for identification with place and communities within it. When students learn to articulate their places and see themselves as members of communities, their education becomes more meaningful to them.

Brooke, a professor at the University of Nebraska–Lincoln, focuses his place-based analyses on the importance of an active citizenry for rural and suburban populations. Though his focus is different from my own as a professor at a public university in New York City, I find his framing for investigating local issues to be important. Drawing upon the work of Wendell Berry, Brooke (2015) begs that we see place as "a mutually interdependent system of relations" (29), and he says place can further be defined as natural (watershed) and human-made (commonwealth). In terms of urban dwelling, I believe it is most important to focus on the latter term, which Brooke defines as "a cultural entity: a network of mutually interdependent cultural systems that work together within a particular political entity" (28). When considering the commonwealth in terms of New York City, we can immediately identify the often imaginative if not literal delineation of neighborhoods and the communities that reside in them, and we can further consider how these neighborhood places change and develop over time due to social and economic factors (I am particularly thinking here in terms of gentrification). The inevitability of change is reflected always in our surroundings and ourselves. Rebecca Solnit (2000), in her history on walking,[1] captures a change in herself and her urban landscape when she discusses walking through her San Francisco neighborhood as a teenager and as an adult:

> I began walking my own city's streets as a teenager and walked them so long that both they and I changed, the desperate pacing of adolescence when the present seemed an eternal ordeal giving way to the musing walks and innumerable errands of someone no longer wound so tight, so isolated,

so poor, and my walks have now often become reviews of my own and
the city's history together. Vacant lots become new buildings, old geezer
bars are taken over by young hipsters, the Castro's discos become vitamin
stores, whole streets and neighborhoods change their complexion. (194)

Solnit (2000) beautifully describes how personality changes with age
and how neighborhoods too do not remain stagnant; she, in effect,
matures with her city. Her walking practices also slow with age, and her
ways of seeing become keener as she notices and appreciates her surroundings. Her reminiscences are descriptive—and, at times in her
narrative, she longs for the old and resists change. Solnit is an active
participant in her milieu. She brings to the forefront the ways her city
of San Francisco is exceptional and diverse, commenting on how "the
buildings of my city contained Zen centers, Pentecostal churches, tattoo
parlors, produce stores, burrito places, movie palaces, dim sum shops.
Even the most ordinary things struck me with wonder, and the people
on the street offered a thousand glimpses of lives like and utterly unlike
mine" (171). Solnit is a woman of the crowd, and this perspective affords
her the ability to document and describe the city she loves. She actually
has edited an Atlas guide for San Francisco (as well ones on New Orleans
and New York). Her writing is memorable because of its aesthetic quality. Solnit is a theorist, but a pragmatic one—a rare combination. She
draws attention to the commonwealth of cities Brooke describes while
at the same time framing her own participation as part of this process of
change. She writes with a kaleidoscopic lens, twisting and forming new
patterns of personal and public reflections. Her style is one students can
learn to reproduce and in the process become more familiar with their
landscapes and the changes that have occurred over time.

Place-based writing should, ideally, be taught in a way that allows for
both expressive (personal) and social (public) student writing. Unlike
many scholars who critique expressive pedagogy, I show in this chapter how the personal is political, just as Thomas O'Donnell argues in
his now seminal essay "Politics and Ordinary Language: A Defense of
Expressivism" (1996). Whenever we describe and name a place and its
meaning to us, we are also at the same time speaking about the collective identity a place has for others. We can also venture to investigate the
social, political, and economic issues in a place through our classroom
practices. A place-based pedagogy that allows for both personal and public writing must recognize the hybrid nature of student voice. Stephen
Parks (2010) discusses his own efforts at place-based writing through
Temple University's outreach programs. He says that through his
experiences, he learned writing "could be seen as a vehicle that would

enable students to use their local experiences as the initial lens to trace how larger cultural and political structures had shaped their identities" (xxii). He further explains that this kind of classroom writing recognizes voice is a hybrid—not solely "authentic," as some expressivists have claimed, and not solely "socially constructed," as social epistemologists have claimed. Rather, classroom practices should operate under the assumption of voice hybridity in which student writing "simultaneously authorize[s] the individual's voiced experience and work[s] collectively to address the larger social and political contexts in which that personal voice exists" (33).

In the rest of this chapter, I outline a place-based curriculum I have developed and taught at the College of Staten Island CUNY, which I believe analyses issues of the commonwealth while also considering the experiences of everyday New Yorkers, including students. It is a curriculum focused on neighborhood change and development through gentrification. The chapter is divided into three sections, based on the unit assignments: photo essay, critical-response essay, and argumentative essay. In each section I provide an overview of the theory, readings, and activities, and in the first and last section I additionally include an analysis of student papers.[2]

PLACE PHOTO ESSAYS

In the CUNY system, several programs encourage college acceptance and retention, college readiness, and support for minority and working-class students—one being ASAP, an accelerated associate degree program that gives qualified students free tuition, a monthly metro card, and bookstore credit if they continue to meet program requirements. This program intends to open the borders of our academic community and improve retention. For two fall semesters, I have worked with these writers. These students are often the first in their families to attend college and so navigate institutions of higher learning as outsiders. I find myself in the position of offering advice on scheduling, time management, and personal issues. There are struggles with attendance and turning in work. There are struggles meeting page limits. But, there are also many positive outcomes that define this work; students learn to read critically, find their voices, and see themselves as writers.

It is important to me—and I think to rhetoric and composition as a field—to not see this work as part of helping "remedial" students gain access to the university, but rather we must consider the ways this student population critically adds to our classrooms. We must seek out narratives of difference that speak back to official university discourses of knowledge-making. Place-based writing, by its nature, values personal experience and accomplishes this inclusive goal for our curriculums.

As many in composition have argued, the politics of remediation displaces writers from the center of the university. Mike Rose (1985) claims that labeling something as "remedial," or in the case of ASAP, as a "special program," serves a hierarchical function—"to keep in place the hard fought for . . . distinction between college and second-ary work" (349)—and, by extension, maintains the border between college-ready and underprepared students. Furthermore, basic writers are pushed from the academic center because their home and work life experiences do not count as knowledge. At my institution in the CUNY system, students—the majority of them commuters, working class, and/or minorities—often feel, as Jonathan Mauk (2003) describes, "unsitu-ated in academic space" (368). Much of our scholarship in literacy and composition studies (Reynolds 2004) critiques the way power circulates in institutions and asks us to imagine how the boundary between institu-tional and home literacies can be less divisive, as this border perpetuates racial and class inequalities.

Rather than expecting basic writers to assimilate to university culture and discourses, professors must create assignments that "conceive the space . . . outside of the classroom as academic" (Mauk 2003, 380). In this way, students become, as Shor (1999) notes, "authorities, agents, and unofficial teachers" (13). Academic practices that normalize knowledge-making and exclude minority and working-class perspectives are the problems to which a place-based writing curriculum responds. Place-based writing, as I have practiced it at CSI CUNY, critically engages urban college students in FYC, asking them to investigate their home communities as sites of analysis, and thus helps transform the university by authorizing student experience.

This chapter offers some pedagogical strategies for teaching place-based writing, specifically to urban populations. In the photo-essay section of the curriculum, students reflect on their neighborhoods, questioning, *How do you define your neighborhood? What are the boundaries of your neighborhood? How do neighborhoods get reputations? How does emo-tion play a role in neighborhood perceptions? Why do you feel connected to—or disconnected from—your neighborhood?* Students work to identify landmarks of significance by mapping, as Brooke and Jason McIntosh (2007) describe, this "active conceptualization of space," which "is a necessary prerequisite to writing *inside, in relationship to,* or *for* a place" (133). Students compose multimodal photo essays that take readers on "tours" of their neighborhoods, offering insight into how they understand their place and the ways it has shaped their characters and perceptions.

As I understand place-based writing, one of the main assumptions is that movement in place is a rhetorical activity that leads to self-development. De Certeau (1988), in the *Practice of Everyday Life*, reminds us that walking is a form of "enunciation," like speech, when he writes that a pedestrian begins

> *appropriation* of the topographical system on the part of the pedestrian (just as the speaker appropriates and takes on the language); it is a spatial acting-out of the place (just as the speech act is an acoustic acting-out of language); and it implies *relations* among differentiated positions, that is, among pragmatic "contracts"; in the form of movements (just as verbal enunciation is an "allocution," "posits another opposite" the speaker and puts contracts between interlocutors into action). (97–98)

Walking, and other forms of movement, then, creates an intimacy and familiarity with place that allows us to name its landmarks—natural and human made. Movers create their city, just as it, in turn, influences and shapes their characters—this process is dialectical. Benjamin (2002) further discusses how, by walking the city streets of Paris, the flâneur is able to transform outside space into the interior: "The city splits for him into its dialectical poles. It opens up to him as a landscape, even as it closes around him as a room" (417). Places become familiar as we experience them in motion; they become a part of our interior life. Wandering in place is thus central to character development (ethos).

Walking, other movements, and interacting with the milieu as the flâneur does—through studying people, through gossip—ties the rituals of movement to a process of knowledge-making. Walking, for example, takes time; thus this form of knowledge-making sees "idleness as a fruit of labor" (Benjamin 2002, 453) and requires a slowing down that—in our contemporary moment—we often cannot afford. Walking is now too often seen as an inconvenience rather than a moment to relish and to learn from.

Walking knowledge is not alien to our students, especially those who come from urban places and walk as a daily form of transportation. Walking is a form of knowledge that is "something experienced and lived through," and therefore it begs us to give it more attention as teachers of discourse (Benjamin 2002, 417). How can writing include elements of the walk? What would such writing look like?

Composition scholars have turned to the image of Benjamin's flâneur in discussing place-based pedagogies. Reynolds (2004) argues that the flâneur is a model for seeing how movement creates a connection between place and identity (71). Intimacy with place is created through meandering. However, there is also a sense that in wandering there is a potential for becoming "lost," even in an intimate place; or perhaps more accurately, the walker recovers a sense of wonderment for that place (Benjamin 2002, 419). Paying close attention to a familiar place—through walking, through other movements, through research, through photography and sketching, through reflective writing—has the potential to make what is familiar to us strange, to reveal the remarkable aspects of place. This wonderment in wandering is an integral part of flâneurie that compositionists often miss; it is also arguably essential to student invention in writing about place.

I follow Rickert's (2013) lead in *Ambient Rhetoric* in recognizing that the work of rhetoric, like walking, is "an embodied and embedded practice"; it is something that emerges from an environment and situation; rhetoric is comprised of "interactive engagements, redolent of a world that affects us" (34). In this vein, students mapped geographical landmarks and considered their bodies and movements within them. Students read Corder's "Late Word from the Provinces" (*Lost* 1988) as a model. Corder reflects on his childhood home in West Texas and describes the landmarks that make up his province and their centrality to his character. He writes, "The cosmos, as I am able to apprehend it, stretches from the Double Mountains northwestward some forty miles to the Big Rock Candy Mountain. On up that road from Apermont, through Swenson, through Jayton, where my family lived" (7). Corder's tie to this region is felt through his many writings, and they show too how he wishes to continue to return to and wander in the region to trace the origins of his character. The world is much larger than West Texas, of course, but Corder reminds readers of how a city block or a regional affiliation can become the measure of comparison for our ways of seeing and being. Corder complicates the notion of this measure-taking as he considers how the idea of province is at once liberatory and confining. Recognizing our limitations of how we experience space/time is essential in mapping the dimensions of our own "province." Corder writes, "We cannot be in all provinces at once, nor hear all melodies at once, nor say all words at once, and there is no final sadness in that. A province . . . is the place you stand to sense and measure your experience" (*Lost* 1988, 50). When students are asked to write about place, it is an invitation to show their own measure-taking to audience(s).

After reading and analyzing Corder's piece, as well as other student essay examples,[3] students literally map their own provinces and take fellow students on a "walking tour" of them. I ask students to reflect on how their character is tied to these areas. Students think about how they can speak to an audience about their places in order to create identification with their readers. I wanted students to continue to ask questions that center the idea of transformative ethos: How do we practice and perform a commodious language in relation to our descriptions on place? How do we get others to listen to us, especially those who have differing life experiences and may not know our places and the communities and issues connected to them?

Student place photo essays identify a larger significance of the place to their lives, describe the place to outsiders, reflect on their emotions in place, consider memories in relation to the place, and include multimedia (pictures and sketches) of the place.

Students learn how to use the rhetorical tools of storytelling, detailed descriptions, and narrative style in order to communicate their experience in a way that is, hopefully, expansive toward readers—to write to be understood is a powerful thing. This statement, again, serves as a form of argument—one based on my experience of personal stories as persuasive. However, I argue that this form of writing is not necessarily meant to be aggressive or antagonistic; rather, the argument, modeled through the narrative, becomes inviting and reveals the reflections and lived experience of the author.

In my classes at CSI CUNY, I note four main topoi students often write through when discussing place. The first is transitioning from being renter to owner of an apartment or home; the second is related to their life at work; the third is narratives of immigration; the fourth is reflecting on urban spaces as sites of escape. In the following sections, I analyze two student essays that exemplify the work life and escape topoi. I comment on the descriptive language these students use to construct their places and their movements within them for the reader. I additionally discuss the ways these students communicate their character and identity development to readers.

In his essay titled "Let's Be Out," Pedro discusses the bond he shares with his friends, Manny and Sean, and their created dreamscape in Ozone Park, Queens. The theme of his narrative is about creating friendships through play. The area in Forest Park they claim as their own is a bandshell and stage. Pedro and Manny are skaters and are always "busting some moves off the platform and whatnot." A public space is thus transformed into a private retreat, a place where the boys can claim agency in their lives.

"Let's Be Out," the essay's title, is a direct quote from Manny; he says it whenever the boys head up to the park. Finding a place of one's own, in public, is a theme of urban living; Pedro talks about how they skate to escape cramped apartments and crowded streets. Pedro describes his journey to the bandshell: "Watch your head and the road, for the pigeons and potholes are a tag team around these parts. As I skate through the loud crowded streets of Jamaica Avenue all around I hear horns, the trains, and people. Can't complete a single thought while plowing through here. As soon as I take a right on 84th Street Forest Parkway, the atmosphere becomes still. Off my board and time to march up the hill. Probably the longest blocks I ever walked, yet there is only three." Pedro describes how time slows down for him in this place and how the atmosphere changes from frenetic to calm. We see him flying by the urban scene on his board and then stepping off it as he walks uphill to the park. Pedro engages the readers through his prose that invites them on his journey through the use of "you" and the specific landmarks he cites, like street names and distances.

In his discussions on the bandshell, Pedro again engages the reader in explaining its significance: "This is the Bandshell. An outdoor little stadium where anything goes, it's up to you what adventure you plan to go with." Again, note how the use of "you" invites the reader into the space and its play. Through his comments, we can see this as a place where creativity and agency flow for Pedro. In fact, when he was composing this essay, he showed me videos he and his friends made of their skating adventures at the park. The images he includes in his narrative further reinforce his strong bonds with his friends and their ties to their bandshell. To further illustrate the idea of place as agency, Pedro comments, "The Bandshell is our getaway from our . . . 'stressful' lives. It's a place where we cannot be told what to do or how to act. When I'm at the Bandshell I become a cartoon. . . . When I'm with my brothers, it's like we have complete control over everything around us." We can read into these lines through the lens of rebellious youth but also through the lens of urban life; his friendships, and by extension the bandshell, keep Pedro grounded in his urban milieu. Pedro and his friends, as young, Puerto Rican men, also see this space as an alternative reality to the one in which their agencies are often restrained. He is able to make the public space a dreamscape where he can "become a cartoon" and live out his desires through play. The essay also shows us how movement to, through, and from places significantly changes our relationship with them. The narrative is not just about teens skating and rebelling in a park, it's also—and maybe more important—about friendship, agency, and creativity.

In "Volunteer Love," Narcy discusses her position in the ER at Staten Island University Hospital. Her narrative's theme is that work is a form of love: in one sense, work is love because it is enjoyable and fulfilling, and in another, her work is an act of love because she wishes to care for and help others. In the narrative, Narcy refers to the hospital as her "happy place," admitting she can stay there for shifts as long as fifteen-hour. She writes, "The day doesn't have enough hours when I'm there. I always knew this was going to be a nice experience, but . . . it never occurred to me that I was going to love it as much as I do. It's been 120 hours and I cherished every minute." Narcy includes pictures of her volunteer badge and several selfies of herself in scrubs doing various tasks, like sitting with patients and preparing health kits.

Being in a hospital originates from Narcy's present desire to help others and her future goal of becoming a medical professional. Narcy takes her volunteer job very seriously. For example, she describes how she advocated to move from volunteering in the maternity ward—where she was doing more clerical tasks, like photocopying—to a spot in the emergency room, where she would have more direct patient contact. She writes, "After a few months . . . the volunteering job became more about paperwork and less about patients. I wasn't volunteering there to gain clerical experience, but to see how it is to work with people who are sick. . . . After a while of thinking about it, I decided I wanted to speak to the person in charge of the volunteering services and ask her to relocate me. She did." Narcy's narrative shows a personal investment in the job and her goals and expectations. She poses herself as an agent of change in her situation.

After this relocation, Narcy began to experience more work with patients, and she sees this work as an act of love. The hospital refers to volunteer outreach with patients as "comfort care," and it is in this area that Narcy excels. She shares, "I sometimes speak with people who are from a similar cultural background as me; I'm Honduran and I moved to the United States 2 years ago. My family and I have had a very hard time, and we still do, but we try our best and push through. . . . I'm fluent in both English and Spanish, so I usually help at the front desk when people who don't speak English need to be registered and seen." Narcy describes how, through sharing stories and experiences, she feels she is making a difference in the quality of care offered to the patients at the hospital. Her background as a Honduran immigrant further helps her relate to patients who share similar life experiences and language.

Narcy envisions a future for herself in the medical field. She dreams of becoming a pediatrician—describing how a career she loves will be satisfying and not feel like work. She writes, "Being a volunteer has given me the best insight ever. . . . It has been real and it makes me believe there is absolutely nothing in the world that I want to do more than help people, cure them, attend them in every way possible, and if I ever get a chance, maybe even save lives." Narcy shows how, through her investment in being at her workplace, she is building a future for herself. The hospital, in many ways, is her place to gain practical experience and knowledge she couldn't from a biology course or an anatomy textbook. As she continues to pursue her studies, it seems the love she learns volunteering—both for the profession and for others—will sustain her.

When students are invited to draw from their personal experience and to consider their own places as sites for analysis, we get to read papers that offer descriptive and thoughtful commentary about their position in the world. The students here, through their analyses of place, show how they folded these places into their own sense of identity; additionally, readers are invited into their worlds. As Corder would say, the student's voices emerged as a presence, and readers were enfolded by their discourses.

Many agree that argumentative writing is the favored mode of composition studies. The field continues to move away from expressive elements in writing, somehow believing that they are not grounded in the social world or that this writing does little to serve students beyond FYC. These are false assumptions. The sad truth is there is very little room in our curriculums for place-based narrative reflection essays. The idle wandering of the flâneur is not the stuff of academic discourse. And, it is hard for WPAs to explain to pragmatic parties why place-based writing matters. Yet, we must argue that place-based writing, and by extension expressive discourse, is essential to student intellectual development. First, it allows them to make sense of their experiences in the world and to see how their perspectives are largely shaped by their geographies. Second, expressive writing does speak to a larger, public audience, and it makes arguments through the ethos and pathos appeal rather than so rigidly relying on academic logos. Indeed, this writing may serve students more than researched argument will, particularly in public debate, where we know "facts" only go so far in persuasion. Third, place-based narrative gives students, particularly basic writers, a way to understand rhetorical identifications with audiences. Finally, this writing happens beyond the walls of the academy; its subjects recall the places we call home, the recipes we make in our kitchens, and the lessons our grandfathers taught us about working the land. There is something about this writing that levels the playing field—that makes students experts and invites them to share their expertise with the university. As I state earlier, this is one of the ways a working-class, minority population can intervene in practices of knowledge-making. These are the reasons to fight to maintain expressive discourse in the college writing curriculum. What is at stake is not trivial. Expressive discourse opens up the university's borders to student experience, increasing the probability of success for basic writers in our writing classes and beyond.

But, perhaps even this pedagogy has a larger motive than the mere exchange of stories. There is something important in knowing how you came to stand where you stand and the lessons you learned along the way. And, isn't there something important in knowing where others have stood and have lived and have learned? Perhaps, then, we can show each other our beautiful people and places and lessons. Perhaps, then, we might start loving each other, or at least liking each other, or maybe just coming to a place of a respectful understanding.

I believe assignments like place-based narrative essays allow students to understand rhetorical identifications. They learn how to appeal to their audiences through descriptive writing that invites readers to walk through the world as students inhabit and see it. The everyday revelations walkers experience are the origins for their character development, and by relating this experience to readers, there is potential for moments of identification as readers become consubstantial with the writer's ways of being.

CRITICAL-ANALYSIS ESSAY

The place-based curriculum practiced in my classroom worked to move from the personal to the public more explicitly, as Stephen Parks describes in *Gravyland* (2010). All my students were currently living in New York City, though some of them were immigrants from other countries, and many in their place-based writings discussed their connections to local NYC neighborhoods, schools, parks, businesses and workplaces, and homes. I wanted them to broaden their lens from thinking about their relationship to the city to considering others' relationships to the city, and I also wanted them to focus on one particular social issue through our course readings: gentrification in New York City.

Students were introduced to the topic through a 2014 report on public housing from the Office of the New York City Comptroller, "The Growing Gap: New York City's Housing Affordability Challenge." The report, written in a style both logical and comprehensible, with several charts and graphs, outlined trends in housing costs and availability from the early 2000s to 2012 in New York City. The story of the housing market was shown in numbers, and the report claimed rent had risen, on average, $600, accounting for every borough in the city, the largest number of these raises being in Manhattan (21). The report tied this rise in cost to a decrease in affordable housing, informing readers that there was "a net loss of 152,751 affordable housing units in New York City's rent stabilization system from 1994–2012" (20) and that "over the last decade, 69.2 percent of the City's rent stabilized housing losses were in the Borough of Manhattan" (21). The report further detailed how this loss in affordable housing had affected low-income individuals and families. Basically, those earning less than $40,000 a year in 2012 "ha[d] seen their incomes stagnate while the supply of rental apartments affordable to them ha[d] evaporated" (25). To be more specific, the report claimed that low-income families continued to have to dedicate a higher percentage of their earnings to housing—in 2000, that average percentage was 33; in 2012, it was 41 (1). One can only imagine, given the upward trends in rent, what the percentages look like at present.

While I find this report helpful to understanding the housing situation in terms of a broad analysis through a use of statistics, it falls short in representing to students the stories of tenants, landlords, low-income families, activists, and others in relation to the changing landscape of New York City's housing market and the effects gentrification has on the city in general. In other words, the report served as an introduction to the topic to get students situated and prepared to read a book of oral histories of New Yorkers published in 2015, D. W. Gibson's *The Edge Becomes the Center: An Oral History of Gentrification in the Twenty-First Century* (2015).

Before reading narratives from the book, students were asked to do several freewrites and participate in discussions based on short video clips related to urban gentrification. For example, students were shown videos and articles from Brooklyn's nonprofit group FUREE, Families United for Racial and Economic Equality, particularly the section on their website dedicated to affordable housing. They watched YouTube clips about gentrification in Bushwick, Brooklyn, which featured interviews with residents, social service workers, and small business owners in the neighborhood as they discussed issues caused by gentrification, such as rising rents. Additionally, students watched a short video done by Buzzfeed, "What It's Like to Get Kicked Out of Your Own Neighborhood," in which the narrator, a young person of color named Kai, tells us about the changes in his neighborhood in San Francisco—the Mission District—and how he and his family could no longer afford to live there because of rising rents. His video brings up race and class issues that surfaced as tensions rose between old residents and new young tech professionals who were moving into the neighborhood, which resulted in a fight between the two groups over recreation space in a local park. Students were asked questions that helped them think about the speakers and their identities and perspectives:

1. Who were the people being interviewed in this clip? Why did their perspectives matter?

2. Were there differing perspectives shown in the clip? Did this lead to a conflict in opinion or tension?

3. How is the change in the neighborhood (or city) being talked about? What is your opinion about these changes?

This inquiry allowed to students to further prepare for the analyses expected of them when they encountered the oral histories in Gibson's book.

The Edge Becomes the Center provides several interviews with people who live and work in neighborhoods experiencing change (including a decrease in housing affordability) because of gentrification, such as Harlem, Bushwick, Park Slope, and Crown Heights. The interviewees are a diverse representation of the New York population, as they are of different professions, classes, races, genders, and ages. In the following sections, I briefly describe some of the selected chapters read in class and the ways the interviewees' stories helped students think about these New Yorkers' connections to place and the phenomenon of gentrification throughout their city.

Stephen Chu, an architect, speaks to Gibson about the evolution of cities as related to his firm's building projects. He discusses being involved in expansions of the NYU campus into the neighborhood in the West Village and how the community board often opposed the changes being made. His job as an architect was to design in consideration of their concerns, such as noise level or pedestrian traffic. Chu describes the inevitability of change in the area because of the campus expansion: "We're hired by an institution that, with or without us, will do something. It's not that without us they just won't do it. So if we have the opportunity to make it better [for the neighborhood], we will" (Gibson 2015, 51). This give and take of community board and architect shows how gentrification sometimes requires loss, yet the loss may lead to, at the very least, a "livable" compromise. Chu seems open to the board and wants to work with them. His philosophy of architecture is one that embraces the concept of "adaptive reuse," as his favorite projects to work on are those for which "there's the existing and there's the new and the new is not trying to copy the old, it has its own language. But there's a dialogue with the existing and not just crashing the new on top of it, or drawing a line. The two want to work together. And I think the history of time plays out in architecture. Visually you can understand that's what's happening" (52). Chu's description is metaphorical; it tries to account for how change is inevitable but also how it can be a beautiful process of dialogue between old and new. His description is also very much in the realm of the real, as we see construction happening all the time in New York City.

In fact, Chu describes how his own neighborhood in Queens is being reenvisioned as abandoned warehouses are being converted into real estate and retail spaces. Neighbors contacted Chu in the hopes that he would sign a petition to block this rezoning; however, he was opposed to their aims. He explains, "When I hear people say, 'Oh, it's changing the character [of the neighborhood],' I ask, 'Is that a bad thing?' It's an evolving process, it's living, right? It's like language. Language changes and so does language use. So does land" (Gibson 2015, 53). Chu, because of his architecture background, finds the possibility of change and rebuilding exciting. He supports the use of a space for living, and an abandoned space, in his view, does not aid in that goal. His perspective gave students a way to view gentrification through building development, which is only one piece of gentrification's complicated influence on NYC neighborhoods, but an important one nonetheless. Chu, overall, represents how he sees change in the city as inevitable—a form of evolution—and supports it because he anxiously wants to see how everything will turn out in his own building projects and the ones in his neighborhood.

Noelia Calero, a tenant for twenty-three years in the same apartment building in Bushwick, offered students a perspective of someone who is being displaced from her neighborhood by a profit-seeking landlord. Her housing complex is rent stabilized. The owner, under the guise of improving their apartment, tore out her family's kitchen and bathroom, leaving them with no access to running water. This was his plan for kicking out the tenants; he figured they would get so fed up with the living conditions they would leave, and once they left, he could raise the rents, possibly double what he is earning now. Noelia, however, will not stand for this bullying and intimidation. She does not want to leave her home, a place she has lived for twenty-three years and for which she has always paid the rent on time. She takes a stand, taking this landlord to court and also speaking about her situation to the media. Noelia frames her decision to stand up through her race and class positionality—she is originally from Nicaragua, and her family could be considered part of America's working class, as she is a clerical assistant and her husband works construction. Noelia is at first shy about appearing on the news but justifies going public: "I think about the other people and other Hispanics, a lot of them don't speak English, or maybe some of them are illegal and they get scared and they leave. But I'm not illegal, I'm a citizen, and I do speak English and you're not treating me like this so I'm not leaving" (Gibson 2015, 234). Noelia speaks about the changing of Bushwick from a predominantly Latinx, working-class community to a white, middle-class community. She witnesses her neighbors and others being displaced by landlord intimidation, or being "priced out" by raising rents. It is interesting to note how she frames her rights through a discourse of citizenship and linguistic mastery of English, showing how, because of these things, she is more able to fight on television and in court than some of her peers. Noelia, like Stephen Chu, was excited about the changes and improvements in her neighborhood at first, citing that the new apartment buildings looked nice, that a new coffee shop opened near her place that she liked, and that there is now less drug trade and less crime overall: "I feel safe walking around my neighborhood. And I thought they're finally fixing Brooklyn." However, she notes these changes and improvements came at the expense of the community already thriving in the neighborhood, saying, "Before it was a lot of Hispanics and a lot of blacks. Now you don't see a lot of them. You see a lot of white people," concluding, because of Bushwick's improvement due to gentrification, that "it's not for us to live in" (235). Noelia's narrative brings race, class, citizenship, and linguistic issues to the forefront of discussions on gentrification, as we see her position (at once marginalized and privileged) in a larger landscape of her neighborhood and New York City as a whole. In general, students sympathized with her situation, and that allowed them to see the social dimensions and consequences of gentrification, even if they agreed with it overall. In FYC terms, students can see the "cons" of the issue, and any sort of complex perspective we can develop on social issues is a step toward racial and class justice, even if it doesn't completely change their opinion outright (I expand on this discussion more in the following section in my analysis of student opinion essays).

Noelia's lawyer, Brent, a young professional from Canada, discusses her case and others he has argued in housing court in relation to tenants' rights. His stance on gentrification is a complicated one, as he is not explicitly for or against it; however, he is concerned for his clients, hoping he can make the government reactive for them (Gibson 2015, 223). Brent points out that gentrification is an issue in which we see the blurring of race and class lines and categories, at least in

New York City. He says, "You start talking class, you start talking about race. Take Crown Heights for a moment. This is predominately an African American neighborhood and it's becoming white. Really, really white. So what does that mean?" (224). He cites other examples and neighborhoods in Brooklyn that are experiencing class and race demographic shifts (Downtown, Park Slope, Bay Ridge). Brent, as a young white professional man, helps clients from diverse backgrounds every day and sees the nature of his class and race privilege, and he is frustrated by the lack of government response and services for his clients. Brent discusses how the courts have a lot of laws to protect tenants but that justice in these courts is slow and sometimes nonexistent. For example, he must be selective in which cases he can take on—because the volume is so high, he only accepts the cases he thinks he has a chance of winning. He says, "Family court, housing court, criminal court—those are all poor people's courts. There's no justice. And I think a lot of people don't understand that" (228). Brent, as a public defender, explains how the justice system stalls cases and even rules against tenants in housing court, despite their being favored in the written "letter of the law." His interview gives a professional perspective to Noelia's story, which is why Gibson placed their narratives next to each other in the book.

Another narrative students read is from a millennial named Shatia Strother, who grew up in Bedford-Stuyvesant and is still residing there with her husband and son. After a successful career in the fashion industry, Shatia decided to refocus her efforts and go into community activism, starting a community garden and food-education workshops for neighbors, as well as going to graduate school to get her master's degree in sociology at NYU. Her motivation for community work, she explains, comes from a place of wanting to see Black people in leadership roles in the community, particularly around food-justice issues—which she feels is an area dominated by white women, who usually come into urban communities to serve people of color. Shatia tells Gibson, "I think there have been long-standing stereotypes and ideas about seeing a white face in authority—and the only authority. There needs to be some measures for correcting that, for saying [to black children], 'There are people who look like you who know things. There are experts who look like you'" (Gibson 2015, 67). She feels that people from the community know the community's concerns the best, explaining that outsiders often assume a deficit or lack of knowledge or need without ever asking the people they are there to "serve." This condescension—and in some ways misunderstanding—from outsiders is something Shatia is working to dispel, drawing upon the strengths of local community members in the development of her nonprofit and its programs.

Shatia feels torn as to her role in gentrification as someone who wants to see improvements in her community. On the one hand, she likes the effects of gentrification on the neighborhood and has befriended some of the new residents, who are for the most part white; but on the other hand, she doesn't like the loss of old neighbors or the ways some of the new ones act. She explains, "The negative impact of gentrification has more to do with the disengagement of people who are moving in . . . my biggest problem is people who move here just because the rent is cheap and they see it as a pit stop to wherever their path is in life" (Gibson 2015, 71). Shatia, having such strong roots in her neighborhood and building her identity around it, wants new residents to feel the same commitment she does; however, she also sees many of her new neighbors as transients who will stay for a year or two and then move on to the next thing—in a sense, they do not contribute to the community though they may benefit from its affordability, convenience, and services. She sees this as not a racial conflict but as a class conflict; so, unlike Brent and Noelia, Shatia believed class supersedes race when it comes to gentrification. As an educated Black woman who is currently in the middle class, and who is also related to wealthy black people who own their own homes in the area, she began to see how Black people could be gentrifiers and describes this revelation:

> I had a very skewed view of gentrification because I never thought of black wealthy people as gentrifiers. It always had this racial connotation to it. And I woke up and realized that gentrification is a class issue, it's not a race issue, and it took all the white faces to move in for it to occur to me that gentrification has been occurring for a long time, it's just now it has a white face (70).

Shatia's narrative gave students the perspective of someone who feels conflicted about gentrification because of her race and class position. She is a change-maker and leader in her community, and in some ways, she sees herself as gentrifier and contributing to the gentrification process through her work with the community garden food-justice programs. She also sees herself as a role model for young Black people especially, and she wants to stay true to her roots and actually listen to the needs of her community.

During class, students completed several low-stakes and no-stakes writing assignments individually and in groups in relation to Gibson's interviewees. For each chapter read, students answered the following questions in group discussion and reported them aloud to the class:

1. What was the interviewee's relationship to their neighborhood? What was their identity (race, class, age, gender, etc.)?

2. What was their situation? Why do you think their perspective was included in this oral history on gentrification?

3. Did they talk about their opinion of gentrification or other social issues? Did they mention race, class, or other identity markers when they talked about issues in their neighborhood?

4. What were two quotes you thought were important from their interview? Why?

Another writing assignment asked students to assume the position of one of the interviewees, write a letter in their voice, share their response with a peer, and then reflect upon the experience:

> Pick one interviewee from the G. W. Gibson book that we have read so far. Pretend you are this person. Compose a letter in their voice. In the letter you must include one quote from their interview. The letter can be addressed to anyone: a family member, a boss, a landlord, etc.
>
> Ex: If I am pretending to be Noelia, I might choose to write a letter to my lawyer expressing my concerns for the upcoming case against my landlord.
>
> Peer-share your letter and reflect on the following:
>
> 1. What were some of the things you had to take into account about the interviewee as you composed the letter?
>
> 2. What is their voice like? What quote did you choose and why?
>
> 3. Do you understand this interviewee's perspective more after doing this activity? How so?

For the final assignment in this unit, the critical-analysis paper, students were asked to analyze two interviewees' narratives. They were to discuss how positionality (race/ethnicity, class, profession, gender, etc.) affects a person's definition of, experience of, and opinion about gentrification. Students were to make a clear argument that convinced readers that they had read the book closely and that they understood gentrification from at least two people's critical perspectives, using evidence (quotations and paraphrases) from the narratives. As they composed, students were asked to consider the following questions as they considered the book broadly:

1. How does the definition of, and opinions about, gentrification change from person to person in Gibson's book?

2. Which narratives were most compelling to you as a reader? Did you find yourself sympathizing or agreeing with some perspectives over others?

3. Did you see any differences or similarities among the narrators/interviewees?

4. What quotes or ideas really stand out to you from the narratives? Can you use those to help you with your paper's argument?

Once they decided upon which interviewees they wanted to write about, they considered their narratives through these questions:

1. Who are two interviewees you are considering writing on for the paper?

2. Why these two? What about their stories is compelling to you? What is their situation?

3. What are their opinions about gentrification? Did they mention race, class, or other identity markers when they talked about the issues? Was their perspective influenced by their identity?

4. Do they relate or differ from each other in any way? How can you talk about both people in one essay? What's the common line of analysis here?

5. What are some quotes you think you might use in the essay? Why? How do these quotes help show the interviewee's perspectives?

This unit's paper brought students closer to a view of gentrification that accounted for both the broad, researched issues—such as housing affordability in the city—and the personal stories of New Yorkers living and working in gentrifying neighborhoods. The oral histories also brought to the forefront economic, social, and racial issues and tensions that are a part of living in the city. Many students identified with the speakers in the book. In some ways, this unit helped bridge their personal experience as New Yorkers, as explored in the first essay, to a public issue. Students struggled with this transition, often finding the second essay difficult to write because of the critical-reading and analysis work expected of them. The third essay, which I discuss in the following section, asked students to write an opinion essay about proposed developments on the North Shore of Staten Island. This local case study gave students a way of expressing their experiences and opinions on gentrification in a developing neighborhood near our campus community.

PUBLIC ARGUMENT: THE WEIGH-IN ESSAY

After learning about gentrification occurring in Brooklyn and Manhattan, students were directed to look at a case study happening near the College of Staten Island in the neighboring community of St. George. Here, in a neighborhood currently comprised of a majority of African American residents in the lower to middle class, the city is set to build several new projects: a giant wheel reminiscent of the London Eye, an outlet mall, a hotel, and luxury apartments (New York City 2011).[4]

Staten Island is often referred to as the Forgotten Borough for several reasons, which is exactly why it is the site being favored for this new development. Though it is the second-largest borough in terms of landmass, it is the least dense in population, which makes Staten Island more suburban than the rest of the city. The island, for the most part, was quite insular until the opening of the Verrazano Narrows Bridge in 1964, which linked it to Brooklyn: "Housing boomed as the island's population grew from 222,000 in 1960 to 352,000 in 1980 and about half a million today" (Gurwitt 2014). Unlike other boroughs, Staten Island only has one rail line along its shore, and many residents rely on cars for travel rather than public transit. The population is generally comprised of working- to middle-class people who are employed in public service (NYFD, NYPD, NY sanitation, etc.) (Dooling, *Huffington Post*, January 23, 2014). It is the least ethnically diverse borough, with the majority of residents identifying as white. And, it is by far the most conservative borough, with the majority of its residents registered as Republican (Gruwitt). The borough is often known for its prescription-drug and heroin-addiction problem, as ads in the SI ferry terminal tell riders about places for rehabilitation on the island (Goodman and Wilson, *New York Times*, May 4, 2014). Additionally, for many years, Staten Island served as New York City's dump. Lucy Lippard (2016), in her *Nonstop Metropolis: A New York City Atlas* contribution titled "Trash in the City," describes the Fresh Kills Landfill as "the receptacle for all of its [the city's] garbage for almost seventy years;" the trash was piled, one load on top of the other, making the landfill the highest point above sea level on the East Coast. Staten Islanders' notions of their borough being "a backwater, the forgotten borough" comes from its many years of being a literal wasteland (143).

I came across these attitudes about Staten Island after I accepted my job at CSI. I considered moving to Staten Island and even looked at several apartments in St. George. I discussed my pending move with a native New Yorker who currently resides in Harlem, and I'll always remember what he said: "Ro, it would be like a minivacation to come visit you. To be honest, I'd probably never come out to see you." Though the ferry connects Staten Island to Manhattan, it is seen as going into another world by most New Yorkers. The separation of the Upper Bay is both a literal and psychological barrier. Many never bother to make the journey, and others (mostly tourists) sometimes ride the ferry to get a free view of the Statue of Liberty and turn right around once on the Staten Island side.

However, with new plans for St. George in the making, Staten Island hopes to change its reputation for being "forgotten" and to attract tourists and newer residents to its North Shore. As the opening of Katherine Clarke's July 23, 2015, *New York Daily News* article claims, "Staten Island wants to be the new Brooklyn." Students in my class read several articles about the zoning plans, which featured interviews from developers, current residents, and Staten Island borough president James S. Oddo. They were asked to consider whether or not they agreed with the proposed changes happening in the borough, specifically on the North Shore, given their previous readings from the course on gentrification. The assignment, an argument research paper, asked students to answer the following questions:

> Do I see the North Shore development as a process of gentrification? How do I personally feel about gentrification?
>
> Do I think these changes will benefit Staten Island? What are the positive and negative consequences of these new developments? How will the new changes affect residents of Staten Island?
>
> Do I find these projects to be an effective use of the area? Will these changes improve the economy of Staten Island/NYC?

As discussed earlier in the chapter, students offered their opinions on a public issue, in this case gentrification, based on their experiences as New Yorkers and careful research. Many of the readings throughout the semester discussed the hopes and fears of those living in gentrifying neighborhoods, as well as those who were a part of the zoning and building of projects. These readings were curated with the aims of critical pedagogy in mind, to foster a type of "critical literacy [that] involves questioning received knowledge and immediate experience with the goals of challenging inequality and developing an activist citizenry" (Shor 1999, 11). Like Brooke (2015), Flower (2008), Long (2008), Parks (2010), Shor (1999), and so many other scholars and teachers who write about social justice, place, and literacy, I too wanted to instill a sense of civic literacy, and perhaps even action, in my students.

I think Shor's definition of critical literacy involves a loftier goal than what is actually achieved on the ground in one semester of first-year writing—at least in my experience of it. This is not a critique of critical pedagogy's goals—which I happen to agree with—but rather a reality check as to how they can translate to the writing classroom. I can't report to you that all my students took up the cause of social justice and fought for tenants' rights, but I do believe—and their writings from the semester show—that they became more aware of the complexities of the controversy of gentrification in New York City. Furthermore, they could speak with assurance about how race and class play a role in uplifting some and marginalizing others in New York in regard to housing security, even if they ultimately agreed with gentrification in general and in St. George in particular. The essays I analyze below come from students who showed this complex understanding through their definitions of gentrification, their understanding of the research, and their articulated positions.

All my students are currently New Yorkers, though some are foreign born, and a good majority of them are Staten Island residents. In these essays from local residents I see the students moving from personal experience to public argument. I want to show through my analysis of their essays how the students worked to reconcile their own experiences with the oral histories of other New Yorkers and their research on the current situation in St. George.

Daniel, a native Staten Islander, focuses on the issues of homelessness and addiction on the island in his essay, offering the perspective that gentrification is a way to better the situation. He sees gentrification as a form of change that "has both pros and cons for the locations and the people that live within them," but in Staten Island's case, he believes, "it is better to try something to help ourselves rather than to stand by and do nothing." Daniel writes in his essay that he has known people who have died of addiction and has witnessed homeless panhandlers by the ferry terminal; these occurrences, he says, might be prevented if the Staten Island economy were given a jump-start through the proposed developments.

Interestingly, Daniel frames his analysis of gentrification through the perspective of class. His definition of the phenomenon does not pass over class struggle but addresses it head on. He writes,

> Gentrification is the act of renovating/moving buildings and people from one location so that the area will be able to meet the standards set by the middle class. What this means is that while some people are removed from their homes due to increased taxes [and rent], there are many others who can benefit from the exposure given to the area. This is the double-edged sword known as gentrification, since the result is potentially both good and bad.

Daniel's description of the process of gentrification shows an awareness of how it can disadvantage and displace those not in the middle class while at the same time improving the neighborhood through new developments and renovations. This awareness of class struggle is something Daniel learned, he writes, through reading Shatia's narrative in Gibson's (2015) *The Edge Becomes the Center*. He describes how her development of a community garden was a part of gentrification in Bed-Stuy, but he also sees it as a change that was brought on by someone in the community who cared. Daniel writes, "When I think about Staten Island benefitting from gentrification, it makes me believe that we could potentially learn from Shatia and her experiences." In what he deems a "perfect world," the initial impact of gentrification will affect some residents, but hopefully this impact can be mitigated through community involvement in keeping social programs and affordable housing so "we would see the fruits of our labor." He says that to disagree with gentrification is, in some ways, to try to stop a change already in motion. To be an active citizen, Daniel writes, we should "not ignore the complications that come with it [gentrification], but instead view [our] situation in the bigger picture and think about what will come with these changes in the future." Through the lens of a young person witnessing problems in the borough, such as addiction and homelessness brought on by economic depression, he sees the solution in economic development. But, through reading the class text, Daniel was able to also articulate how development must be community driven and consider resident opinions and working-class struggles.

Another student, Kye, lives on the North Shore with her family, who are middle-class homeowners. She views the problem of gentrification through both race and class, ultimately stating she takes a "neutral stance" on the proposals because "as a young Black woman [she] also see[s] how the changes being made to the North Shore can cause unrest for the minority groups in that neighborhood."

Kye discusses how, as homeowners in the area, she and her family will benefit from the changes through a rise in property values and a higher quality of living. She writes about how the new luxury condos, ferris wheel, and mall are a way of attracting "the young crowd from Brooklyn that want the feel of Brooklyn but cannot afford it"; as a young person, she admits she is excited to see her neighborhood, "a once 'forgotten' or looked down upon place," change "into an upbeat, desirable place to live, creating new businesses, and attracting a new group of people." But her excitement begins to wane when she considers the way her neighborhood is now. Describing it as an "affordable" place, she fears that when the "gentrifiers," the typically "young, white, and 'artsy' group of people," move into the neighborhood, they will bring Brooklyn rent prices with them. The gentrifiers, she says, will be getting everything they want—a trendy neighborhood for less. But for current residents, she paints a different picture. She questions the proposed changes:

> That side of Staten Island is predominantly Black and most of that community may not be able to remain in that area after the price of their rent begins to get higher. People will lose their businesses, their jobs, and

possibly even their homes. Knowing what the repercussions may be for some of the people by the North Shore is extremely conflicting for me especially as a young Black woman. What good are the changes being made to the North Shore if the people near it cannot afford it?

Kye reasons that changes caused by gentrification often exclude minority and working-class people. She questions the motives of the projects if local residents cannot afford to ride the wheel or shop at the outlet mall. In a poem she wrote for the class, she expresses her uncertainty over her position in the issue further:

> Am I right for desiring stores with curb
> Appeal
> Or wrong because shopping there for some
> Isn't real
> I believe we should enjoy the fruits of our
> Labor
> But should it be at the detriment to my
> Neighbor?

Kye, ultimately, draws on her own positionality in this argument paper, seeing Shatia's narrative from Gibson's book as one she can relate to. Because Shatia is a middle-class African American resident in a gentrifying Brooklyn neighborhood, she sees gentrification as both a class and race issue. Kye agrees with Shatia because "people like her [Shatia's] great-aunt, herself, and me are examples of African Americans that may either be gentrifiers or be able to handle the effects of gentrification." She further adds that this knowledge gives her an unsettling feeling: "[I know] that while I can go to the North Shore and enjoy it someone else that I can identify myself with is without a home because of it." Kye shows how race and class are inextricably linked and how identification across racial lines can occur even if there is a class difference. Her "neutral" stance on gentrification mirrors Shatia's perspective, as she sees her neighborhood overall improving—and likes those improvements—but also takes issue with the exclusionary price points those improvements created.

Kye, like many students in the class, admitted she "didn't give gentrification much thought," but after reading the required texts, she—and many of her classmates, no matter the ultimate stance they chose to adopt—saw gentrification as a "multi-layered process" that doesn't offer a simple solution or have pro/con sides. We should strive to foster this dialectical thinking in the composition classroom, as I think it is the first step toward Shor's definition of critical literacy. Ultimately, we want students to view issues through a perspective that allows them to see and critique racial and class inequality.

RHETORIC IS FOR LIFE

An ideal place-based curriculum in first-year writing, I believe, should engage students to consider their personal relationship to place, particularly through mapping and movement, as well as explore the idea of place as a context for social-political struggles and research and develop informed opinions on local issues. The curriculum should center their experiences as writers and ask them to consider how to express their character to audiences. In this way, the curriculum serves both expressivist and social-epistemic pedagogical agendas, allowing for students to develop their writing for multiple genres, contexts, and audiences.

In the version of a place-based curriculum discussed throughout this chapter, my class focused on one urban issue: gentrification. However, place-based curricula should be tailored to area-specific issues and communities surrounding the college. It is also imperative to include the opinions and experiences of local residents, whether these perspectives are gleaned through a book of oral histories, as used in my curriculum, a memoir or set of nonfiction texts, newspaper articles, or even interviews with locals as a research assignment. A place-based curriculum gets students to see their experiences and contexts as something to explore, research, and write about.

When considering current trends in the field of rhetoric and writing, I worry that the value of an expressive, place-based curriculum is lessened. When considering the most recent WPA Outcomes Statement (Council of Writing Program Administrators 2019), I am completely shocked—as I am sure other compositionists are—that there is no mention of student development of local or cultural literacy, no mention of the ethos appeal (or any of the rhetorical appeals for that matter), and only one mention—very briefly—of voice, which is only in reference to a stylistic aspect of the writing (tone) in the "Rhetorical Awareness" section of the statement. To me, the WPA Outcomes Statement—a guiding document for our field often used to explain the field's purpose to others—values the present turn toward cognition, genre theory, and TFT (teaching for transfer).[5] These pedagogical emphases and practices align well with a job-preparation agenda, and furthermore, work to homogenize student learning by decontextualizing and disembodying students in terms of their home communities, privileging the academic community and its knowledges. In other words, a student's local knowledge and experience are not valued in this statement. In short, I find the WPA Outcomes Statement to be a document too conservative in intention and unhelpful for instilling in students a form of self- and critical literacy that allows them to participate in their communities with intent to garner results and change. What is a rhetorical education, I question, without an ethical dimension?

To me, it is interesting how college writing teachers are quick to critique standardizing curricula in high schools, citing a wholesale approach to pedagogy and an extreme emphasis on results-based examinations. For example, Brooke (2015) cautions high-school teachers in his recent book that "National standards and a core curriculum serve a migratory, placeless model of education serving a largely migratory business sector." These same comments can also apply to FYW curriculums that too heavily focus on practical skills, disciplinary rhetoric, and multimodal production at the mitigation or even exclusion of expressive and social writing and research. Brooke contrasts standards-based curricula in high schools to place-conscious ones, saying that a place-conscious pedagogy "serves an educational model of an active citizenry" (235). Writing studies in college should do more than merely teach the strategies of rhetoric—"negotiating purpose, audience, context, and conventions" (Council of Writing Program Administrators 2014)—so students can achieve personal advancement in their disciplinary fields and eventually in their workplaces. I fear that if rhetoric and composition as a field continues to place emphasis on professionalization through writing, we (teachers of composition) will continue to serve a neoconservative agenda.

This book argues that we must pay more attention to the vine in the air-conditioning vent to allow for a curriculum that places material and place-based writings at the center of rhetorical practice for students. Students should ask and answer existential and ethical questions about the nature of place, their relationship to it, what happens in it, and the communities that are a part of it. In first-year writing curriculums, students should be encouraged to make sense of their world through reading, movement, and writing, not merely to be responsive to the constructed knowledge of academic disciplines and the demands of a capitalist workplace. Only then can we really develop and practice a rhetoric of transformative ethos.

Rh=Life. Rhetoric is life. Rhetoric is for bringing us back to the nature of what it means to be human, and it helps us answer the existential questions about our being. Rhetoric is for understanding character. Rhetoric is for wandering and embracing movement as epistemology.

Rhetoric is for learning how to discern an ethical, right path. Rhetoric is for learning how to communicate your perspectives to others. Rhetoric is for creating identification(s) through differences in race, class, gender, and so forth. Rhetoric is for fostering empathy. Rhetoric is for imagining and creating a more just world. Rhetoric, in short, allows us to be with others.

APPENDIX 1

WRITING ON THE MATERIAL

The Object, the Souvenir, and the Collection

This assignment asks you to adopt the position of a cultural critic. More specifically, you are interested in the potentiality of material objects to affect the human psyche. However, rather than offering an objective statement about contemporary materiality, you should write to reveal your own development, or lessons learned, from the artifact(s) of your life.

Like Jim Corder in "The Glove," you will be in search of the primary artifact(s) and/or text(s) of your life. It can be argued that Corder's main reason for writing this essay is to answer the question, "When and how and why did I begin to learn that rhetoric of my boyhood that had remained?" (22). Corder investigates his "rhetoric"—or the stories and lessons he learned from material culture—to make sense of his identity. His story reveals lessons on sport, specifically in regards to "truths" about masculinity, class, and race relations in West Texas around the 1930s and 40s. The "baseball story," Corder concedes, may be generic and universal; but he also argues that stories are essential to our living experience even if they are mythical, fantastical, and archetypal. Stories reveal our living space and time because they "remain as memory and energy," they "persist" (85).

What stories can you think to tell from your childhood in relation to the material culture of your time? How might the material reveal your character? What lessons and emotions do artifacts instill and reveal about your living?

Your essay should include:

1. A detailed focus and description on *at least* one material artifact. Your description should try to make the artifact "come alive" for readers. Be sensitive to the descriptive use of anthropomorphism in your paper.

2. A brief history of your object (this will require some research on its manufacture, production, and popularity). You may also research a topic related to the object beyond these suggestions, such as Corder did with baseball.

3. A story that reveals the object's significance in your life. The writing should include moments of reflection as to the cultural lessons on identity you experienced through your relation with the object and its larger

DOI: 10.7330/9781646420636.c005

milieu—so, for example, how Corder was able to translate the materiality of the glove to the game of baseball, to boyhood lessons on masculinity, class, and race.

4. A discussion of the object in relation to time, very similar to the place assignment, with an eye toward the past, present, and/or future of the object.

ASSIGNMENT DETAILS: Your essay should follow MLA format and citations. 4–6 pages double-spaced, including Works Cited page.

Material Object Rubric:

The writer maintains a focus on at least one material object or collection. The writer describes the object(s) in great detail to the point that the reader can "see" the object(s) in their mind.

_____ / 15

The writer's prose tells a detailed narrative in relation to their object/collection through the recalling of particular events and an explanation of their relationship with the object/collection over several years.

_____ / 10

The writer provides a history for their object. They *may* discuss its significance in relation to family, especially if the object is an heirloom. Most important, though, the author engages research on the object's manufacture, production, and/or popularity. This requires the writer to have *at least* two sources. The writer expertly weaves research into their narrative to the point where the research feels essential to the story.

_____ / 20

The writer includes moments of reflection in their narrative to convey cultural lessons on identity they experienced through relation with the object/collection and its larger context. These lessons may be related to gender, race, class, and other facets of identity.

_____ / 20

The writer's voice is distinct. The writer's personality comes across through the words, and their tone is appropriate given the topic. A reader feels they can believe this narrator; in other words, they find the narrator credible. Voice is created through the details offered, the story, the style, and the organization.

_____ / 20

The writer shows they have a command of language. There are very few errors in the piece. The sentence structure is complex and varied. The prose is engaging and thoughtful.

_____ / 15

APPENDIX 2

GENTRIFICATION IN NEW YORK CITY
A Sample Place-Based Writing Curriculum

ASSIGNMENT 1: PLACE-NARRATIVE
REFLECTION AND PHOTO ESSAY

This essay is a narrative reflection on your neighborhood, more broadly defined as province. Don't feel limited to a few streets. You can branch out a bit more to include old schools, parks, or other landmarks you believe are local and important to you.

You are reflecting on your neighborhood in order to show readers something about where you grew up. You will also be thinking about how your neighborhood relates to your identity development. Some questions to ask in composing this essay include, What memories do you have around certain places in your neighborhood? What are/were your routines and rituals? Who were/are you with? How long have you lived there? How do you feel connected to these place(s)?

Think about Images:

This is not just a written reflection. I want you to use original and found images: present or past photos, drawings, and/or maps to accompany your words. So, think of this as a photo essay (similar to making a story on Instagram, but with a few more words).

I want you to include *at least five visuals* in your essay.

The story should make sense with the images—so the words and pictures need to work together. You should also consider how each section relates to the other ones.

Think about Audience:

Remember, you are familiar with your place. You know it well. You are an insider. But, most of your readers will be outsiders to your place. You need to keep your perspective as an insider but also adopt the perspective of an outsider in your descriptions. How would you endeavor to describe your place to readers? What details will you focus on? The placement of objects? The layout of the landscape? The weather at certain times of year? What are the smells of your place? The noises? Try to use figurative language—metaphor, simile, and personification—in your descriptions.

DOI: 10.7330/9781646420636.c006

Think about Emotions and Memories:

You'll want to talk about how this place evokes many emotions in you. Usually emotions are related to memories. You may want to talk about how your emotions have changed over time in and toward this place. You want your readers to get a sense of this place's significance for you through a description of your emotional experience.

Also, you might comment on how your province has changed over time. Why has this change occurred? How do you feel about it?

Think about Purpose:

You should ask yourself, Why am I composing on this place in particular? What do I want my readers to understand about this place, about my life, about life in general, after they finish my piece?

WORD COUNT AND FORMAT: Your narrative should be 750–1,000 words. The formatting, though, is up to you. Since I want you to use images, you can take advantage of any software you know of that allows you to embed images alongside words (text).

ASSIGNMENT 2: CRITICAL-RESPONSE ESSAY

Assignment Goals:

   Analyze complex text(s) through close reading and discussion.

   Construct a clear and logical progression of ideas in support of a thesis (the thesis that invites readers to understand the meaning of the texts as you do).

   Integrate plentiful textual evidence to support your thesis.

   Include personal reflections to the text (when appropriate). and

   Practice reading, writing, and revision strategies

PERCENTAGE OF COURSE GRADE: 25%

The Texts:

Selections from D. W. Gibson's *The Edge Becomes the Center: An Oral History of Gentrification in the 21st Century.*

The Project:

"I set out to understand how gentrification affects lives and not far into my trip I realized the word gentrification is useless—rendered so by overuse, too broad to adequately capture a huge range of *disparate experiences, contexts, and ultimately, meanings*" (highlighted for emphasis, D. W. Gibson, 10).

As Gibson says above, gentrification means different things to different people. We have talked about the stakeholders—or people who hold a vested interest—in this issue; these include residents (tenants), landlords, developers, gentrifiers, activist groups, etc. As our class discussions revealed, there is more than one opinion on this issue and more than one definition of gentrification.

MAIN ARGUMENT: In this paper, you will discuss how positionality (race/ethnicity, class, profession, gender, etc.) affects a person's definition, experience of, and opinion about gentrification.

You will choose *at least 2* people's stories from the texts in this unit and write an analysis of their narratives. **Note: this can be a compare-and-contrast essay or a straight-up analysis of each person**.

In this critical response, you will make a clear argument. Your argument should convince readers that you have read the text(s) closely and that you understand gentrification from at least 2 people's critical perspectives based on the readings. **You will quote from the texts extensively in order to show this understanding**.

Some Questions to Consider as You Write:

1. How does the definition of, and how do opinions about, gentrification change from person to person?

2. Which narratives were most compelling to you as a reader? Did you find yourself sympathizing or agreeing with some perspectives over others?

3. Did you see any differences or similarities among the narrators/ interviewees?

4. What quotes or ideas really stand out to you from the narratives? Can you use those to help you with your paper's argument?

How Do You Convince Readers?

1. You must articulate a **clear, concise** thesis statement that you develop throughout the paper.

2. You must have **no fewer than four** textual references (quotes) in your paper.

3. *Developing* means you must synthesize both the primary texts and your insights. This requires you to be a rigorous reader. Remember to use the annotation skills learned this semester. You should pick quotes judiciously as you write. This means you must avoid scattering quotes throughout the paper with little explanation or context (e.g., "quote-dropping").

4. Your paper should not read as a summary of text but rather should be analytical. Your writing, in other words, should further your argument and not tell your reader what the texts are about. "And then this happened, and then this happened . . ." is BORING.

5. You must also cite the source you use throughout the paper both in the text and on a separate Works Cited page.

Tips on the Thesis:

1. Make sure your thesis statement answers a <u>why</u> and <u>how</u> question.

2. Ensure that your thesis makes a claim about the subject that needs proving (i.e., use of evidence from the text).

3. Provide the reader with a clearly focused lens through which to view the subject.

Tips on Organization:

1. Forecast your essay in the introduction through a roadmap.

2. Make transitions between ideas so your argument flows in a logical order

3. Each paragraph should include original assertion(s), quote(s), and explication(s)

Tips on Expression and Conventions:

1. Vary your sentence structure—not all long or short sentences, not all simple or complex sentences.

2. Make sure your tone is academic but not stilted—don't use big words for the sake of using big words.

3. Read your paper out loud!! This will help you catch awkward sentences and hear the rhythm of your writing.

4. When using direct quotes, include the page number.

5. Discuss texts in the present tense: Woolf *suggests* that . . .

YOUR AUDIENCE: Write your analysis for an academic audience that is generally, but not closely, familiar with the texts. For example, the audience may have read the text a long time ago.

LENGTH: 4 to 5 double-spaced, typed pages

FORMAT: MLA, double spaced, and Works Cited page

ASSIGNMENT 3: "WEIGH-IN" ESSAY

Assignment Goals:

- ✓ Analyze complex texts through close reading, discussion and viewing.
- ✓ Construct an argument with a thesis that offers your opinion on an issue you are exploring from the texts in the course.
- ✓ Integrate plentiful textual evidence to support your thesis (your paper should include *at least two of the texts* we read/viewed in class and should have *at least four quotes—one must be from the Gibson book*).
- ✓ Include personal reflection as it relates to your argument.
- ✓ Practice reading, writing, and revision strategies.

PERCENTAGE OF COURSE GRADE: 30%

The Texts:

D. W. Gibson *The Edge Becomes the Center: A History of Gentrification in the 21st Century* **(at least one quote needed from this book)**

Several articles on the North Shore/St. George Development (see Blackboard)

and/or other works of literature/films of your choice

The Project:

Now that you have performed a close reading of our texts, you are being asked to write an analysis in which you make a clear argument—your essay should offer your opinion on a debatable issue in the readings (at least two sources engaged).

More specifically, **you should offer your opinion** about the changes proposed for Staten Island's North Shore/St. George.

Some questions you might ask yourself include:

> Do I see the North Shore development as a process of gentrification? How do I personally feel about gentrification?

> Do I think these changes will benefit Staten Island? What are the positive and negative consequences of these new developments? How will the new changes affect residents of Staten Island?

> Do I think this is an effective use of the area; will these changes improve the economy of Staten Island/NYC?

You will need to rely on the **authority** that comes with being a *careful reader, discussion member, and critic.* Remember, you are being asked to convince the readers of this paper that your argument (opinion) is valid. An important factor in assessment of your essay is its ability to engage readers with thoughtful observations.

How do you convince readers?

1. You must articulate a **clear, concise** thesis statement (your opinion), which you develop throughout the paper.

2. You must have no fewer than two textual references in your paper.

3. *Developing* means you must synthesize both the primary texts and your insights. This requires you to be a rigorous reader. Remember to use the annotation skills learned this semester. You should pick quotes judiciously as you write. This means you must avoid scattering quotes throughout the paper with little explanation or context (e.g., "quote-dropping").

4. Your paper should not read as a summary of texts but rather should be analytical.

5. You must also cite the sources you use throughout the paper **both in the text and on a separate Works Cited page**.

Tips on the Thesis:
1. Compose a statement that is clear and concise.

2. Make connections to the texts you are citing in your argument.

3. Remember that the thesis should answer a question!

Tips on Organization:
1. Forecast your essay in the introduction through a roadmap.

2. Make transitions between ideas so your argument flows in a logical order

3. Each paragraph should include original assertion(s), quote(s), and explication(s)

Tips on Expression and Conventions:
1. Vary your sentence structure—not all long or short sentences, not all simple or complex sentences.

2. Make sure your tone is academic but not stilted—don't use big words for the sake of using big words.

3. Read your paper out loud!! This will help you catch awkward sentences and hear the rhythm of your writing.

4. When using direct quotes, include the page number.

5. Discuss texts in the present tense: Gibson *suggests* that . . .

YOUR AUDIENCE: Write your "weigh-in" essay for an academic audience that is generally, but not closely, familiar with the texts. For example, the audience may have read/watched the text a long time ago.

LENGTH: MLA format, 6–7 double-spaced, typed pages, and a separate Works Cited page

ASSIGNMENT 4: PUBLIC ARGUMENT

Part I: Rewind and Reenvision: Creating a Public Argument

Assignment Goals:
✓ Reflect upon past research and writing for the weigh-in essay (**REWIND!**) and present your knowledge and opinion about your topic (**SI North Shore development**) in a different visual/spatial genre that would be intended for a public audience of stakeholders (**REENVISION!**).

✓ Apply your understanding of the rhetorical situation (audience, purpose, context) and rhetorical appeals (ethos, pathos, logos) in order to create a public argument.

✓ **Choose** a particular visual/spatial genre for your project and **Analyze** an example of it in order to **Compose** effectively in it.

✓ Be creative: work to create visual and spatial arguments that target a particular audience.

The Project:

Now that you have thoroughly and carefully researched and formed an opinion—and written about that opinion in the weigh-in essay—on the development **(gentrification)** of the North Shore in Staten Island, you are going to create a public argument for an audience connected to the topic.

Think of ALL the stakeholders associated with gentrification: long-time residents, new residents (gentrifiers), landlords, small businesses, community organizations, developers and investors, politicians, tourists, etc. You should choose a **TARGET AUDIENCE** for your project among these stakeholders.

Think of all the possible genres in which you can choose to compose to make an argument: poster, flyer, brochure, meme, blog, video, t-shirt, song, poem, board game, diorama, etc. The sky is the limit! This is a chance for you to be creative and draw on your strengths—are you good at drawing? Photography? Composing music? Writing? Something else? You should choose a **GENRE** to analyze and compose in for this project.

Consider the Following:

Think about the genre: It is said that "the medium is the message." What genre is best to choose for your particular argument? What are effective examples of that genre? How do you persuade your target audience through using the medium you have chosen?

Think about the situation: What made you concerned about this issue? What circumstances surround the issue? How can you address the rhetorical situation (writer, audience, purpose, context) carefully in your public argument?

Decide on your purpose: Do you want to persuade your audience to be concerned about your topic? Change the readers' minds about a current viewpoint? Ask the readers to take action, or support a change you're suggesting? How will you influence the community affected?

Decide how to present yourself: As a writer, what kinds of information about yourself should you reveal to the reader to persuade them to listen to you? Do you have any authority to speak on the issue? What examples, ideas, or personal experiences could you include to help build your credibility?

Decide on your audience: To whom will you address this public argument? If you know your purpose, decide on the audience for the argument that can best help you achieve that goal. Who will disagree? What will they say? How will you respond? Imagine a conversation with those voices. To make a convincing argument, you must recognize differing views on the issue.

Think about your tone: As you decide on appropriate style and language choices for your argument, keep in mind the readers you are trying to reach. Will satire or humor move them? Will they "get it?" Or would it be more appropriate to take a serious tone?

Part 2: Reflecting on Rhetorical Choices

For the second half of your final, you will write a reflective essay, at least 750 words (**3–4 pages**), discussing the strategies you used in composing the public argument. You should focus on how you targeted a new audience through the genre you chose. For this assignment, you had to compose in a new genre for a new audience—what decisions did you have to make to do this? What was your process of composing?

In this essay, you should:

1. Consider the visual/spatial genre you chose and how you used the model text to help you compose.

   • Based on your model text and the one you composed for this assignment, what makes a good example in your genre? How did you meet the expectations of your new genre?

2. Explain your target audience in your reenvisioned text.

   • What were some specific considerations or choices you made given your audience for the public argument—who were they and how were you trying to convince them?

3. Describe how you thought through your argument differently from the weigh-in essay to the public argument.

   • How did you have to use your sources and knowledge in each assignment? What was your thesis in the weigh-in and how did that come through (or not) in the public argument? How did you translate one project into the other?

4. Discuss your audience, context, and purpose for your public argument. Analyze how you applied rhetorical appeals (ethos, pathos, logos) in your public argument.

   • How did you appeal to the emotions and/or logic of your audience? What tone did you use in approaching them? What did you want them to feel or do after they encountered your text?

NOTES

INTRODUCTION

1. CUNY is calling this increase in course load the "15/30 plan." There are several web pages, videos, and posters produced by CUNY around our campuses explaining the reasoning behind the campaign. Here is an example of a video from the campaign: https://www.youtube.com/watch?v=U6judDYbF50.

2. I don't disagree with accelerating remediation through corequisite models of composition. However, I think this model places too much emphasis on (and faith in) the idea of efficiency and less emphasis on the ideas of persistence and retention, particularly in thinking about populations who have historically been marginalized in the university.

3. See Chris Gallagher's discussion on competency-based education (CBE) in *Composition in the Age of Austerity* for a further explanation of this trend toward extreme outcomes assessment on the postsecondary level (2016, 21–34).

4. See James S. Baumlin and Tita French Baumlin, eds., *Ethos: New Essays in Rhetorical and Critical Theory* (1994); James S. Baumlin and Keith D. Miller, eds. *Selected Essays of Jim W. Corder Pursuing the Personal in Scholarship, Teaching, and Writing* (2004); Mike Duncan and Star Vanguiri, eds., *The Centrality of Style*, Fort Collins, CO: WAC Clearinghouse and Parlor Press (2012); Theresa Enos and Keith D. Miller, eds., *Beyond Postprocess and Postmodernism: Essays on the Spaciousness of Rhetoric*, Mahweh, NJ: Erlbaum (2003); Theresa Enos, "Voice as Echo of Delivery, Ethos as Transforming Process" (1994); Kathleen Blake Yancey, ed., *Voices on Voice: Perspectives, Definitions, Inquiry*, Urbana, IL: NCTE, 1994.

5. See Kenneth Burke, *A Rhetoric of Motives* (1969); Edward P. J. Corbett, *Classical Rhetoric for the Modern Student* (1965); Sonja K. Foss and Cindy L. Griffin, "Beyond Persuasion: A Proposal for an Invitational Rhetoric" (1995); Michael S. Halloran, "Aristotle's Concept of *Ethos*, or If Not His Somebody Else's" (1982); Michael Hyde, ed., *The Ethos of Rhetoric* (2004); Thomas Rickert, *Ambient Rhetoric: The Attunements of Rhetorical Being* (2013).

6. Halloran's work on ethos describes the term as a "habitual gathering place" where public life and culture develop (1982, 60), which is similar to what I am getting at in this section.

7. Nedra Reynolds considers this idea in her article "*Ethos* as Location: New Sites for Understanding Discursive Authority," *Rhetoric Review* 11.2 (1993): 325–38. Her book *Geographies of Writing: Inhabiting Places and Encountering Difference* (2007) is helpful in understanding place-based writing in the field, but it does not create a theory of ethos development and geography, as I do in my book.

8. For a comprehensive history of open admissions at City College, I recommend reading Conor Tomás Reed's "'Treasures That Prevail': Adrienne Rich, the SEEK Program, and Social Movements at the City College of New York, 1968–72" (2013).

9. I use the word *female* here to denote sex assigned at birth only.

10. This paragraph is somewhat facetious, but I am trying to point out that there are fads in the teaching of writing that have later been seen as less than desirable by

the field. Some readers will know I am referring here to studies done in the 1970s and 80s that recorded students on tape as they composed to reveal their thought processes while writing. This pseudoscientific methodology was critiqued because it did not take into account the social and contextual realities of the writer(s). See Linda Flower and John Hayes (1981) as one of the most famous examples of this protocol.

11.   Western supremacy, the rhetorical tradition's nursemaid, has certainly performed the same kind of exclusions and normalization throughout its history. Thus, it is hard to fathom how neoconservatism could be equal to or more pernicious than the primacy of Western thought that continues to overshadow our thinking in academia, and by extension, rhetoric and writing studies. This book project, however, isn't offering an extensive critique of the rhetorical tradition. In some ways, my project is trying to show how some ideas from that tradition can be repurposed for our own time and leveraged in potentially progressive ways. As you read the following chapters, you will see an extensive critique of Aristotelian rhetoric, favoring approaches that privilege emotion and character development over logic and objectivism.

12.   An overwhelming amount of scholarship supports this statement. See Jacqueline Jones Royster (1996), Victor Villanueva (2004), and Vershawn Ashanti Young (2009), three influential articles in our field on the supremacy of these aspects in university culture and writing.

13.   See the CCCC resolution "Students' Right to Their Own Language" (NCTE 1974).

14.   Asao Inoue's keynote address at CCCC 2019 (2019a), "How Do We Language so People Stop Killing Each Other, or What Do We Do about White Language Supremacy?" addressed these issues of white supremacy in writing instruction head on and additionally led to more discussion on WPA-L.

15.   This subheading references an early primer for understanding the teaching of writing, Erika Lindemann's *A Rhetoric for Writing Teachers* (2001). This book was one of my introductions to the field of rhetoric and composition. Its insistence on understanding the rhetorical tradition and teaching writing in a rhetorical frame offers an important foundation for teacher-scholars.

16.   For a discussion of rhetoric as a study of ethics, see Judy Holiday's (2009) "In[ter]vention: Locating Rhetoric's Ethos."

17.   My dad, Robert Carlo, earned a BA in literature from Southern Connecticut State University. From there, he worked as a telephone operator at Southern New England Telephone (SNET) and—as he was raising my sister and me—he continued to earn promotions and retired from a middle-management position the summer before I left for graduate school in 2008, after around thirty years at his company. He now works part time as a substitute teacher in local elementary schools. I'm grateful to my father for being a loving person, for supporting my decision to go on to academia and helping me physically move to Arizona and later to New York. I would not be the person I am today without the support of both my parents and extended family.

18.   See Inoue's discussion of white racial habitus as a haunting presence in academia in chapter 2 of his latest book, *Labor-Based Grading Contracts: Building Equity and Inclusion in the Compassionate Writing Classroom* (2019b).

CHAPTER 1: FINDING A TRANSFORMATIVE DEFINITION OF ETHO

1.   Theresa Enos asks this same question in one of her articles on transformative ethos: *Voice as Echo of Delivery, Ethos as Transforming Process* (1994, 189).

2. When I invoke the word *habit*, I mean to suggest ways of being we learn through processes of socialization. Habit is not natural, in other words, but practiced. Beyond Aristotle's discussion in the *Nichomachean Ethics*, it may be helpful to look to Pierre Bourdieu's (2006) notion of "habitus," in which he asserts that the development of the modern subject is one in which "[s]ocial subjects [are] classified by their classifications, distinguish themselves by the distinctions they make, between the beautiful and the ugly, the distinguished and the vulgar, in which their position in the objective classifications is expressed or betrayed" (324). The learning of classification and the behavior associated with those preferences is a part of habit.

3. This "shared reality" can sometimes be a good thing, but sometimes it can go bad—for example, didn't Trump supporters believe in a "shared reality" that somehow made immigrants the Other? I'm unsure all shared realities lead to ethical outcomes, in other words.

4. When I reference *dwelling*, I am primarily thinking of Heidegger's (2013b) use of the word in several of his writings. "Dwelling," as a term, has what he calls "a double demand" because, in a literal sense, it means a place where people live and build houses and other structures, but it also has a higher, more abstract meaning to Heidegger that is related to Being. The second definition is connected to the idea that we need to feel a sense of belonging (with a community and/or place) before we can build, or dwell, in a literal sense. This type of dwelling as belonging is a prerequisite of dwelling as literal settlement; dwelling as belonging is poetic, as "the nature of poetry" creates a mindset for "a letting-dwell," and this is a "distinctive kind of building," one that does not raise buildings literally but rather creates the conditions for such acts (213).

5. See Holiday's 2009 article for a discussion of how rhetoric is a source of ethics due to its inventive and character-appealing qualities.

6. Provisionality can, in some ways, hurt the Other—especially if they are a person who stands without, or with less, privilege. Not everyone stands or is afforded authority when they speak, so provisionality can undermine someone who has been traditionally marginalized and thus needs to make a polemical statement. It is hard to account for this in my writing, but I think this caveat is very important to our national state of affairs.

7. I find the work of José Esteban Muñoz (1999) to be illuminating here, as he discusses queer subject formation as dependent upon the "survival" strategy of disidentification with white, heterosexual norms, whereby "the minority subject practices [disidentification] in order to negotiate a phobic majoritarian public sphere that continuously elides or punishes the existence of subjects who do not conform to the phantasm of normative citizenship" (4).

CHAPTER 2: FINDING AND COLLECTING

1. Although my discussion in this chapter is specifically on the positionalities of the finder and the collector, I find Jacques Derrida's concept of messianicity in *Archive Fever* (1996)—or, the idea of gathering materials for the future in the hope of a once-unknown object or figure emerging—to be generative to a discussion on the ways the material functions rhetorically. The impulse to shape the understanding and discourse of the past for the future is one that potentially requires the persuasive force of material things, and things, in some ways, serve as evidence of a constructed archival narrative. As Derrida (1996) writes, the impulse to archive comes from "the question of the future itself, the question of a response, of a promise, and of a responsibility for tomorrow" (36). Corder's sentiment to preserve his artifacts

for the future echoes Derrida's—though, again, I would not consider Corder an archivist but rather someone who embodies the positionality of the finder and collector.

2. Alice Brand's body of scholarly work particularly relates, as she has always advocated for the study of emotion in the writing process in the field of rhetoric and composition. In "Writing and Feelings: Checking our Vital Signs" (1990) specifically, she does a quantitative analysis of her student reflections to explore emotions in her classroom. Dale Jacobs and Laura Micciche's edited collection *A Way to Move* (2003) is one of the more recent edited collections for scholarship on emotion in rhetoric and composition studies, especially Gretchen Moon's chapter on how contemporary writing textbooks treat the topic of emotion and Ellen Quandahl's chapter on Aristotelian interpretation of emotion in rhetoric. Lastly, T. R. Johnson's article "School Sucks" (2001) discusses the ways institutional schooling of emotion, especially through the privileging of academic discourse, can make writing a painful process for students; he offers suggestions for a renegade rhetorical pedagogy he hopes will instill a sense of pleasure for students in composing processes.

3. I borrow this particular structure from Jane Bennett's books *Vibrant Matter: A Political Ecology of Things* (2010) and *The Enchantment of Modern Life: Attachments, Crossings, and Ethics* (2001). She develops her theory of materiality through subsections that, for lack of a better term, serve as storied case studies.

4. When I reference the idea of material stories, I mean the narrators are discussing material objects in their writing. Often, these stories are told to connect the object to an experience, and often these stories reveal something about the narrator's character.

5. Return to Burke's discussion "Introduction: The Five Key Terms of Dramatism" in *A Grammar of Motives* for more detail on what I mean by emphasizing different terms based on context. I specifically find Burke's metaphor that the pentadic terms are fingers on a hand helpful here—my key terms of the material are connected at the palm but separate in their functions, like fingers (1969, xxii).

6. This material story is paraphrased from Jim Corder's chapter "The Glove" from *The Heroes Have Gone: Personal Essays on Sport, Popular Culture, and the American West* (2008).

7. Corder's emphasis on invention in his writings is related to the idea of becoming. For him, invention is a constant process—a writer cycles back and forth between invention and structure (see "From Rhetoric to Grace" [1984]). Corder, then, recognizes how invention is essential to ethos, as repetition of the cycle reveals new information and reflections about our characters. I think a finder must have an open posture, playing through this cycle of invention when interacting with the material.

8. Nostalgia for the past isn't always a positive thing—though Corder views it as such. What I mean by this warning is that present statements like "Make America Great Again" try to use nostalgia to reach from the past into the present, but in this case, the nostalgia is tinged with white supremacy, patriarchy, and heterosexism. Going back into history to dig up the vestiges of the colonial past isn't a project worth doing and can—I think rightly—discredit a feeling of nostalgia and can also actively work to divide people and perpetuate violence against people who don't fit the norm of the "past/present."

9. Roland Barthes (1980) is very explicit at the end of the book about this public and private divide as a part of consuming and connecting with images: "I must, by a necessary resistance, reconstitute the division of *public* and *private*. I want to utter interiority without yielding intimacy. I experience the Photograph and the world in which it participates according to two regions: on one side the Images, on the

other my photographs; on the one side, unconcern, shifting, noise, the inessential (even if I am abusively deafened by it), on the other the burning, the wounded" (98). These two experiences are representative of the terms *studium*—the public language of photography—and the *punctum*—photography's interior, private language.

10.   For further reference on how Barthes sees his project as having a phenomenological origin, please refer to pages 21, 43–45, 84, 89, 98 of *Camera Lucida* (1980). I specifically like the passage where he states, "As *Spectator* I was interested in Photography only for 'sentimental' reasons; I wanted to explore it not as a question (a theme) but as a wound: I see, I feel, hence I notice, I observe, and I think" (21). The ending clause, where each sentence starts with "I," shows how this project is rooted in subjectivity. For indeed, as Barthes describes, we cannot feel another's wounds; only our body and our mind are the sites of pain and trauma.

11.   Barthes believes not all photographs inspire a wound, or punctum. For him, a photo must reveal the truth of its subject for it to be emotionally moving. He writes, "'Not a just image, just an image,' Godard says. But my grief wanted a just image, an image which would be both justice and accuracy—*justesse*: just an image, but a just image" (1980, 70). The search, then, was for a just image of his mother that would show her essence and bring her back "to life," rather than what the typical photo does, which is to continually remind its viewer of the subject's mortality. Barthes refers to the photograph as a form of death in several passages in *Camera Lucida*; for further reference please see pages 14–15, 79, and 92–93

12.   I don't mean to present a binary of white audience and Black/Other audience in analyzing hooks's work. I do think she does speak to white people and then to a large, diverse audience of Other (though, sometimes she speaks to an African American/African diaspora audience specifically). Overall, hooks's writing is intersectional, and I don't wish to perpetuate binary thinking through parsing out the particulars of her messaging in this section.

13.   Please see appendix 1 for a sample assignment and rubric dedicated to material analysis and storytelling.

CHAPTER 3: MOVEMENT

1.   See Rickert's chapter 7 "On Ambient Dwelling" in *Ambient Rhetoric* (2013). Here he claims that when we think through the lens of ontology, we must view affect as "worldly; it must go beyond human doing" (239).

2.   As discussed in the introduction, by dwelling I mean to suggest both a literal construction of homes and buildings and a more abstract state of mind in the creation of community.

3.   In *Ambient Rhetoric* (2013), Rickert continually asserts that the subject/object binary has dissolved. I have tried to catalogue each section of the book in which he uses the word "dissolve" or "dissolution" in reference to the subject/object binary. These passages can be found on pages xii, 1, 43, 82, 84, 104, 169, 171, and 221. Rickert must make this argument for his book because he claims that ontological understanding of being shifts agency away from humans and distributes it across all assemblages in an environment. Everything is connected, so there is no division. I am somewhat uncomfortable with this complete shift for several reasons—one being that I don't think ontological inquiry is the lens we should privilege as rhetoricians to the exclusion of epistemological and phenomenological inquiry. Several arguments in the book are unsettling because of this privileging of ontology—one being the complete denial of the existence of the

idea of worldview (xvi, 223); perhaps white males can claim there is no such thing as positionality, but to say so is to minimize the struggles and oppressions under-privileged groups face because of their identity. The term *worldview* is one way of expressing these struggles and oppressions. The other argument I find problem-atic is the shift away from intentionality in rhetoric (x); though I understand the need to qualify intentionality in the postmodern age, I am hesitant to cast it aside completely, especially when thinking about an author's stylistic choices and voice. I still find that type of analysis important to the study of rhetoric despite it being seemingly passé to some scholars.

4.   Derrida (1995) discusses the dialectic between the sensible and the mythical: "But on the other hand, in the order of becoming, when one cannot lay claim to a firm and stable *logos*, when one must make do with the probable, then myth is the done thing; it is rigor" (112).

5.   Corder's narratives come from the perspective of white rural poverty. These narra-tives, when we view them through the lens of critical race studies and also consider white privilege, do not represent a marginalized population. Yet, there is something to be said, I think, about the exclusion of the white poor in university culture, particularly in English studies and its valued texts. As Corder writes, "Epic, tragedy, adventure, and romance would not admit many I loved. And I was angry. I am still angry. Why, when we defined heroism, did we exclude my father? My mother? Why are the sweet, zesty, gentle, cantankerous people of our lives excluded [from the literary canon]?" (*Little Sorrows* n.d., 95).

6.   It is important to note here that *cosmos* is seen as a subjective term. Cosmos refers to a form of order and harmony; its opposition is *chaos*. Cosmos as a term can and should be thought about in plural ways. West Texas is not my cosmos, and it might not be the cosmos for many readers. Corder (1988) invites us to think about our own cosmos/province in this chapter (50) and thus offers his cosmos as an example in his writing for the reader to begin inventing and reflecting on their own.

7.   It is important to note that the *Encyclopedia of Rhetoric and Composition* (Enos 1996) does not contain the term *chora*, but there is an entire entry on and there are sev-eral references to *topoi* in the volume.

8.   See Ana Munster's *Materializing New Media: Embodiment in Information Aesthetics* (2005) for a discussion on the history of the concept of the fold.

CHAPTER 4: FOR AN AFFECTIVE, EMBODIED, PLACE-BASED WRITING CURRICULUM

1.   In *Wanderlust: A History of Walking* (2000), Rebecca Solnit devotes all of chapter 11 to walking in the city. In the following chapter, 12, she focuses on walking in Paris specifically. Readers interested in the figure of the *flâneur* will find her reflections valuable.

2.   Please see appendix 2 for all assignment sheets discussed in this chapter.

3.   Students additionally read James Chisholm and Brandie Trent's (2013) essay "Digi-tal Story-Telling in a Place-Based Composition Course," which includes an analysis of a digital place-based essay written by a high-school student. This article provides a good model and additional theory to discuss in class.

4.   This unit was taught in spring 2017. As an update, the SI wheel project was aban-doned in spring 2019, as the investors pulled out of the project, though many of the luxury residential buildings have already opened and the Empire Outlets opened in Summer 2019; the luxury hotel remains under construction and has not announced an opening.

5. Kathleen Blake Yancey, Liane Robertson, and Kara Taczak's book on teaching for transfer, *Writing across Contexts: Transfer, Composition, and Sites of Writing* (2014), has become one of the most popular pedagogical texts about first-year composition, as many writing programs have been quick to adopt its model assignments and join the listserv and CCCC SIG set up by the authors.

REFERENCES

Adler-Kassner and Elizabeth Wardle, eds. 2015. *Naming What We Know: Threshold Concepts in Writing Studies.* Logan: Utah State University Press.

Ahmed, Sara. 2014. *The Cultural Politics of Emotion.* London: Routledge.

Aristotle. 1939. *Nichomachean Ethics.* Translated by Harris Rackham. Perseus Digital Library.

Aristotle. 1991. *On Rhetoric: A Theory of Civic Discourse.* Translated by George A. Kennedy. New York: Oxford University Press.

Bachelard, Gaston. 1994. *The Poetics of Space: The Classic Look at How We Experience Intimate Places.* Translated by Maria Jolas. Boston: Beacon.

Baker-Bell, April. 2020. *Linguistic Justice: Black Language, Literacy, Identity, and Pedagogy.* New York: NCTE Routledge.

Barthes, Roland. 1977. "The Death of the Author." In *Image-Music-Text,* 49–55. Translated by Stephen Heath. New York: Hill and Wang.

Barthes, Roland. 1980. *Camera Lucida: Reflections on Photography.* Translated by Richard Howard. New York: Hill and Wang.

Barthes, Roland. 2010. *Mourning Diary: October 26, 1977–September 15, 1979.* Translated by Richard Howard. New York: Hill and Wang.

Baumlin, James. "Toward a Corderian Theory of Rhetoric." 2003. In *Beyond Postprocess and Postmodernism: Essays on the Spaciousness of Rhetoric,* edited by Theresa Enos and Keith D. Miller, 25–58. Mahwah, NJ: Earlbaum.

Baumlin, James S., and Tita French Baumlin, eds. 1994. *Ethos: Essays in Rhetorical and Critical Theory.* Dallas: Southern Methodist University Press.

Baumlin, James S., and Jim W. Corder. 1990. "Jackleg Carpentry and the Fall from Freedom into Authority in Writing." *Freshman English News* 18 (1): 18–25.

Baumlin, James, and Keith D. Miller. 2008. Afterword in *The Heroes Have Gone: Personal Essays on Sport, Popular Culture, and the American West,* by Jim W. Corder, 169–81. Kansas City, MO: Moon City.

Bazerman, Charles, and Howard Tinberg. 2015. "Text Is an Object Outside of Oneself That Can Be Improved and Developed." In *Naming What We Know: Threshold Concepts of Writing Studies,* edited by Linda Adler-Kassner and Elizabeth Wardle, 61. Logan: Utah State University Press.

Benjamin, Walter. 1969. "Unpacking My Library: A Talk about Book Collecting." In *Illuminations,* 59–67. Edited by Hannah Arendt. Translated by Harry Zohn. New York: Shocken.

Benjamin, Walter. 2002. *The Arcades Project.* Translated by Howard Eiland and Kevin McLaughlin. Boston: Belknap.

Benjamin, Walter. 2006. *Berlin Childhood around 1900.* Translated by Howard Eiland. Boston: Belknap.

Bennett, Jane. 2001. *The Enchantment of Modern Life: Attachments, Crossings, and Ethics.* Princeton: Princeton University Press.

Bennett, Jane. 2010. *Vibrant Matter: A Political Ecology of Things.* Durham, NC: Duke University Press.

Bernstein, Susan Naomi. 2016. "Occupy Basic Writing: Pedagogy in the Wake of Austerity." In *Composition in the Age of Austerity,* edited by Nancy Welch and Tony Scott, 92–105. Logan: Utah State University Press.

DOI: 10.7330/9781646420636.c007

Blankenship, Lisa. 2019. *Changing the Subject: A Theory of Rhetorical Empathy.* Logan: Utah State University Press.

Bourdieu, Pierre. 2006. "Distinction: A Social Critique of the Judgment of Taste." In *Media and Cultural Studies: Keyworks,* edited by Douglas Kellner and Meenakshi Gigi, 249–52. Durham, NC: Wiley-Blackwell.

Brand, Alice. 1990. "Writing and Feelings: Checking Our Vital Signs." *Rhetoric Review* 8 (2): 290–308.

Brooke, Robert, ed. 2003. *Rural Voices: Place Conscious Education and The Teaching of Writing.* New York: Teacher's College Press.

Brooke, Robert, ed. 2015. "Introduction." In *Writing Suburban Citizenship: Place-Conscious Education and the Conundrum of Suburbia.* Syracuse, NY: Syracuse University Press.

Brooke, Robert, and Jason McIntosh. 2007. "Deep Maps: Teaching Rhetorical Engagement through Place-Conscious Education." In *The Locations of Composition,* edited by Christopher J. Keller and Christian R. Weisser, 131–49. Albany: SUNY Press.

Burke, Kenneth. 1968. *Language as Symbolic Action.* Berkley: University of California Press.

Burke, Kenneth. 1969a. *Grammar of Motives.* Berkley: University of California Press.

Burke, Kenneth 1969b. *A Rhetoric of Motives.* Berkley: University of California Press.

Burke, Kenneth. 1993. "Definition of Man." In *Professing the New Rhetorics: A Sourcebook,* edited by Theresa Enos and Stuart Brown, 40–62. Englewood Cliffs: Pearson.

Carlo, Rosanne. 2016. "Keyword Essay: Place-Based Literacies." *Community Literacy Journal* 10 (2): 45–56.

Casey, Edward. 1993. *Getting Back into Place: Toward a Renewed Understanding of the Place World.* Bloomington: Indiana University Press.

Casey, Edward. 1998. *The Fate of Place.* Berkeley: University of California Press.

Chandler, Sally. 2007. "Fear, Teaching Composition, and Students' Discursive Choices: Re-Thinking Connections between Emotions and College Student Writing." *Composition Studies* 35 (2): 53–70.

Charlton, Colin, Jonikka Charlton, Tarez Samra Grabin, Kathleen J. Ryan, and Amy Ferdinandt Stolley, eds. 2011. *GenAdmin: Theorizing WPA Identities in the Twenty-First Century.* Anderson, SC: Parlor.

Chisholm, James S., and Brandie Trent. 2013. "Digital Storytelling in a Place-Based Composition Course." *Journal of Adolescent and Adult Literacy.* 57 (4): 307–18.

Complete College America. n.d. "Complete College America: City University of New York (CUNY)." Accessed May 5, 2019. https://completecollege.org/project/cuny-mo mentum/.

Conners, Robert J. 1992. "Dreams and Play: Historical Method and Methodology." In *Methods and Methodology in Composition Research,* edited by Gesa Kirsch and Patricia Sullivan, 15–36. Carbondale: Southern Illinois University Press.

Coole, Diana, and Samantha Frost. 2010. *New Materialisms: Ontology, Agency, and Politics.* Durham, NC: Duke University Press.

Corbett, Edward P. J. 1965. *Classical Rhetoric for the Modern Student.* 1st ed. New York: Oxford University Press.

Corder, Jim W. 1984. "From Rhetoric to Grace: Propositions 55–81 about Rhetoric, Propositions 1–54 and 82 et seq. Being as Yet Unstated; Or, Getting from the Classroom to the World." *Rhetoric Society Quarterly* 14 (5): 15–28.

Corder, Jim W. 1985. "Argument as Emergence, Rhetoric as Love." *Rhetoric Review* 4 (1): 16–32.

Corder, Jim W. 1988. *Lost in West Texas.* College Station: Texas A&M University Press.

Corder, Jim W. 1989a. *Chronicle of a Small Town.* College Station: Texas A&M University Press.

Corder, Jim W. 1989b. "Hunting for Ethos Where They Say It Can't Be Found." In *Selected Essays of Jim W. Corder: Pursuing the Personal in Scholarship, Teaching, and Writing,* edited by James S. Baumlin and Keith D. Miller, 202–20. Urbana, IL: NCTE.

Corder, Jim W. 1992. *Yonder: Life on the Far Side of Change.* Atlanta: University of Georgia Press.

Corder, Jim W. 1993a. "At Last Report, I Was Still Here." In *The Subject Is Writing: Essays by Teachers and Students,* edited by Wendy Bishop, 261–66. Portsmouth, NH: Boynton/ Cook.

Corder, Jim W. 1993b. "Tribes and Displaced Persons: Some Observations on Collaboration." In *Theory and Practice in the Teaching of writing: Rethinking the Discipline,* edited by Lee Odell, 271–88. Carbondale: Southern Illinois University Press.

Corder, Jim W. 1995. "Notes on a Rhetoric of Regret." *Composition Studies/Freshman English News* 23 (1): 94–105.

Corder, Jim W. n.d., circa late 90s. *Little Sorrows: An Essay on Changing Rhetorics.* Unpublished Typescript. Roberta Corder's House. Fort Worth, TX.

Corder, Jim W. n.d., circa 1990s. "A Portable Flea Market." Unpublished handwritten and typescript. Roberta Corder's House. Fort Worth, TX.

Corder, Jim W. n.d., circa 1990s. "A Remnant." Unpublished handwritten journal and typescript. Roberta Corder's House. Fort Worth, TX.

Corder, Jim W. 2004. "Varieties of Ethical Argument, with Some Account of the Significance of Ethos in the Teaching of Composition." In *Selected Essays of Jim W. Corder: Pursuing the Personal in Scholarship, Teaching, and Writing,* edited by James S. Baumlin and Keith D. Miller, 60–101. Urbana, IL: NCTE

Corder, Jim W. 2009. *On Living and Dying in West Texas: A Postmodern Scrapbook.* Edited by James S. Baumlin and Eric Knickerbocker. Kansas City: Moon City.

Council of Writing Program Administrators. 2019. "WPA Outcomes Statement for First-Year Composition (3.0), Approved July 17, 2014." http://wpacouncil.org/aws/CWPA /pt/sd/news_article/243055/_PARENT/layout_details/false.

de Certeau, Michel. 1998. *The Practice of Everyday Life.* Berkeley: University of California Press.

Deleuze, Gilles. 1986. *Foucault.* Translated by Sean Hand. London: Athlone.

Deleuze, Gilles, and Felix Guatarri. 2005. *A Thousand Plateaus: Capitalism and Schizophrenia.* Translated by Brian Massumi. Minneapolis: University of Minnesota Press.

Derrida, Jacques. 1995. *On the Name: Meridian Crossing Aesthetics.* Edited by Thomas Dutoit. Translated by David Wood, John P. Leavy, and Ian McLeod. Berkley: Stanford University Press.

Derrida, Jacques. 1996. *Archive Fever: A Freudian Impression.* Chicago: University of Chicago Press.

Derrida, Jacques, and Peter Eisenman. 1997. *Chora L Works: Jacques Derrida and Peter Eisenman.* New York: Monacelli.

Drew, Julie. 2001. "The Politics of Place: Student Travelers and Pedagogical Maps." In *Ecocomposition: Theoretical and Pedagogical Approaches,* edited by Christian R. Weisser and Sidney I. Dobrin, 57–68. Albany: SUNY Press.

Duffy, John. 2015. "Writing Involves Making Ethical Choices." In *Naming What We Know: Threshold Concepts of Writing Studies,* edited by Linda Adler-Kassner and Elizabeth Wardle, 31. Logan: Utah State University Press.

Duffy, John, John Gallagher, and Steve Holmes. 2018. "Virtue Ethics." *Rhetoric Review* 37 (4): 321–92.

Duncan, Mike and Star Vanguiri, eds. 2012. *The Centrality of Style.* Fort Collins, CO: WAC Clearinghouse and Parlor Press.

Elbow, Peter. 2005. "A Friendly Challenge to Push the Outcomes Statement Further." In *The Outcomes Book: Debate and Consensus after the WPA Outcomes Statement,* edited by Susanmarie Harrington, Keith Rhodes, Ruth Overman Fischer, and Rita Malenczk, 177–191. Logan: Utah State University Press.

Enos, Theresa. 1994. "Voice as Echo of Delivery, Ethos as Transforming Process." In *Composition in Context: Essays in Honor of Donald C. Stewart,* edited by W. Ross Winterowd and Vincent Gillespie, 180–195. Carbondale: Southern Illinois University Press.

Enos, Theresa, ed. 1996. *Encyclopedia of Rhetoric and Composition: Communication from Ancient Times to the Information Age*. London: Routledge.

Enos, Theresa. 2013. "From Invention, Voice, and Ethos to Neo-Epideictic Time and Space." *Rhetoric Review* 32 (1): 4–7.

Theresa Enos, and Keith D. Miller, eds. 2003. *Beyond Postprocess and Postmodernism: Essays on the Spaciousness of Rhetoric*. Mahweh, NJ: Erlbaum.

Eppley, Karen. 2011. "Teaching Rural Place: Pre-Service Language and Literacy Students Consider Place-Conscious Literacy." *Pedagogies: An International Journal* 6 (2): 87–103.

Fisher, Walter K. 1989. *Human Communication as Narration: Toward a Philosophy of Reason, Value, and Action*. Columbia: University of South Carolina Press.

Flower, Linda. 2008. *Community Literacy and the Rhetoric of Public Engagement*. Carbondale: Southern Illinois Press.

Flower, Linda, and John R. Hayes. 1981. "A Cognitive Process Theory of Writing." *College Composition and Communication* 32 (4): 365–87.

Foss, Sonja K., and Cindy L. Griffin. 1995. "Beyond Persuasion: A Proposal for an Invitational Rhetoric." *Communication Monographs* 62: 1–18.

Foucault, Michel. 1969. "Authorship: What Is an Author?" *Screen* 20 (Spring): 13–34.

Frost, Randy O., and Gail Steketee. 2010. *Stuff: Compulsive Hoarding and the Meaning of Things*. New York: Houghton.

Gaillet, Lynne Lewis, and Michelle F. Eble. 2015. *Primary Research and Writing: People, Places, and Spaces*. New York: Routledge.

Gallagher, Chris W. 2016. "The Trouble with Outcomes: Pragmatic Inquiry and Educational Aims." *College English* 75 (1): 42–60.

Gibson, D. W. 2015. *The Edge Becomes the Center: An Oral History of Gentrification in the 21st Century*. New York: Overlook.

Goldblatt, Eli. 2007. *Because We Live Here: Sponsoring Literacy beyond the College Curriculum*. New York: Hampton.

Grassi, Ernesto. 1993. "Rhetoric and Philosophy." In *Professing the New Rhetorics: A Sourcebook*, edited by Theresa Enos and Stuart C. Brown, n.p. Pearson.

Gunn, Josh. 2008. "For the Love of Rhetoric, with Continual Reference to Kenny and Dolly." *Quarterly Journal of Speech* 94 (2): 131–55.

Gurwitt, Rob. 2005. "How Dense Can You Get?" *Governing: The Future of States and Localities*, August 2005. https://www.governing.com/mag/August-2005.html.

Halloran, Michael S. 1982. "Aristotle's Concept of Ethos, or If Not His Somebody Else's." *Rhetoric Review* 1 (1): 58–63.

Hawhee, Deborah. 2004. *Bodily Arts: Rhetoric and Athletics in Ancient Greece*. Austin: University of Texas Press.

Heidegger, Martin. 1993. "Building, Dwelling, Thinking." In *Basic Writings*, edited by David Farrell Krell, 343–64. New York: Harper Collins.

Heidegger, Martin. 2008. "Origin of the Work of Art." In *Basic Writings*. Rev. and expanded ed. Edited by David Farrell Krell, 139–212. New York: Harper Collins.

Heidegger, Martin. "Language." 2013a. In *Poetry, Language, Thought*, translated by Albert Hofstadter, 185–208. New York: Harper Perennial Modern Classics.

Heidegger, Martin. 2013b. ". . . Poetically Man Dwells . . ." In *Poetry, Language, Thought*, translated by Albert Hofstadter, 209–56. New York: Harper Perennial Modern Classics.

Heidegger, Martin. 2013c. "What Are Poets For?" In *Poetry, Language, Thought*, translated by Albert Hofstadter, 87–140. New York: Harper Perennial Modern Classics.

Holiday, Judy. 2009. "In[ter]vention: Locating Rhetoric's Ethos." *Rhetoric Review* 28 (4): 388–405.

Holmes, Ashley. 2016. *Public Pedagogy in Composition Studies*. CCCC Studies in Writing and Rhetoric Series. Urbana, IL: NCTE.

hooks, bell. 1994. *Teaching to Transgress: Education as the Practice of Freedom*. New York: Routledge.

hooks, bell. 1996. *Bone Black: Memories of Girlhood.* New York: Holt.

hooks, bell. 2009. *Belonging: A Culture of Place.* New York: Routledge.

Hsu, Jo V. 2018. "Reflection as Relationality: Rhetorical Alliances and Teaching Alternative Rhetorics." *College Composition and Communication* 70 (2): 142–168.

Hyde, Michael, ed. 2004. *The Ethos of Rhetoric.* Charleston: University of South Carolina Press.

Inoue, Asao. 2019a. "How Do We Language So People Stop Killing Each Other, Or What Do We Do about White Language Supremacy?" Keynote address at the Conference on College Composition and Communication, Pittsburgh, PA March 14.

Inoue, Asao. 2019b. *Labor-Based Grading Contracts: Building Equity and Inclusion in the Compassionate Writing Classroom.* Fort Collins, CO: WAC Clearinghouse and University Press of Colorado.

Jacobs, Dale, and Laura Micciche. 2003. *A Way to Move: Rhetorics of Emotion and Composition Studies.* Portsmouth, NH: Heinemann.

Johnson, Nan. 1984. "Ethos and the Aims of Rhetoric." In *Essays on Classical Rhetoric and Modern Discourse,* edited by Robert J. Connors, Lisa Ede, and Andrea A. Lunsford, 98–114. Carbondale: Southern Illinois University Press.

Johnson, T. R. 2001. "School Sucks." *College Composition and Communication* 52 (4): 620–50.

Kinloch, Valerie. 2010. *Harlem on Our Minds: Place, Race, and the Literacies of Urban Youth.* New York: Teacher's College Press.

Kinneavy, James L. 1979. "The Relation of the Whole to the Part in Interpretation Theory and in the Composing Process." In *Linguistics, Stylistics, and the Teaching of Composition,* edited by Donald McQuade, 292–312. Akron, OH: Department of English, University of Akron.

Kirsch, Gesa E., and Liz Rohan, eds. 2008. *Beyond the Archives, Research as Lived Process.* Carbondale: Southern Illinois University Press.

Kynard, Carmen. 2013. "Literacy/Literacies Studies and the Still-Dominant White Center." *Literacy in Composition Studies* 1 (1): 63–65.

Larson, Ann. 2016. "Composition's Dead." In *Composition in the Age of Austerity,* edited by Nancy Welch and Tony Scott, 163–76. Logan: Utah State University Press.

Lindemann, Erika. 2001. *A Rhetoric for Writing Teachers.* New York: Oxford University Press.

Lippard, Lucy. 2016. "Trash in the City." In *Nonstop Metropolis: A New York City Atlas,* edited by Rebecca Solnit and Joshua Jelly-Schapiro. Berkeley: University of California Press.

Livingston, Jenny, dir. 1990. *Paris Is Burning.* New York: Off-White Productions.

Long, Elenore. 2008. *Community Literacy and the Rhetoric of Local Publics.* West Lafayette, IN: Parlor and WAC Clearinghouse.

Lorde, Audre. 1984. "The Master's Tools Will Never Dismantle the Master's House." In *Sister Outsider: Essays and Speeches by Audre Lorde,* 110–113. Berkeley: Crossing.

Lucretius, Titus. 2008. *Of The Nature of Things.* Translated by William Ellory Leonard. Project Gutenberg Ebook. http://www.gutenberg.org/ebooks/785.

Lugones, Maria. 1987. "Playfulness, World-Travelling, and Loving Perception." *Hypatia* 2 (2): 3–19.

MacFarlane, Robert. 2016. *Landmarks.* New York: Penguin.

Malenczyk, Rita, Susan Miller-Cochran, Elizabeth Wardle, and Kathleen Blake Yancey, eds. 2018. *Composition, Rhetoric, and Disciplinarity.* Logan: Utah State University Press.

Massey, Doreen. 2005. *For Space.* London: SAGE

Mathieu, Paula. 2005. *Tactics of Hope: The Public Turn in English Composition.* Portsmouth, NH: Boynton/Cook.

Mathieu, Paula, George Grattan, Tim Lindgren, and Staci Shultz. 2012. *Writing Places: A Longman Topics Reader.* 2nd ed. New York: Pearson.

Mauk, Jonathan. 2003. "Location, Location, Location: The 'Real' (E)states of Being, Writing, and Thinking in Composition." *College English* 65 (4): 368–88.

McNeill, William. 2006. *The Time of Life: Heidegger and Ethos.* New York: SUNY Press.

Merleau-Ponty, Maurice. 1968. *The Visible and the Invisible.* Edited by Claude Lefort. Translated by Alphonso Lingis. Evanston, IL: Northwestern University Press.

Meyer, Jan, and Ray Land. 2003. "Threshold Concepts and Troublesome Knowledge: Linkages to Ways of Thinking and Practising within the Disciplines." *Enhancing Teaching-Learning Environments in Undergraduate Courses.* ETL Project, Occasional Report 4, 1–12. http://www.etl.tla.ed.ac.uk/docs/ETLreport4.pdf.

Micciche, Laura. 2007. *Doing Emotion: Rhetoric, Writing, Teaching.* Portsmouth, NH: Boynton/Cook.

Miller, Arthur. 1974. "Aristotle on Habit and Character: Implications for The Rhetoric." *Speech Monograph* 41 (4): 309–16.

Miller, Bernard Alan. 2011. *Rhetoric's Earthly Realm: Heidegger, Sophistry, and the Gorgian Kairos.* Anderson, SC: Parlor.

Muñoz, José Esteban. 1999. *Disidentifications: Queers of Color and the Performance of Politics.* Minneapolis: University of Minnesota Press.

Muñoz, José Esteban. 2009. *Cruising Utopia: The Then and There of Queer Futurity.* New York: New York University Press.

Munster, Anna. 2005. *Materializing New Media: Embodiment in Information Aesthetics.* Hanover: Dartmouth College Press.

National Council of Teachers of English, Conference on College Composition and Communication. 1974. "Students' Right to Their Own Language." http://cccc.ncte.org/library/NCTEFiles/Groups/CCCC/NewSRTOL.pdf.

New York City Department of City Planning, New York City Economic Development Corporation. 2011. "Staten Island North Shore Land Use and Transportation Study." http://www1.nyc.gov/site/planning/plans/north-shore/north-shore.page.

O'Donnell, Thomas. 1996. "Politics and Ordinary Language: A Defense of Expressivism." *College English* 58 (4): 423–39.

Office of the New York City Comptroller. 2014. "The Growing Gap: New York City's Housing Affordability Challenge." http://comptroller.nyc.gov/wp-content/uploads/documents/Growing_Gap.pdf.

O'Neill, Eugene. 2002. *Long Day's Journey Into Night.* Edited by Harold Bloom. New Haven: Yale University Press.

"Open Educational Resources." 2020. The City University of New York. Accessed June 23, 2020. https://www.cuny.edu/libraries/open-educational-resources/.

Owens, Derek. 2001. *Composition and Sustainability: Teaching for a Threatened Generation.* Urbana, IL: NCTE.

Parks, Stephen. 2010. *Gravyland: Writing Beyond the Curriculum in the City of Brotherly Love.* Syracuse, NY: Syracuse University Press.

Perelman, Chaim, and Lucy Olbrechts-Tyteca. 1991. *The New Rhetoric: A Theory of Argumentation.* South Bend, IN: University of Notre Dame Press.

Perl, Sondra. 1980. "Understanding Composing." *College Composition and Communication* 31 (4): 363–69.

Plato. 1913. *Phaedrus.* Translated by Christopher G. Smart. Perseus Digital Library.

Plato. 2013. *Timaeus.* Translated by Benjamin Jowett. The Project Gutenberg EBook.

Ramsey, Alexis E., Wendy B. Sharer, Barbara L'Eplattenier, and Lisa S. Mastrangelo, eds. 2010. *Working in the Archives: Practical Research Methods for Rhetoric and Composition.* Carbondale: Southern Illinois University Press.

Reed, Conor Tomás. 2013. "'Treasures That Prevail': Adrienne Rich, the SEEK Program, and Social Movements at the City College of New York, 1968–72." In *"What We Are Part Of": Teaching at CUNY 1968–74: Adrienne Rich Part II,* edited by Iemanjá Brown, Stephania Heim, erica kaufman, Kristin Moriah, Conor Thomás Reed, Talia Shelev, Wendy Tronrud, and Ammiel Alcalay. Lost and Found, the CUNY Poetics Document Initiative, Series 4, No. 3, Pt. 2.

Restaino, Jessica. 2019. *Surrender: Feminist Rhetoric in Love and Illness.* Carbondale: Southern Illinois University Press.

Reynolds, Nedra. 2007. *Geographies of Writing: Inhabiting Places and Encountering Difference.* Carbondale: Southern Illinois University Press.

Reynolds, Nedra. 1993. "*Ethos* as Location: New Sites for Understanding Discursive Authority." *Rhetoric Review* 11 (2): 325–38.

Riccio, Anthony. 2006. *The Italian American Experience in New Haven.* Albany, NY: SUNY Press.

Rice, Jeff. 2007. *The Rhetoric of Cool: Composition Studies and New Media.* Carbondale: Southern Illinois University Press.

Rich, Adrienne. 1980. "Teaching Language in Open Admissions (1972)." In *On Lies, Secrets, and Silence: Selected 1966–1978 Prose*, edited by Adrienne Rich. New York: Norton.

Rickert, Thomas. 2013. *Ambient Rhetoric: The Attunements of Rhetorical Being.* Pittsburgh: University of Pittsburgh Press.

Rivers, Nathaniel. 2016. "Geocomposition in Public Writing and Rhetoric Pedagogy." *College Composition and Communication* 67 (4): 576–606.

Robertson, Liane, and Kara Taczak. 2018. "Disciplinarity and First-Year Composition: Shifting to a New Paradigm." In *Composition, Rhetoric, and Disciplinarity*, edited by Rita Malenczyk, Susan Miller-Cochran, Elizabeth Wardle, and Kathleen Blake Yancey, 185–205. Logan: Utah State University Press.

Roozen, Kevin. 2015. "Writing Is a Social and Rhetorical Activity." In *Naming What We Know: Threshold Concepts for Writing Studies*, edited by Linda Adler-Kassner and Elizabeth Wardle, 17–19. Logan: Utah State University Press.

Rose, Mike. 1985. "The Language of Exclusion: Writing Instruction at the University." *College English* 47 (4): 341–59.

Royster, Jacqueline Jones. 1996. "When the First Voice You Hear Is Not Your Own." *College Composition and Communication* 47 (1): 29–40.

Ryan, Kathleen J., Nancy Meyers, and Rebecca Jones, eds. 2016. *Rethinking Ethos: A Feminist Ecological Approach to Rhetoric* Carbondale: Southern Illinois University Press.

Sieburth, Richard. 1989. "Benjamin the Scrivener." In *Benjamin: Philosophy, History, Aesthetics*, edited by Gary Smith, 13–37. Chicago: University of Chicago Press.

Shipka, Jody. 2011. *Toward a Composition Made Whole.* Pittsburgh: University of Pittsburgh Press.

Shipka, Jody. 2015. "On Estate Sales, Archives, and the Matter of Making Things." *Provocations: Reconstructing the Archive.* Logan: Utah State University Press, Computers and Composition Digital Press.

Shor, Ira. 1999. "What Is Critical Literacy?" *Journal of Pedagogy, Pluralism, and Practice* 1 (4): 2–32.

Sirc, Geoffrey. 2002. *English Composition as a Happening.* Logan: Utah State University Press.

Solnit, Rebecca. 2000. *Wanderlust: A History of Walking.* London: Penguin.

Solnit, Rebecca. 2005. *A Field Guide to Getting Lost.* New York: Penguin.

Sontag, Susan. 1973. *On Photography.* New York: Picador.

Stewart, Susan. 1993. *On Longing: Narratives of the Miniature, the Gigantic, the Souvenir, the Collection.* Durham: Duke University Press.

Strickland, Donna. 2011 *The Managerial Unconscious in the History of Composition Studies.* CCC Studies in Writing and Rhetoric. Carbondale: Southern Illinois University Press.

Tolbert, Linda, and Paul Theobald. 2006. "Finding Their Place in the Community: Urban Education outside the Classroom." *Childhood Education* 82 (5): 271–74.

Ulmer, Gregory. 2002. *Internet Invention: From Literacy to Electracy.* New York: Pearson.

Villanueva, Victor. 2004. "'Memoria' Is a Friend of Ours: On the Discourse of Color." *College English* 67 (1): 9–19.

Waite, Stacey. "The Unavailable Means of Persuasion: A Queer Ethos for Feminist Writers and Teachers." In *Rethinking Ethos: A Feminist Ecological Approach to Writing*, edited by

Kathleen J. Ryan, Nancy Meyers, and Rebecca Jones, 71–88. Carbondale: Southern Illinois University Press.

Walter, E. V. 1988. *Placeways: A Theory of Human Environment*. Chapel Hill: University of North Carolina Press.

Walker, Paul. 2010. "(Un)earthing a Vocabulary of Values: A Discourse Analysis for Eco-composition." *Composition Studies* 38 (1): 69–87.

Weisser, Christian R., and Sidney I. Dobrin. 2001. *Ecocomposition: Theoretical and Pedagogical Approaches*. Albany: SUNY Press.

Welsh, Nancy, and Tony Scott. 2016. "Introduction." In *Composition in the Age of Austerity*, edited by Nancy Welch and Tony Scott, 3–20. Logan: Utah State University Press.

Williams, Tennessee. 2011. *The Glass Menagerie: The Deluxe Centennial Edition*. Edited by Tony Kushner. New York: New Directions.

Wyschogrod, Edith. 1998. *An Ethics of Remembering: History, Heterology, and Nameless Others*. Chicago: University of Chicago Press.

Yancey, Kathleen Blake. 2018. "Mapping the Turn to Disciplinarity: A Historical Analysis of Composition's Trajectory and Its Current Method." In *Composition, Rhetoric, and Disciplinarity*, edited by Rita Malenczyk, Susan Miller Cochran, Elizabeth Wardle, and Kathleen Blake Yancey, 15–35. Logan: Utah State University Press.

Kathleen Blake Yancey, ed. 1994. *Voices on Voice: Perspectives, Definitions, Inquiry*. Urbana, IL: NCTE.

Yancey, Kathleen Blake, Liane Robertson, and Kara Taczak. 2014. *Writing across Contexts: Transfer, Composition, and Sites of Writing*. Logan: Utah State University Press.

Young, Richard E. 1992. "Rogerian Argument and the Context of the Situation: Taking a Closer Look." In *Rogerian Perspectives: Collaborative Rhetoric for Oral and Written Communication*, edited by Nathaniel Teich, 109–21. Norwood, NJ: Ablex.

Young, Vershawn Ashanti. 2009. "Nah, We Straight: An Argument Against Code-Switching." *JAC* 29 (1): 49–76.

Young, Vershawn Ashanti, Rusty Barrett, Y'Shanda Young Rivera, and Kim Brian Lovejoy. 2018. *Other People's English: Code-Meshing, Code-Switching, and African American Literacy*. Anderson, SC: Parlor P.

Young, Vershawn Ashanti. 2019. "Performance Rhetoric, Performance Composition." 2019 CCCC Annual Convention: Call for Program Proposals. http://cccc.ncte.org/cccc/conv/call-2019.

ABOUT THE AUTHOR

Rosanne Carlo is an assistant professor in rhetoric and composition at The College of Staten Island CUNY where she primarily teaches first-year writing and MA courses on the teaching of writing. Her research interests include rhetorical theory, ethos and voice, material rhetorics, and place-based writing. Rosanne codirects the writing-across-the-curriculum (WAC) program at the college and aids the CSI Writing Program in professional development on the teaching of writing for MA student teachers, adjunct instructors, and full-time faculty. She also coleads a writing partnership at CSI with local high schools called #SIWrites: Engaging in College and Career Preparation. Rosanne's other scholarly work can be found in the *Community Literacy Journal*, *Composition Forum*, *Intraspection*, the *Journal for the Assembly on the Expanded Perspectives on Learning*, *Rhetoric Review*, and the *Writing Instructor*.

INDEX